The Dark Side of
Samuel Pepys

The Voluptuary
'God forgive me, I could not think it too much; which is a strange slavery that I
stand in to beauty, that I value nothing near it.'
The Diary of Samuel Pepys 6th September 1664

* * *

The Wife Beater
'Thereupon she giving me some cross answer I did strike her over her left eye
such a blow as the poor wretch did cry out and was in great pain.'
The Diary of Samuel Pepys 19th December 1664

* * *

The Philogynist
'God forgive me, I do still see that my future is not to be quite conquered, but
will esteem pleasure above all things. … music and women I cannot but give way
to, whatever my business is.'
The Diary of Samuel Pepys 28th February 1666

* * *

The Voyeur
'After dinner I by water alone to Westminster to the parish church, and there did
entertain myself with my perspective glass up and down the church, by which
I had the great pleasure of seeing and gazing at a great many very fine women. …'
The Diary of Samuel Pepys 26th May 1667

* * *

The Groper
'… my wife, coming up suddenly, did find me embracing the girl with my hand
under her skirts. …'
The Diary of Samuel Pepys 25th October 1668

* * *

The Rapist
'Alone with her, I tried to do what I wanted, and against her struggles I did it,
though not to my satisfaction.'
The Diary of Samuel Pepys 20th December 1664

* * *

The Dark Side of Samuel Pepys

Society's First Sex Offender

Geoffrey Pimm

PEN & SWORD
HISTORY

First published in Great Britain in 2017 by
Pen & Sword History
an imprint of
Pen & Sword Books Ltd
47 Church Street
Barnsley
South Yorkshire
S70 2AS

ISBN 978 1 52671 729 0

A CIP catalogue record for this book is available from the British Library

Typeset in Ehrhardt by
Mac Style Ltd, Bridlington, East Yorkshire
Printed and bound in the UK by TJ International Ltd,Padstow
PL28 8RW

Pen & Sword Books Limited incorporates the imprints of Atlas,
Archaeology, Aviation, Discovery, Family History, Fiction, History,
Maritime, Military, Military Classics, Politics, Select, Transport,
True Crime, Air World, Frontline Publishing, Leo Cooper,
Remember When, Seaforth Publishing, The Praetorian Press, Wharncliffe
Local History, Wharncliffe Transport, Wharncliffe True Crime
and White Owl.

For a complete list of Pen & Sword titles please contact
PEN & SWORD BOOKS LIMITED
47 Church Street, Barnsley, South Yorkshire, S70 2AS, England
E-mail: enquiries@pen-and-sword.co.uk
Website: www.pen-and-sword.co.uk

Contents

Introduction		vii
Acknowledgements		x
Chapter 1	Pepys' World	1
Chapter 2	Pepys the Celebrity	12
Chapter 3	Full Forty Times Over	15
Chapter 4	Better to Marry than to Burn	19
Chapter 5	A Woman's Place	23
Chapter 6	A Pretty Dutch Woman	29
Chapter 7	Sunday Recreations	33
Chapter 8	Servant Girls	39
Chapter 9	A Pretty, Conceited Woman	46
Chapter 10	Haberdasherie & Hanky-Panky	54
Chapter 11	A Most Modest Woman	78
Chapter 12	My Dear Mrs. Knipp	84
Chapter 13	A Very Pretty Wench & Her Mother	92
Chapter 14	The Carpenter's Wife & Other Assignations	100
Chapter 15	A Pretty Companion	118
Chapter 16	Caught Red-Handed	123
Chapter 17	The Storm Continues Unabated	126
Chapter 18	Hell Hath No Fury	130
Chapter 19	Some That Got Away	139

Chapter 20   Last Love   143

Chapter 21   Shame & Remorse?   147

Chapter 22   Postscript   155

Appendix A: The School of Venus   157
Appendix B: The Bagwells   161
Appendix C: Full Forty Times Over (full libretto)   162
Appendix D: Ladies of Pepys' acquaintanceship   164
Appendix E: Female Servants in Pepys' Household During the Diary Period   174
Bibliography   178
Index   180

Introduction

Ask his contemporaries what they thought of Samuel Pepys and they would have told you that he was an upright and God-fearing citizen, renowned for his integrity, hard work and unblemished reputation. By dint of unswerving application to his duties he had risen from humble (if well-connected) beginnings to be amongst the most powerful men in the land, known and respected by everyone with whom he came into contact, including even King Charles II himself. Without Samuel Pepys, England may not have had the navy that, for centuries after his death, would preserve the country from foreign invasion and secure the greatest empire the world had ever known. The historian Arthur Bryant writing in 1938 described it as 'his supreme achievement – that by virtue of which his country still rules the sea.' As Secretary of the Royal Navy, a Member of Parliament, Master of Trinity House and President of the Royal Society, Pepys exerted his influence over every aspect of seventeenth century public life.

And yet we know from his personal diary, into which he carefully recorded every daily event in his public and private life over a period of more than nine years from January 1660 to May 1669, that there was a darker and much less reputable side to his character. For reasons which will almost certainly forever remain a mystery, Samuel Pepys recorded in unabashed and graphic detail, behaviour that might make even a modern case-hardened tabloid journalist blush. At first glance, it appears that it was never intended that the world at large would have access to this document – the whole text was written in shorthand, whilst very personal (and potentially highly embarrassing) episodes were first written in a strange mixture of foreign languages, before being transcribed into their encoded format, what modern code-breakers might call 'double encryption'.

All the various translators of the diary have shied away from including plain English renditions of these episodes in their editions. Pepys's diary was first made available to the general public during the nineteenth century, both in a notoriously bowdlerized edition by Lord Braybrooke and in a more accurate but censored version by Henry B. Wheatley, which he published over a number of years in seventy-three volumes. It was the early 1970s before a complete edition was published by Latham and Matthews, and even then, the offending passages were only rendered into their strange mix of foreign languages, without translation or explanatory notes.

Henry Wheatley also wrote two additional works on the subject; *Samuel Pepys and the World He Lived In* published in 1889 and *Pepysiana* subtitled *Additional Notes on the Particulars of Pepys' Life and on some Passages in the Diary*. The Victorians were notoriously shy when it came to discussing the subject of sex, and Mr Wheatley was no exception. Pepys' diary is full of women and his relationships with them – thirty-one female domestic servants alone are mentioned in varying degrees of detail, including an affair with one that very nearly destroyed his marriage. In *Pepysiana* fifty-one pages are devoted to notes about 'Friends and Acquaintances' yet 'Women' occupy rather less than a single page, in which Pepys is largely blameless and the characters of a few women are viciously assassinated; for example: 'Mrs. Betty Lane, afterwards Mrs. Martin, who figures so largely in Pepys's pages, is the most objectionable of all. There is no evidence that she had any virtue to lose, and her conduct throughout is very revolting.'

However, in a couple of matters, Wheatley allows a mild criticism of Pepys' behaviour; With regard to the affair with Mrs Bagwell, which lasted for much of the diary period, 'it appears that Pepys actually did seduce her, and that in a way much to his discredit.' The affair with the maid Deb Willett, whom Pepys systematically and forcibly seduced and which nearly destroyed his marriage, is described as affording 'a very curious illustration of Pepys's code of morals.'

Whilst a student at Cambridge, Pepys probably had access to a work by Thomas Shelton called *A Tutor to Tachygraphy* in which the author enumerates some of the advantages of writing by his shorthand method, among them being 'secrecy, brevity, celerity and perpetuity.' Shelton went on to add a paragraph that must have appealed greatly to the young Pepys: 'Sometimes a man may have occasion to write that which he would not have everyone acquainted with, which being set down in these Characters, he may have them for his own private use only.'

However, if it was never intended for other eyes, but for 'his own private use only' why did Pepys go to the trouble of collecting the pages of the diary into tooled leather bindings and catalogue them into what is acknowledged to be one of the greatest of surviving seventeenth-century libraries? At this distance in time it is unlikely that we will ever find the answers to these questions and thereby discover his real motivation. Nevertheless, his motives for keeping such a detailed history of his life for nearly a decade remain a subject ripe for speculation. It has been suggested that it was the product of a puritanical urge to record (and thereby correct) his moral lapses, but these only represent a relatively small percentage of the total record. Others suggest that it was motivated by an historian's desire to record the momentous events of his time, yet when he began to keep the diary, he was a relatively humble clerk and many of the great events of the seventeenth century that he was to witness, participate in and record had not yet occurred or were even foreseen. It has even been suggested that he was attempting to render those lascivious memories less immediately part of his own consciousness thereby rendering them all the more titillating in the later reading; yet again these instances represent only a small proportion of the diary, so can hardly represent its *raison d'etre*.

Whatever his motives in keeping the diary, the encryption afforded by his knowledge of Shelton's method suited his needs admirably, for away from the respectability of his professional life, he set down private opinions that polite convention would have suppressed. Moreover, he faithfully recorded acts of moral turpitude that in later centuries might have caused his name to be blazoned across the newspapers and in some instances, most probably lead him to be arraigned in the courts. During the diary period, he had sexual encounters of one sort or another with around fifty women other than his wife. At one end of the scale of improper behaviour he was a voyeur, even in church peeping at women through his telescope – gowns were cut lower than at any other time in history either before or since. He was a groper, assaulting his wife's maids even in his own parlour and other women, pregnant or not, whenever and wherever he could – even on more than one occasion in his wife's presence as the ladies sat either side of him in a coach.

Further up the scale of inappropriate behaviour, he unashamedly used his position in public life to further the careers of subordinate men, in return for enjoying the sexual favours of their wives. Finally at the very top of the scale of sexual offences, women who still remained uncooperative after blandishments, money, or their husbands' advancement had failed to secure his lascivious objectives, found themselves physically forced into satisfying his lust, in a manner that modern courts would have no problem at all in finding to be rape.

Whilst on a visit to the notorious Bartholomew Fair in 1668, Pepys came upon a trained mare performing tricks at the instigation of her master, to the applause of the watching crowd. The showman instructed the horse 'to go to him of the company that most loved a pretty wench in a corner.' The mare unhesitatingly ambled over and to the amusement of the crowd, nuzzled Pepys. Unabashed, he flicked a shilling (5p) to the showman and turned and kissed an unknown pretty girl who stood next to him. (Diary 1st September 1668).

In the society of loose morals that was restoration England, led by a libertine king and court, Samuel Pepys, the celebrated member of the establishment and respectable pillar of society, took every opportunity that came his way to 'love a pretty wench in a corner' or at very least to kiss them and put his hand up their skirts.

Acknowledgements

With thanks to my sister in law, novelist Nicola Slade, for her advice and encouragement.

Extracts from the diary of Samuel Pepys edited and translated by Robert Latham and William Matthews reprinted by permission of Peters Fraser & Dunlop (www.petersfraserdunlop.com) on behalf of the estate of Robert Latham.

Chapter 1

Pepys' World

There can be almost no one, in the western world at least, that does not know the name Samuel Pepys. His daily personal diary, kept meticulously for almost a decade, remains not just a primary source of information on some of the most important events of the seventeenth century, but a fascinating window into the customs, morals and mores of the English restoration period. Through the pages of the journal, we see the world with his eyes; through his lips we taste the food he ate and through his nostrils smell the odours that pervaded the London streets and houses of his day, most of which, in an age long before closed drains and the invention of the water closet, would utterly disgust modern sensibilities.

The lack of sanitation and no knowledge of virology meant that life expectancy was comparatively short, with the average falling between 35 and 40 years, largely from diseases the origins of which were not understood and for which no effective treatments existed – Pepys' own wife Elizabeth died from typhoid fever at the age of 29. However, this low life expectancy takes into account the fact that up to a half of all children died before the age of 16. If one survived to the age of 30, life expectancy rose to 59.

The seventeenth century was already one-third gone when Samuel made his appearance in the world in February 1633, his parents' fifth child. His ancestors had first been yeoman farmers in the fens of Cambridgeshire, with various lands around Cottenham and including the manor of Impington. In 1618 the sister of Samuel's Cambridgeshire grandfather, Paulina (already widowed early in life) married a brother of the 1st Earl of Manchester, Sir Sydney Montagu, a genteel connection that was later to prove so beneficial to the rising young Samuel Pepys. As the century progressed several other members of the wider Pepys family rose to become pillars of the establishment. In 1625 his great uncle Talbot Pepys was Recorder and then for a short while MP for Cambridge. His father's first cousin, Sir Richard Pepys, was elected MP for Sudbury in 1640, Baron of the Exchequer in 1654, and finally Lord Chief Justice of Ireland in 1655. But Samuel's immediate antecedents were considerably more humble. His father John was a tailor who had married one Margaret Kite, the sister of a butcher from Whitechapel in London. In many ways, it was an apparently ill-matched pairing – a pious, Bible-reading, gentle artisan and a shrewish, illiterate wash-maid. Nevertheless, they obviously had something in common, as eleven children issued from their union over a period of fourteen years.

The London in which young Samuel was to establish himself was tiny compared with the modern metropolis; a conurbation of 475,000 in 1670 (Prof. Ian Mortimer 'The Time Traveller's Guide to Restoration Britain' Bodley Head 2017), extending for about 3 miles from Westminster Abbey in the west to the Tower of London in the east. A single bridge connected it to the thin strip of urbanization on the south bank that contained Shakespeare's Globe Theatre and Southwark Cathedral. From the higher vantage points of the city one could readily glimpse the green fields of the surrounding countryside, easily accessible on foot when the smells and the hubbub of the city became unbearable.

John Pepys had his tailoring business in Salisbury Court, accessed through a narrow cobbled lane from Fleet Street, on the western edge of the city and close to the northern bank of the Thames, where many of the rich and famous had their grand dwellings. Samuel was born literally above the shop, in one of the two bedrooms that comprised the top floor of the narrow three-storey timbered house, a dwelling typical of the city that was to all but disappear thirty-three years later in the famous conflagration of 1666. The house, in common with all in the neighbourhood, would have reeked by modern standards. In the absence of any lavatorial facilities that would be familiar to the twenty-first century, the house would have been equipped with several chamber-pots, some waiting to be emptied – either by being poured from the window into the street below or in better houses, taken down to the cellar and emptied into what was known as the 'house of office', a latrine containing a receptacle for the household's human waste, there to wait upon its occasional removal by the 'night-men', a job so unpleasant that its operatives often denied their occupation, the lingering traces of their work so evident that people saw the truth, allegedly giving rise to the origin of the expression 'you're taking the piss!'. If not emptied regularly, the results could be disgusting to say the least:

> This morning one came to me to advise with me where to make me a window into my cellar in lieu of one which Sir W. Batten had stopped up, and going down into my cellar to look I stepped into a great heap of turds by which I found that Mr. Turner's house of office is full and comes into my cellar, which do trouble me, but I shall have it helped. (Diary 20th October 1660)

This was not the only time Pepys was incommoded by the lavatorial arrangements of his neighbours:

> … at night home and up to the leads; but were, contrary to expectation, driven down again with a stink, by Sir. W Pen's emptying of a shitten pot in their house of office close by; which doth trouble me, for fear it do hereafter annoy me. (Diary 30th April 1666)

Sometimes, even a convenient receptacle was not utilized – Dr Johnson once famously defecated into his hosts' fireplace. Pepys did the same on at least one occasion when in urgent need and a suitable receptacle was not to hand:

> … and so I to bed, and in the night was mightily troubled with a looseness (I suppose from some fresh damp linen that I put on this night), and feeling for a chamber-pott, there was none, I having called the mayde up out of her bed, she had forgot I suppose to put one there; so I was forced in this strange house to rise and shit in the chimney twice; and so to bed and was very well again. (Diary 28th September 1665)

Even Pepys, who must have been inured to the ever pervading stench, must occasionally have found it unbearable, but was pleasantly surprised by the efficiency of the 'night-men': '… thence home; where my house of office was emptying, and I find they will do it with much more cleanness than I expected.' (Diary 28th July 1663)

However, the next day, it is clear that his expectations were ill-founded: '… and so home and there going to Sir W.Batten (having no stomach to dine at home, it being yet hardly clean of last night's turds).' (Diary 29th July 1663)

With no running water or toilet paper, clothes would quickly have become soiled, and as the laundry was generally only done once a month, dirty linen of all descriptions would either continue to be worn or piled up until the appointed wash-day arrived. Pepys records lying in bed with his wife, reminiscing about the time in their life before they could afford a maid and '…how she used to make coal fires and wash my foul clothes with her own hand for me, poor wretch, in my little room.' (Diary 25th February 1667)

Personal hygiene was no better. Pepys only once records being totally immersed in water, when he visited the facilities in the city of Bath, where he regarded the immersion of so many people in a single body of water as distinctly unhygienic:

> Up at four o'clock, being by appointment called up to the Cross Bath, where we were carried one after one another, myself, and wife, and Betty Turner, Willet, and W. Hewer. And by and by, though we designed to have done before company come, much company come; very fine ladies; and the manner pretty enough, only methinks it cannot be clean to go so many bodies together in the same water. (Diary 13th June 1668)

Sometimes, personal hygiene was so lacking that even contemporaries noticed it: '… the fine Mrs. Middleton is noted for carrying about her body a continued sour base Smell that is very offensive, especially if she be a little hot.' (Diary 3rd October 1665)

That other famous diarist of the seventeenth century, John Evelyn, (with whom Pepys was friends for more than forty years) decided in August 1653 that he would experiment with washing his hair annually – presumably a routine that he followed thereafter whether it needed it or not!

But the worst pollution of all came from the coal which provided the whole city with its fuel, both for domestic heating and industrial processes, large numbers of which were conducted in people's homes. In 1661, John Evelyn published a paper which railed against this 'prodigious annoyance' entitled *Fumifugium or The Inconvenience of the Aer and Smoake of London dissipated*. He describes with startling clarity the effect on the city's population, familiar to anyone who lived through the London smogs of the nineteenth and twentieth centuries:

> … her Inhabitants breathe nothing but an impure and thick Mist, accompanied with a fuliginous and filthy vapour, which renders them obnoxious to a thousand inconveniences, corrupting the Lungs, and disordering the entire habit of their Bodies; so that Catharrs, Phthisicks, Coughs and Consumptions, rage more in this one City, than in the whole Earth besides.

These foul emissions must have contributed significantly to the death toll of children, which the contemporary 'Bill of Mortality' records as being half of all those born in the city failing to achieve two years of age. Apart from coal, everyday rubbish, together with human and animal waste, comprised a major health hazard. The River Thames itself formed the main artery of the sewage system, with open street drains emptying into the dozen or more rivers that then flowed through the city. Everything went into these drains, not just human and animal sewage. Butchers threw the remains of their carcasses into the waters, the bodies of dead dogs and cats were plentiful, and no doubt more than a few human corpses wound their way into eternity along this route. One of the largest of these rivers, the Fleet, was so notorious that it moved several poets to compose odes to its revolting condition. Ben Jonson, who died in 1637, imagined a journey along its length in a poem entitled 'On the Famous Voyage':

> How dare your dainty nostrils (in so hot a season,
> When every clerk eats artichokes and peason,
> Laxative lettuce, and such windy meat),
> 'Tempt such a passage? When each privy's seat
> Is filled with buttock, and the walls do sweat
> Urine and plasters? When the noise doth beat
> Upon your ears of discords so un-sweet,
> And outcries of the damned in the Fleet?

Nearly a century later, matters had not improved. In 1728 Alexander Pope was to write: 'To where Fleet-ditch with disemboguing streams, rolls the large tribute of dead dogs to Thames.'

Neither was it just dead dogs that floated into eternity by this route: 'I was much troubled today to see a dead man lie floating upon the waters; and had done, (they say) these four days and nobody takes him up to bury him, which is very barbarous.' (Diary 4th April 1662)

Even as early as the fourteenth century, the nineteen-arched single bridge over the river with its 200 buildings (some of them seven-storeys high) contained a multi-seated public latrine which overhung the bridge parapets and discharged directly into the river below; as did the many private latrines reserved for the bridge residents, shopkeepers and bridge officials.

It would be more than the smells of seventeenth-century London that twenty-first century Britons would find repugnant. Everyday sights would also revolt modern sensibilities. This was a time when the punishment for almost any crime that did not carry the death sentence was corporal in nature and was invariably administered in public. Whipping of both sexes with a cat o' nine tails and branding or boring through the tongue with a red-hot iron were high on the tariff, together with the maiming of the nose or the amputation of ears. As if these penalties were not sufficiently cruel, they were often coupled with the unfortunate recipient spending several hours trapped by the neck and wrists in the pillory or by the ankles in the stocks. Thus the sufferer was obliged to stand for as many hours as the sentence demanded, their heads exposed to whatever the mob cared to hurl at them. These missiles might be relatively harmless, rotting fruit and vegetables being a favourite choice, or if the felon was unpopular, they might equally well have been rocks and stones and deaths are recorded as having ensued from a bombardment of this sort. Refinements in the cruel application of this punishment included the nailing of the culprit's ears to the board. At the end of the period of suffering, the ears were either slit to free them from the nails, or amputated altogether.

The seventeenth-century poet John Taylor, writing in 1630, describes the necessarily extensive provision of the facilities required to inflict these punishments upon the hapless miscreants of London: 'In London, and within a mile, I ween, There are jails or prisons full eighteen, And sixty whipping-posts and stocks and cages.'

The execution of felons was effected either by public hanging, or in the case of male traitors, by hanging, drawing and quartering (unless you were nobility, in which case you were mercifully decapitated!): 'This morning, Mr. Carew was hanged and quartered at Charing Cross – but his quarters by a great favour are not to be hanged up.' (Diary 15th October 1660)

Female traitors were merely burned alive, but it was not necessary to be a female spy to incur this penalty – plotting to murder one's husband was prosecuted as 'petit treason'. The penalty for men involved the cutting down of the miscreant whilst still alive, before disembowelling and then burning the still-warm entrails under the nose of the victim. The trunk was then dismembered and beheaded and the gory components exhibited in various parts of the city. Pepys (who at the age of 15 had witnessed the decapitation of King Charles I outside the Banqueting House in the Palace of Whitehall) watched just such a procedure when Major-General Harrison, one of the signatories of Charles' death warrant, was thus executed for treason in October 1660. Difficult though it might be to believe now, these events were seen as great public entertainment and have been described elsewhere as 'the pornography of the age'. Pepys recorded that: '… he [Harrison] was presently cut down and his head and his heart shown to the people, at which there was [sic] great shouts of joy.'

Oliver Cromwell, who led the Protectorate after King Charles's execution, had died at the age of 59 in September 1658, thought probably to have been from septicaemia following a urinary infection. However, his relatively early demise from natural causes did not enable him to escape the ignominy demanded by the law for those convicted of treason. His body was exhumed on the 30th January 1661 and hanged by the neck on the public gibbet at Tyburn (close by what is now Marble Arch in London) all morning and most of the afternoon.[1] At four o'clock it was cut down, the cadaver decapitated and the head stuck on a pole outside Westminster Hall. Pepys must often have seen the gruesome relic on the many occasions he visited the building, as it remained there for the next twenty years until it eventually blew down in a storm.

In the diary, Pepys never mentions joining the baying crowds salivating over the bloody flogging of half-naked men and women, an everyday occurrence in his day, often administered with excessive cruelty. The notorious seventeenth century Judge Jeffries, having sentenced a woman to be publicly whipped, famously instructed the hangman to: '… pay particular attention to this lady. Scourge her soundly, man. Scourge her till the blood runs down. It is the Christmas season; a cold season for madam to strip in. See, therefore, man, that you warm her shoulders thoroughly.'

---

1. It is worth noting that there is a question as to whether or not the body mutilated at Tyburn was in fact that of Cromwell. These doubts arose because it was assumed that between his death in September 1658 and the exhumation of January 1661, Cromwell's body was buried and reburied in several places to protect it from royalists out for revenge. It has been variously suggested that his bodily remains are actually buried in London, Cambridgeshire, Northamptonshire or Yorkshire, but that's another story.

However, the public administration of justice was by no means the only form of public entertainment available in Pepys' London. He describes his visits to see what to modern eyes would be equally barbaric amusements, many of which had been recently re-introduced after being officially banned under the Puritan rule of the Commonwealth. One of these was the 'sport' of baiting bulls with dogs:

> And after dinner with my wife and Mercer to the Beare Garden, where I have not been I think of many years, and saw some good sport of the bull's tossing of the dogs – one into the very boxes. But it is a very rude and nasty pleasure. (Diary 14th August 1666)

Also recently re-introduced was the equally bloody sport of cock-fighting:

> Being directed by sight of bills upon the walls, did go to Shooe Lane to see a cocke-fighting at a new pit there – a sport I was never at in my life...... I soon had enough of it; and yet I would not but have seen it once, it being strange to observe the nature of those poor creatures, how they fight till they drop down dead upon the table and strike after they are ready to give up the ghost – not offering to run away when they are weary or wounded past doing further. (Diary 21st September 1663)

Another very popular public entertainment was prize-fighting with swords, often between amateurs, the principal venue for which was the Bear Garden in Southwark, on the south side of the Thames:

> Then abroad by [?] and stopped at the Bear-garden stairs, there to see a prize fought; but the house so full, there was no getting in there; so forced to [go] through an alehouse into the pit where the bears are baited, and upon a stool did see them fight, which they did very furiously, a butcher and a waterman. The former had the better all along, till by and by the latter dropped his sword out of his hand, and the butcher, whether not seeing his sword dropped or I know not, but did give him a cut over the wrist, so as he was disabled to fight any longer. (Diary 28th May 1667)

Pepys was well able to make his own entertainment. In 1667 he acquired a 'perspective glass' or what we call a telescope. Amazingly, he took the instrument to church and spent the service ogling women:

> After dinner I by water alone to Westminster to the parish church, and there did entertain myself with my perspective glass up and down the church, by which I had the great pleasure of seeing and gazing at a great many very fine women.... (Diary 26th May 1667)

Women's formal dress in the seventeenth century would have afforded Pepys much to ogle at. Although skirts reached to the ground, necklines were often cut so low that often a diaphanous kerchief (*fichu* in French) was required in order to preserve some modicum of public decency, the breasts accentuated by being pushed upwards by the long-fronted stiffened bodice.

However, of all the available public entertainments, Samuel most loved the theatre and visited it at any and every opportunity. The Puritans had closed all theatres in 1642 and they remained closed until the restoration of King Charles II. By 1660, there were two companies of licensed players in London, but the roles of women had always previously been played by boys, something that was to change dramatically in the first few years of the restored playhouses: 'I to the Theatre, where was acted Beggars bush – it being very well done; and here the first time that ever I saw Women come upon the stage.' (Diary 3rd January 1661)

It was of course, possible to make one's own entertainment. Then as now, people got drunk and behaved in a hooligan-like manner, which on this occasion, seems also to have involved some cross-dressing by the participants:

> And so we supped, and very merry. And then at about 9 a-clock to Mrs. Mercers gate, where the fire and boys expected us and her son had provided abundance of Serpents and rockets; and there mighty merry…….till about 12 at night, flinging our fireworks and burning one another and the people over the way. And at last, our business being most spent – we went into Mrs. Mercers, and there mighty merry, smutting one another with Candlegresse and soot, till most of us were like devils; and that being done, then we broke up and to my house, and there I made them drink; and upstairs we went, and then fell into dancing (W. Batelier dancing well) and dressing, him and I and one Mr. Banister. … like women; and Mercer put on a suit of Toms like a boy, and mighty mirth we had. … Thus we spent till 3 or 4 in the morning, mighty merry, and then parted and to bed. (Diary 14th August 1666)

Finding out what was going on by way of entertainments in Pepys' London would not have been as easy as it is today. Not only does the seventeenth century obviously predate by more than two centuries any form of electronic communication, it predates until what was recently the most universally accepted method of reporting newsworthy events; the newspaper. The first regular daily newspaper *The Daily Courant* would not appear until 1702, barely a year before Pepys died. Current events in his small world would have been largely conveyed by word of mouth; publication of information in written form was effected either by small pamphlets that were distributed only when some event worthy of notice had occurred, or as in the case of public executions, was expected, or on crude penny broadsheets known as 'Broadside Ballads': 'Ballads! my masters, ballads! Will you ha' o' the newest and truest matter in all London? I have of them for all choices, and over all arguments too.'

Broadside Ballads were the tabloids of their age, often performed by an itinerant musical performer, and usually containing scurrilous or indecent subject matter delivered to the accompaniment of obscene gestures. Performances could be observed at markets and fairs, or in the new coffee houses; the first of which appeared in London in 1652. The singer would carry copious supplies of the printed ballad and having secured the attention of his audience, perform the work up to the point where it became really interesting, whereupon he would stop and demand that his listeners purchase a copy, before proceeding to the denouement. (Modern television follows a similar process today, by grouping advertising segments closer together as the drama approaches its climax.) News of a different sort was peddled across the river in Southwark – the 'red-light' district of Samuel's day, where working girls would entice customers with 'a ripe selection of filthy songs'. Pepys amassed an extensive collection of such printed ballads, more than 1,800 of which are still to be found in his library, preserved in Magdalene College, Cambridge.

If the diary is to be believed, the modern diner might find the seventeenth-century diet, at least for the wealthier classes, very light on fruit and vegetables and very heavy on protein and carbohydrate. Pepys makes frequent references in the diary to his food but almost never mentions anything green in his descriptions, which are confined almost exclusively to meat and fish (exceptions being a reference to the first green peas of the year and on another occasion 'the Spargus' (i.e. asparagus) garden': '... I had a pretty dinner for them – viz; a brace of stewed carps, six roasted chicken, and a jowl of salmon hot, for the first course – a Tanzy and two neats'[2] [i.e. calves] tongues and cheese the second.' (Diary 22nd March 1662)

Nevertheless, we can be reasonably sure that fruit and vegetables formed part of the average diet. Ben Johnson mentions 'artichokes and peason' as well as 'laxative lettuce' whilst John Evelyn wrote a whole book on the subject entitled *Acetaria, a Discourse of Sallets* in which he analyses the benefits or otherwise of vegetables and herbs according to the medical theories of the day. He gives a number of recipes for the eating, pickling and dressing of greenstuffs as well as a table of when to harvest various plants, so it is reasonable to suppose that his readers were well acquainted with the use of such foodstuffs, although some authorities of the time were cautious about their use:

---

2. A 'tansy' was an omelet of eggs and cream flavoured with the herb of the same name and thought to be beneficial for afflictions of the digestive tract including stomach ache and poor appetite. However, in any quantity it is known to be toxic and was sometimes used in times past to induce a miscarriage.

Be carefull in your diet. Eat noe meatte but flesh as is of an easy digestion: as mutton, veale, lambe, capon, chicken or the like: Avoide all raw salletts, or fruites: But for sallets use capers washed in warme water. And sallett of broome budds, or Asparagus or the topps of young hopps are good. Or Cowslipp flowers candiyed and mixed wth a little vinegar. Or rosemary flowers with a little vinegar and sugar. (Doctor's letter dated 1628 – Glamorgan Records Office, MS D/DF V/202)

In an age long before refrigeration and in the absence of winter feed such as turnips to sustain cattle through the barren months, most animals were slaughtered between September and December. In order to maintain supplies throughout the winter, meat had to be either dried, powdered [i.e. salted] or pickled. This inevitably left a strong taste of whatever process had been employed in its preservation, so that when it was cooked, it has been suggested that the addition of strong spice was required to make it palatable. True or not, the extensive use of spices can be clearly seen in a recipe from *The French Cook* of 1653 for Neats' [i.e. calves] tongues: 'Take your Tongues, and season them with Pepper, Salt and Nutmeg, then Lard them with great lard, and steep them all night in Claret-Wine, Wine-Vinegar, slic't Nutmegs and Ginger, whole Cloves, beaten Pepper and Salt.'

Whether or not Pepys ate what would now be considered to be a healthy diet must remain a subject for conjecture. We do know however, that he was a martyr for most of his life to severe constipation. We also know that he suffered from a young age from stones in his bladder, evinced by continual pain and blood in the urine. The condition was probably inherited – his mother suffered from the same complaint:

'And there found my mother still ill of the stone and hath just newly voided one, which she hath let drop into the Chimny; and could not find it to show it me.' (Diary 6th December 1660)

The symptoms became so bad that he decided to undergo surgery and consulted Thomas Hollier, a leading surgeon of the day. The severity of Pepys' condition can be judged from the fact that surgery was known to be exceedingly dangerous and survival rates were low. Hygiene was extremely poor, and with no knowledge of bacteria, disease was thought to be spread by *miasmers*; poison gasses emanating from the open sewers. These were combated by carrying a perfumed sponge under the nose. The surgeon operated in his everyday clothes, and surgical instruments were often left lying on the floor. As an anaesthetic, patients would either sniff opium-soaked sponges or drink large quantities of alcohol, which had little numbing effect and the patient still had to be tied down during the operation, or, as Pepys was, strapped upright into an open-seated chair. It was common for the patient to die from loss of blood or infection from the filthy conditions. After an operation instruments would not be put into water, as that would make them rust, so rather than wash them, they would simply be wiped with a cloth and the surgeon would then move on to his next patient.

Pepys underwent the operation in the bedroom of his cousin's house on 26th March 1658 and the stone was successfully removed, an unlikely deliverance which he celebrated with a dinner on the anniversary of the day for many years thereafter – some sources calculate that up to 80 per cent of patients did not survive long after an invasive operation. Pepys was still suffering from stones in his urinary system at the very end of his life, and indeed they may have contributed in no small measure to his death: '… upon opening his body…there was found in his left Kidney a nest of no less than 7 stones, of the most irregular Figures your imagination can frame, and weighing together 41/2 ounces. …' (Letter from nephew John Jackson to John Evelyn 28th May 1703)

In many respects, the seventeenth century is a continuation of the medieval world, in religion, medicine, law and social structure. Yet it is the century when enormous changes in natural philosophy and science take place and can truly be said to be the dawn of the modern world, when medieval alchemy gives way to chemistry and astrology evolves into astronomy. By its close, a revolution had occurred and science had become an established mathematical, mechanical, and empirical body of knowledge. In mathematics came logarithms and calculus, in physics electricity and the Laws of Motion. Ingenious invention abounded – the first calculating machines appeared, as did the submarine (at least in theory) and the slide-rule. Horizons were expanding not only on the earth, but the heavens could be observed for the first time in close up through the invention of the telescope. In 1638, Dr John Wilkins writes *The Discovery of a World in the Moone* with a prophetic appendix entitled *The Possibility of a Passage Thither*. At the other end of the scale, the previously unsuspected microcosm of the world invisible to the naked eye was revealed for the first time through the lenses of Robert Hooke's microscope. It is the century that gave us Newton, Descartes, Galileo and Pascal.

If we find much of Pepys' world daunting and strange, the one aspect of human behaviour and human frailty that we can immediately recognise is the one associated with sex. Much of Pepys' London had long-established and overt sexual connections; in the thirteenth century, St Pancras had a 'Gropecunt Lane' while Smithfield boasted a more romantically titled 'Love Lane'. However, for centuries the same area harboured a red-light district centered around 'Cock Lane'. Pepys was the first to acknowledge his own fallibility in this respect: '…music and women I cannot but give way to, whatever my business is.' (Diary 28th February 1666)

This then was the world into which Samuel Pepys was born and in which he lived his life, a life that would be largely spent in the company of the great and the good (and the not so good) of his day; wealthy, respected and influential, but with very human flaws and fallibility – truly the life of a celebrity.

Chapter 2

Pepys the Celebrity

The end of the twentieth century and the beginning of the twenty-first has seen an unprecedented rise in the cult of the celebrity. Many have achieved fame by simply being famous (and in most cases accruing great wealth as a result) without contributing much to the greater good. It is thought by many that the cult of the celebrity has perverted children's aspirations and that a generation of children has grown up believing that education and hard work are not important in achieving success.

This book is predicated on the assumption that Samuel Pepys can be thought of as a celebrity. For many, his only claim to fame is that he kept a diary, yet given his many and varied achievements, it would be difficult to argue that in his day he could hardly be regarded as otherwise. However, how he achieved this status is in stark contrast to the route that many have followed in the present age.

Samuel was a grammar school boy who, in common with many others fortunate to have been educated in that way, made it to the highest ranks of influence and privilege. He first attended the grammar school in Huntingdon and then, when the English civil war came to an end, he returned to London and St Paul's School, where he was an enthusiastic and diligent scholar, his application being rewarded with an exhibition to Magdalene College, Cambridge. In fact, he was also awarded a similar exhibition to Trinity Hall, where he would have studied law. In fact, this opportunity was never taken up, either because he could not afford it, or because he had no enthusiasm for a legal career – we will probably never know which. Thus at the then advanced age of 18 (14 was a common age in the seventeenth century for university entrance) Samuel Pepys went off to Cambridge.

He graduated with a Bachelor of Arts degree in March 1654, after which he apparently went home to live with his parents, as many a newly graduated scholar does to this day. At some point in the next two years – we do not know exactly when – Pepys began working as a government clerk in the Exchequer, a position found for him by Edward Montagu, not just a distant relation, but significantly a close confident of Oliver Cromwell. As Pepys was married in December 1655, it is reasonable to suppose that by this date he was gainfully employed. He continued in this employment until 1660, when a changing political climate caused almost all the Exchequer clerks to be sacked and others employed in their place. Pepys, however, remained long enough in his job to be able to resign when his life took a new and momentous direction.

In June 1660, with a reputation for diligence and reliability, and not a little sponsorship from his influential relation, Montagu, who had been recently appointed Master of the Wardrobe in the newly established court of King Charles II, Samuel found himself with the position of Clerk of the Acts with the Navy Board at a salary of £350 per year, no small sum at that time. Not only was there the substantive salary and the opportunity to earn very much more by way of gifts (generally what we would now describe as bribes), but the job came with accommodation by way of a house (or at least part of a large Navy Board building which had been sub-divided into five residencies) in Seething Lane, near the Tower of London.

Samuel's luck did not stop there. In September, Montagu, now the Earl of Sandwich, secured him a second job, albeit part-time, as a clerk at the Privy Seal Office. With a double income and a rent-free house, Pepys was on his way, the beginning of a period of ever more lucrative advancement. In September 1660 he was made a Justice of the Peace, and then on 15 February 1662 he was admitted as a Younger Brother of Trinity House. On 30 April he received the freedom of the city of Portsmouth. Through Lord Sandwich, he was involved in the administration of the short-lived English colony at Tangier, having joined the Tangier committee in August 1662 when the colony was first founded, and subsequently became its treasurer in 1665. He was appointed to a commission of the Royal Fishery on 8 April 1664. All these appointments required the granting of favours, the dispensation of money or the issuing of contracts, all activities that generated substantial wealth in the seventeenth century, even for a basically honest man like Samuel Pepys.

In October 1665 (incidentally a year in which he quadrupled his fortune) he was appointed surveyor-general of victualling for the navy, a position which alone brought in a further £300 a year, at a time when the average working class man or woman's income was, depending upon your occupation, between £5 and £12 per annum.

In the same year, he was elected a Fellow of the Royal Society, a body established by Royal Charter which grew out of the meetings twenty years earlier of natural philosophers to promote knowledge of the natural world through observation and experiment. He was destined to become President of the Society in 1684. In the fourteen years between 1673 and 1687, Pepys was to sit three times as a Member of Parliament. In 1685 James II granted a royal charter which named Pepys, already the Secretary for the Admiralty, as the first Master of the Trinity House, a body which had first come into being under King Henry VIII to improve the art and science of mariners, '… make our trusty and well beloved Samuel Pepys Esquire, Secretary of our Admiralty of England, to be the first and present Master of the said Guild.'

Pepys was not only a successful man in his chosen career. The same application that he demonstrated at school was reflected in whatever activity he chose to pursue, including the pursuit of the opposite sex. Women were not the only consuming passion in his life, although after his career, they probably ranked the foremost of his several obsessions. Alongside his constant need for sexual gratification (at least in the first half of his life) he maintained a passionate interest in music (an interest he almost certainly inherited from his father) and he composed, sang and played a variety of instruments, including the lute, viol, violin, flageolet, recorder and spinet. In some of these he attained more than a passing degree of proficiency – his lessons on the flageolet came from the master of that instrument in his day, Thomas Greeting. The familiar portrait of Samuel painted in 1666 by John Hayls, shows him holding the manuscript of his song 'Beauty Retire'. To the beauty of both women and music, he himself acknowledged that he found both irresistible: 'God forgive me, I could not think it too much; which is a strange slavery that I stand in to beauty, that I value nothing near it.' (Diary 6th September 1664)

Pepys' third great passion was for books. As an undergraduate, he had tried his hand at writing and had produced a romance entitled 'Love a Cheate'. It obviously did not meet the standards he set himself, or perhaps contained material which might have caused him embarrassment, as when he chanced upon the manuscript some years later in his life, he threw it on the fire. His classical education, coupled with an innate curiosity about art and science – 'with child to see any strange things' (Diary 14th May 1660) led him to become a life-long bibliophile. His collection of more than 3,000 volumes is preserved intact to this day in a purpose-built library in Magdalene College, Cambridge University and remains one of the most important surviving libraries of the seventeenth century. Apart from the bound volumes of the diary, there are 60 medieval manuscripts, including works by William Caxton and Wynkyn de Worde, more than 1,800 printed ballads and unique priceless survivors such as the personal autographed almanac of Sir Francis Drake, all beautifully preserved in bespoke tooled leather bindings. The books are preserved in the bespoke book cases or 'presses' that Pepys had made to his own specification.

Pepys made the bequest of his library to Magdalene College conditional upon none of the books from the collection being sold and no additional ones added. The building in which they are housed took thirty-three years to complete, due to a lack of money – Pepys himself putting his hand in his pocket on three separate occasions. Construction was eventually completed in 1703. On the front of the building is the inscription *Bibliotheca Pepysiana 1724*, being the date of arrival of the library; above it are Pepys's arms and his motto taken from Cicero's 'De Republica': *Mens cujusque est quisque* – The Mind is the Man. Pepys could hardly have chosen a more appropriate motto for himself.

Chapter 3

Full Forty Times Over

The first woman to influence the young Pepys was of course, as it is for all men, his mother. Margaret Kite was an uneducated wash-maid, the daughter of a butcher whom his father John Pepys had married in 1626. Although the diary contains 128 references to his mother, the entries are generally brief and give us no clue about Pepys' relationship with her or how he felt about her. Most usually she is simply mentioned as being present when he visits his father, and instances that contain any insight into her character or their relationship are rare. However, Pepys was a well-educated man who must at times have found his mother's lack of sophistication irritating, as is clear from his diary entry relating to an occasion when he stumbled upon his parents in the middle of a domestic row:

> So to my father, and there finding a discontent between my father and mother about the maid (which my father likes and my mother dislikes), I staid till 10 at night, persuading my mother to understand herself, and that in some high words, which I was sorry for, but she is grown, poor woman, very froward. So leaving them in the same discontent I went away home, it being a brave moonshine, and to bed. (Diary 1st April 1661)

When she died in 1667, Pepys' main concern seems to be less about his recent bereavement than about the cost of the funeral: '… vexed about two or three things … at the charge which my mother's death for mourning will bring me when all is paid.' (Diary 3rd April 1667)

The expenditure is still exercising his mind two days later when he is obliged to settle the accounts:

> … up and down, to pay all my scores occasioned by this mourning for my mother – and emptied a 50l bag; and it was a joy to me to see that I am able to part with such a sum without much inconvenience – at least, without any trouble of mind. (Diary 6th April 1667)

His mother only makes one further and rather strange appearance in the diary, after which she disappears from the narrative for ever; on the night of the 28th/29th June 1667 Pepys is awoken by a disturbing dream in which his father, sister and mother meet him at the gate of his office and his mother tells him that she lacks a pair of gloves. In the dream, Pepys decides that his mother is not dead after all, and should anyone make enquiry, they would be told that it was his mother-in-law who had passed away. He goes back to sleep, only to begin another strange (and possibly Freudian) dream:

> Then I dreamed that I had great pain of the stone in making water, and that once I looked upon my yard [penis] in making water at the steps before my door, and there I took hold of a thing and pulled it out, and it was a turd. ...
> (Diary 29th June 1667)

When he went up to Cambridge in his mid teens, Pepys was 5 feet 1 inch in height (155 centimetres), short even for the seventeenth century, when the average height for men was 5 feet 5 ¾ inches (167 centimetres), with thick lips and large enquiring eyes. Nevertheless, he was probably already possessed of the ability to mix easily with all sorts and conditions of men (and women), with a ready wit, a thirst for knowledge and a combative nature in debate. As a Cambridge undergraduate, Pepys was a good scholar and came down from university with a good degree. There must however have been temptations; the regime in the university was puritanical and college rules were strict – students were not allowed to gamble, attend dances or other popular entertainments such as the Sturbridge fair. Nevertheless, we know from an entry in the college register for 21st October 1653 that Pepys and another scholar were solemnly admonished by the Dean for 'having been scandalously over served with drink the night before.' Nothing changes in student life.

From his earliest years, there is little doubt that Pepys took pleasure from watching women, seeking out their company at any opportunity, and that this predilection was well established by the time he went up to university. To what extent he succumbed to their charms whilst a student is difficult to say, although there must have been temptations for a well-set-up young man, away from home for the first time. We know of some of the women with whom he came into contact whilst an undergraduate; there was Goody Mulliner who lived opposite Magdalene College and from whom he apparently purchased prunes. There were the sisters Archer; Mary, who married a fellow student, and more especially Betty, whom Pepys tells us: '... I did admire at Cambridge ... and many times we had her sister Betty's health, whose memory I love.' (Diary 25th November 1661)

It is clear that Pepys also became closely acquainted with less respectable women, as he recollects upon a subsequent visit in later years:

> ... and before night did come to Bishop Stafford, where Louther and his friend did meet us again and carried us to the Raynedeere, where Mrs. Aynsworth (and lived heretofore at Cambridge and whom I knew better than they think for, doth live – it was the woman that, among other things, was great with my Cosen Barmston of Cottenham, and did use to sing to him and did teach me Full Forty Times Over, a very lewd song) doth live, a woman

they are very well acquainted with, and is here what she was at Cambridge, and all the good-fellows of the country come hither. (Diary 7th October 1667)

What she had been at Cambridge was a procuress who had been publicly whipped out of town at the cart's tail by the university authorities in punishment for her wicked ways. She subsequently took over the Rein Deer Inn at Bishop's Stortford, where, despite having driven her out of Cambridge under the sting of the lash, the Vice-Chancellor and some heads of colleges stayed on their way to London and where they were 'nobly entertained'. She was obviously more than a casual acquaintance to Pepys, and knew him well enough to teach him lewd songs. The diary continues:

… we to supper and so to bed, my wife and I in one bed and the girl in another in the same room. And lay very well, but there was so much tearing company in the house, that we could not see my landlady, so I had no opportunity of renewing my old acquaintance with her. (Diary 7th October 1667)

One wonders what form such a renewal might have taken. Pepys had no better luck on a subsequent occasion on which he stayed at the inn: 'And so away to Bishops Stafford, and there dined and changed horses and coach at Mrs. Aynsworth's; but I took no knowledge of her.' (Diary 23rd May 1668)

The lyrics of the song Mrs Aynsworth taught Pepys, which he describes as being 'very lewd' comes down to us via a document entitled 'Merry Drollery' dated 1661; the lewdness is very much of the double-entendre variety and pretty innocuous by modern standards (See Appendix A for full text):

There's a breach readymade, which still open hath been,
With thousands of thoughts to betray it within,
If you once but approach you are sure to get in,
Then stand not off coldly,
But venter on boldly,
With weapon in hand.

Other women flit across the pages of the diary without revealing to what extent, if any, they contributed to the sexual education of the young Pepys. There is the London neighbour from Salisbury Court, Elizabeth Whittle, for whom as a boy he confesses that he had 'a great opinion' and flattered her by making anagrams on her name. (She was destined to become the grandmother of Charles James Fox, the great anti-slavery campaigner). Whilst visiting his well-to-do cousin, John Pepys, on Epsom Downs, he meets one Mrs Hely, with whom he implies that he experienced his first stirrings of sexual affection: 'Down to Minnes Wood with great pleasure view my old walks…where Mrs. Hely and I did use to walk and talk, with whom I had the first sentiments of love and pleasure in a woman's company.' (Diary 26th July 1663)

She was clearly not averse to a little familiarity as he tells us that he began the walk by '… discourse and taking her by the hand – she being a pretty woman', though to what else, if anything, she was not averse we will probably never know. To what extent Pepys was successful or otherwise with women in his younger days we can only guess at. That he had an eye for attractive ladies is evidenced by his marriage to Elizabeth – physically attractive but without any domestic skills or a dowry. Whatever her physically attractive characteristics, they were obviously insufficient to keep the young Pepys satisfied. In the diary period, it becomes very obvious that he is continually on the lookout for the opportunity to engage in some extra-marital fun and games:

> So over the water to Westminster hall, and not finding Mrs. Lane, with whom I purposed to be merry, I went to Jervas's and took him and his wife over the water to their mother Palmer's (the woman that speaks in the belly [i.e. a ventriloquist], and with whom I have two or three years ago made good sport with Mr. Mallard, thinking because I had heard that she is a woman of that sort that I might there have lit upon some lady of pleasure (for which God forgive me), but blest be God there was none, nor anything that pleased me. … (Diary 4th August 1663)

The diary period covers nearly a decade of Pepys' life from the age of twenty-seven. Despite being married to the physically attractive Elizabeth, he had several long-term mistresses and engaged in casual affairs with maidservants, barmaids and companions along with the wives, daughters and mothers of friends and colleagues. He found or engineered opportunities to fondle, grope and kiss most attractive women with whom he came into contact, in their homes, the backrooms of inns, in carriages, in theatre stalls, church pews or even whilst assisting the wife of an admiral and long-standing acquaintance when she got her feet wet:

> … we did send for a pair of old shoes for Mrs. Lowther, and there I did pull the others off and put them on, and did endeavour para tocar su thigh [to touch her thigh] but ella [she] had drawers on, but yo did besar la and tocar sus mamelles [I did kiss her and touch her breasts], elle [she] being poco [very] shy, but doth speak con [with] mighty kindness to me that she would desire me pour su marido [for her husband] if it were to be done. Here staid a little at Sir W. Penn's, who was gone to bed, it being about 11 at night, and so I home to bed. (Diary 10th May 1668)

The wearing of 'drawers' [knickers or panties as we might now know them] was a new habit in the seventeenth century, so not something that would inhibit Pepys' underskirt explorations very often. It was no doubt a fashion many of the ladies with whom Pepys became acquainted might have wished they had adopted.

Chapter 4

Better to Marry than to Burn

'But if they cannot contain, let them marry: for it is better to marry than to burn' says Corinthians Chapter 1 verse 9. In seventeenth-century England, despite an increased interest in pornography, sexual morals played a vitally important role in society and the institution of marriage provided a necessary outlet for the baser human instincts. In the family unit, the man ruled over wife, children and servants, commanding them in their duties and disciplining them wherever and whenever he considered it necessary.

In a society strongly influenced by (although by no means always adhering to) Puritan values, the social status of a married person afforded a woman some inherent respectability. In any event, the difficulty for a woman of finding ways to make an independent living meant that finding and securing a husband was a matter of great importance.

Pepys was 22 when he met the 14-year-old Elizabeth St Michel, his wife to be. Her father Alexandre was the disinherited son of the High Sheriff of Bauge, who had come to England as a minor courtier to Henrietta Maria, the betrothed of Charles I. Dismissed after a fight with a cleric over a religious argument, he had married Dorothea, the daughter of an Irish knight. Although she had come with a substantial dowry, he had squandered this attempting to regain his French estates, been imprisoned as a mercenary and robbed of what little money remained. The family again returned to France with Alexandre commanding a company of English foot soldiers sent to assist the French in the siege of Dunkirk. With the father away at the wars, the family lived in Paris for some three years, until Madame St Michel fell under the influence of the papists and the strongly protestant Alexandre whisked them all back to England.

We are unaware of how Pepys came to know them – it has been suggested that they may have attended the same church, and the young Samuel would undoubtedly have noticed the budding Elizabeth, already a beauty with a fair skin and well-developed breasts – we will discover in due course that (in the days long before women's skirts revealed their legs) Pepys was very much a 'breast man'. By the time of their meeting, the St Michel family was living in genteel poverty in Westminster. Alexandre lived by his wits, money donated by friends and four shillings (twenty pence) a week from the French church in London. He had turned his mind to 'whimsies and propositions', inventing perpetual motion machines as well as processes for curing smoking chimneys, purifying water, moulding bricks and raising sunken ships, all of them completely useless.

Elizabeth may have been a great beauty, but she was as poor as a church mouse. Later in life, Pepys was to read and re-read *Advice to a Son* by Francis Osborne, written in 1656. Osborn's advice was that putative husbands should be certain of getting a good dowry with their brides: 'The best of husbands are servants' he wrote, 'but he that takes a wife wanting money is a slave to his affection, doing the basest of drudgeries without wages.' Poor though she might have been, there is no doubt that Elizabeth considered herself to be an aristocrat. Pepys may have been enraptured by her voluptuous beauty, but outside the bedroom she was a poor catch as a wife, never having been taught the skills of household management or the virtues of thrift and frugality. All through their married life, they were perpetually at loggerheads over her inability to keep accounts, maintain a clean and tidy house, or manage the servants.

Notwithstanding these shortcomings, Samuel Pepys and Elizabeth were married in church on 10 October 1655, two weeks before her fifteenth birthday. The wedding breakfast was eaten at a tavern on Fish Street Hill, but England was then a republic and the couple were not legally married until a civil ceremony had taken place, which was duly held in the presence of a magistrate on 1 December.

Their married life began in Pepys' rooms in the lodging of Sir Edward Montagu and three years would pass before they were able to move into a small house of their own in Axe Yard, where they lived on twenty shillings (one pound) a week. Sometime during this period there occurred a serious falling-out of the young couple and it appears that the pair separated for a while and Elizabeth moved out of the matrimonial home. As this episode predates the diary period, we do not know the details – Pepys, who hated to be reminded of it, described the occurrence later on as 'our differences'. The cause of the marital disharmony can only be guessed at, but it may well have given rise to some involvement with the law, or at very least, some litigious correspondence, as on the 13th August 1661, the diary entry reads:

> After dinner I went to my father's, where I found him within, and went up to him, and there found him settling his papers against his removal, and I took some old papers of difference between me and my wife and took them away.
> (Diary 13th August 1661)

Certainly, it led to a temporary separation, with Elizabeth going into lodgings with a Mrs Palmer at Charing Cross. Then as now, difficulties in marriage can arise from a variety of causes. It may have been over money, as Pepys was used to accounting for every penny spent and all through their married life, kept his wife short of funds. However, in this early period Elizabeth was used to having very little and knew that her husband, although he had a modest regular income, was not a wealthy man. Perhaps it was Pepys' jealousy, an emotion that Elizabeth was later to describe as his 'old disease'. All through their life together, Pepys suspected his wife of having affairs and indeed several men made improper suggestions to her, which she apparently rebutted in the most robust manner. Ironically, whilst he behaved in a most despicable way throughout their married life, there is no evidence whatever that Elizabeth was ever unfaithful to her husband.

The problems may have arisen – as many marital problems do – in the bedroom. Pepys was clearly a highly sexed young man with powerful appetites, and the marital satisfaction of these was inhibited from the outset by Elizabeth's gynaecological problems. These continued throughout their married life, as the diary records:

'When I came home I found my wife not very well of her old pain in the lip of her chose which she had when we were first married.' (Diary 2nd August 1660)

Elizabeth Pepys health was an ongoing issue throughout the diary period. She often suffered from a recurring abscess, now believed to be a Bartholin's cyst, which often made sexual relations difficult for the couple. The Bartholin's glands are a pair of pea-sized glands found just behind and either side of the lips that surround the entrance to the vagina and which secrete the fluid that acts as a lubricant during sex. The fluid travels down tiny tubes, called ducts, into the vagina. If the ducts become blocked, they can fill with fluid and expand to form a cyst which later develops into a painful abscess: 'This day my wife hath been troubled with her boyles in the old place, which doth much trouble her.' (Diary 21st October 1660)

'My wife hath been so ill of late of her old pain that I have not known her this fortnight almost, which is a pain to me.' (Diary 31st October 1660)

Certainly, something made the usual intimate relations between husband and wife much less regular than then or now might be considered normal: '…lay with her tonight – which I have not done these 8 or 10 days before.' (Diary 14th April 1661)

… and sometimes, an even longer period elapsed without sexual congress: '… she took notice that I had not lain with her this half-year. …' (Diary 2nd August 1667)

Pepys rectifies this shortly thereafter, but he thinks it to be only three months since they had sexual intercourse:

My wife waked betimes to call up her people to washing, and so to bed again; whom I then hugged, it being cold now in the mornings, and then did la otra cosa con her [the other thing with her] which I had not done con ella [with her] for these tres meses [three months] past, which I do believe is a great matter toward the making her of late so indifferent towards me, and with good reason; but now she had much pleasure, and so to sleep again. (Diary 12th August 1667)

Whatever the reasons for the difficulties in their marriage, and in spite of the breach caused by Pepys' extra marital affairs, they remained together throughout the rest of the diary period. Shortly after the diary ended, Mr and Mrs Pepys travelled together to Paris with her brother Balty. It is not known exactly what itinerary they followed on their trip, but upon their return, Elizabeth developed a severe fever. A letter to a friend dated 2 November 1669 captures the severity of Elizabeth's illness and shows that Pepys was already facing the possibility of her death:

SIR. I beg you to believe that I would not have been ten days returned into England without waiting on you, had it not pleased God to afflict mee by the sickness of my wife, who, from the first day of her coming back to London, hath layn under a fever so severe as at this hour to render her recoverie desperate. ... (Letter from Samuel Pepys to John Evelyn 2nd November 1669)

Elizabeth died on November 10, 1669. Pepys did not attend any Navy Board activities for nearly four weeks. He never re-married, although a female companion apparently shared the rest of his life until his death more than thirty years later, in a relationship so close that many of his contemporaries including John Evelyn, sometimes – perhaps in a Freudian slip – referred to her as Mrs Pepys. He was able to acknowledge her in his will in terms that reveal what a close relationship it had been, although why they never married is likely forever to remain a mystery. (See Chapter 20 'Last Love')

Chapter 5

A Woman's Place

Any historical exploration involving the relationship between men and women, especially as far back as the seventeenth century, must take account of the fact that women's place in society was radically different from our modern concept. To begin with, women were seen as being much weaker than men, both physically, morally and intellectually, and in that perception, western society had the support of the Christian religion. Under common law, women had no rights at all (other than some allowed for under ancient custom). A woman's status could be defined in only one of three ways; maid, wife or widow. There was no such thing as a 'career woman', in spite of the fact that many women earned a living in the retail trades, as did several who came under the lustful eye of Mr Pepys.

Women were certainly the victims of what would now be regarded as sexual harassment or even minor sexual assault, of which Pepys was an inveterate practitioner at any opportunity:

> … Betty Mitchell … did stay to endeavour to meet with her and carry her home; but she did not come, so I lost my whole afternoon. But pretty, how I took another pretty woman for her, taking her a clap on the breech [a slap on the bottom], thinking verily it had been her. (Diary 1st October 1666)
> … we did send for a pair of old shoes for Mrs. Lowther, and there I did pull the others off and put them on, and did endeavour to touch her thigh but she had drawers on, but I did kiss her and touch her breasts.… (Diary 10th May 1668)

Virginity was seen as a virtue in those of pre-marital age, but once that age was passed, women who remained unmarried were regarded with suspicion, and the term 'old maid' has always been a pejorative one. As an unmarried maiden, a woman's rights were subordinated to her father, who could dispose of her in marriage as he chose. It is no accident of language that the traditional marriage ceremony still includes the question 'who giveth this woman to be married to this man?'

In the higher echelons of society the young woman commonly had little or no say in the choice of a partner, and should she object to the arrangement made for her, she was unlikely to receive much sympathy or support, even from her mother.

When the diarist John Evelyn's daughter eloped in 1685, he wrote to Pepys: '... confess it harder to me, than had been her Death, which we should have less regretted.' (Letter to Samuel Pepys from John Evelyn dated 29th July 1685)

In 1617, Frances Coke, the 14-year-old daughter of the jurist Sir Edward Coke, refused to be betrothed to the 26-year-old Sir John Villiers, who, by the by, was subject to occasional bouts of insanity. Her mother, Lady Elizabeth Hatton (she had retained her title from her first marriage) had her daughter tied to the bedposts and whipped until she consented to the match.

In seventeenth-century England, marriage and sexual morality held a pivotal place in society. The family centered on a married couple representing the basic social, economic and political unit. The rule of a husband over his wife, children and servants was seen as analogous to the king's reign over his people – part of a hierarchy ordained by God. A woman was seen as the weaker vessel, physically, intellectually, morally and spiritually inferior, whose moral frailty the Bible told us had been instrumental in bringing about mankind's fall from grace.

In this climate the status of a married person gave women respectability and social standing, so finding a husband was a matter of great importance. This could be legally achieved at a very early age by today's standards – 12 years of age for girls and 14 years of age for boys. Moreover, it was possible in the higher echelons of society for the couple to become engaged at the now unbelievably early age of 7.

The ability to run a household efficiently was seen to be a highly desirable quality in a woman – puritans often talked of 'helpmates' in this context. Where self-selection of a mate was permitted (generally amongst the lower classes) romantic love and sexual attraction played no less a part in choosing a partner than they do today. Pepys seems to have married for these latter reasons alone – his poorly educated wife Elizabeth came from a family of impoverished Catholic immigrants and her father was a continual source of embarrassment to him, both socially and financially, throughout their marriage.

Inextricably linked with marriage was the tricky issue of sexuality. Marriage provided the only vehicle in which the seventeenth-century woman could legitimately express her sexual desires. Infidelity in marriage was severely punished, as was incest. The Rump Parliament, which passed a series of draconian laws between 1649 and 1653, even imposed the death penalty upon conviction for either offence (although as far as we know the penalty was never imposed). Girls were expected to remain virgins until after the wedding day, although some sources claim that 25 per cent of seventeenth-century Englishwomen were pregnant at the time of their wedding! Thereafter it was considered a husband's duty to ensure his wife's fidelity by circumventing any situation that might tempt his wife to stray from the path of virtue.

Any deviation from the proscribed norm in terms of sexual behaviour might bring down the full weight of the law upon the unfortunate woman's head. There was clearly a universal perception (at least among men) that women who were sexually promiscuous deserved a flogging, a remedy prescribed and applied from Biblical times. Neither did women have to engage in prostitution to suffer the painful consequences. Women whose only crime was to engage in a sexual liaison outside marriage were considered fit to be whipped. The following anonymous verse was found on a piece of paper in the Essex Assizes Michaelmas Sessions Roll for 1583 – whether it is by the hand of a slighted lover or a jealous wife is a matter of conjecture:

> Here dwelleth an arrant bichant whore
> Such one as deserves the cart
> Her name is Margaret Townsend now
> The horn shows her desert.

(The reference to the cart refers to the fact that public whippings were often carried out with the victim being dragged through the streets tied to the tailboard of such a vehicle whilst the lash was applied, considered to be a more severe punishment than a whipping at the post. The magistrate would specify the route to be taken – the longer the journey, the more severe the punishment. Some routes could take an hour or more to complete.)

In the days before any form of reliable birth control, the results of any illicit unions were often only too plain to see. The Quarter Sessions of Devonshire in 1598 ordered that all mothers of bastard children should be whipped and this soon became common practice throughout the country. The Puritans tried to eliminate all situations where the sexes might encounter temptation by banning pageants and all forms of entertainment, including dancing and the theatre, both of which were considered inventions of the devil. Once respectably married, a woman's husband replaced her father in governance: 'Teach her to live under obedience, and whilst she is unmarried, if she would learn anything, let her ask you, and afterwards her husband.' (Sir Ralph Verney 1613–1693 'At Home')

Whatever money or belongings she owned became the property of her spouse, whom she had promised to 'love, honour and obey'. If she failed or refused to obey her husband, he was legally entitled to beat her until she complied with his wishes, colloquially with a stick no thicker than his thumb: 'A dog, a woman, a walnut tree; the more they're beaten the better still they be.' (1670 J. Ray – English Proverbs)

If, in these circumstances, the marriage proved to be an unhappy one, women were not allowed to sue for divorce, and only after 1670 could men pursue such a course, but it required a private Act of Parliament, putting it out of the question and out of reach for all but the very wealthiest in the land. By the mid-nineteenth century, only 200 people had ever attempted it, and only six of these were women.

A substitute option was declaring the marriage invalid, but to do this, it had to be proved that the marriage was defective in some way; impotence in the man or frigidity in the wife or the revelation that the couple were related. Declaring the marriage invalid gave both partners an opportunity to remarry but the wife lost all her inheritance and any children by the union were proclaimed illegitimate. Another way out an unhappy marriage was a legal separation 'from bed and board' (i.e. bed and table). This alternative was only possible in cases of proven adultery or extreme cruelty. Contrary to declaring the marriage invalid, the separation did not affect the wife's inheritance nor the legitimate status of the children. However, the disadvantage was that the marriage remained undivided and the separated partners could not remarry.

In the seventeenth century, the majority of married women (unless they had married a landless labourer) would have set up home in the countryside where most of the population lived and made a living by farming and husbandry. A husbandman would have had a 'smallholding' i.e. a very small farm, which took two people to run effectively. The housewife would generally be expected to be in charge of the poultry and the dairy. She would raise the chickens, milk the cows and make butter and cheese. She would sell her surplus eggs, chickens, cheese, and butter at market. She would brew the ale that the family drank – water was considered (and in reality was) unsafe to drink and in her spare time spin wool or flax for the family's use.

The majority of the professions such as law or medicine were forbidden to women. However, a woman of good character could become a midwife. This was a prestigious career for a woman, requiring to be licensed by the bishop and then as now engendered the respect of the community she served. A woman who was married to a tradesman or craftsman would often be involved in the family business, since businesses in the seventeenth century were most often conducted from home, as was the tailoring business of Pepys' father. It was by no means unknown for a widow to continue running a business after her husband died. Neither was it unknown for a woman to be in business on her own account (as was Pepys' mistress Mrs Betty Martin), most usually associated with the haberdashery or gloving trades, but also with inn keeping and brewing, and from the Restoration, the theatre and the stage.

A woman who failed to find a husband and had no business of her own had very limited choices when it came to making a living. The commonest job for a poor single woman would be in domestic service, which inevitably meant living with the family she worked for and generally being treated as a junior member of the family. Pepys tellingly opens his diary with the phrase: 'I lived in Axe yard, having my wife and servant Jane, and no more in family than us three.' (Diary: Introductory note January 1660)

Alternatively, she might find employment in selling food and drink or as a laundress. In the countryside, she might find employment on the local farms, milking or feeding animals. None of the jobs was skilled and all were badly paid – Pepys recorded one of his maids as earning £2 per year plus her keep.

Shoplifting was first designated a crime in the seventeenth century and often involved women stealing readily concealed items such as lace, gloves, ribbons etc. which could be easily sold. Penalties were harsh however – thefts of as little as a couple of shillings (10 pence) would result in a public whipping, and anything of greater value in seven years transportation to the colonies or even death by public hanging. Of course, the alternative living available to women was to join the oldest profession and many did. During the seventeenth century, the most notorious area for prostitution in the port of London was Ratcliffe Highway – a road lying to the north of the Wapping waterfront. It was described in 1600 by John Stow as: '… a continual street, or filthy straight passage, with alleys of small tenements or cottages builded [sic] inhabited by sailors and victuallers.'

Sailors from ships moored in the Pool of London flocked to the Highway. Most were single men with plenty of cash to spare after long voyages. They were looking for drink and women, and the taverns and brothels along its length provided for their every need. One of the most notorious (and most successful) of such women in the diary period was Damaris Page. She was born in Stepney around 1620, became a prostitute in her teens and married a man called William Baker in 1640. During the subsequent fifteen years she moved from being a prostitute to become a 'madam' running two brothels, one catering for ordinary seamen and the second more up-market establishment for naval officers and those who could afford more expensive, up-market prostitutes. It even catered for royalty, as Pepys observed: '… the Duke of York was mighty merry at that of Damaris Page's, the great bawd of the seamen.' (Diary 25th March 1668)

Damaris also had a lucrative sideline procuring sailors for the navy. At a Trinity House dinner on 7 June 1669, according to a scandalised note by Pepys, Sir Edward Spragge told him that as long as she lived '… hee was sure hee would not lack Men. This among others Mr Evelin heard & took notice of it to mee with great affliction'. (Pepys: Navy White Book)

For the next 200 years, upon marriage, the husband and wife became one person under the law, the property of the wife being surrendered to her husband, and her legal identity would cease to exist. The subordinate status of women in England would not improve until the introduction of the Married Women's Property Act of 1882. This Act altered the common law doctrine of covertures to include the wife's right to own, buy and sell her separate property. Wives' legal identities were also restored, as the courts were forced to recognise a husband and a wife as two separate legal entities, in the same manner as if the wife was a single woman. For the first time, married women became liable for their own debts, and to hold stock in their own name. However, even in the twenty-first century, battles still rage over equal pay, and during the traditional marriage ceremony, the woman is still 'given away' by her father or nearest male relative!

Chapter 6

A Pretty Dutch Woman

On 23 March 1660 Pepys boards a ship to Holland with his employer, Edward Montagu, to bring Charles II home from exile; his specific job, other than being secretary to his boss, was the procurement of 'a rich barge' in which to ferry the king ashore. He was to be away from home and wife until the end of May. Even on the day of his departure, he cannot resist the opportunity to ogle a pretty woman, although on this occasion, his plan was frustrated:

> 'Shelston … had brought his wife, which he said was a very pretty woman, to the Ship tavern hard by for me to see, but I could not go.' (Diary 23rd March 1660)

Six months later we know that Shelston, who was a grocer, was seeking gainful employment from Pepys: 'Home, where Mr. Snow came to see me; and with him one Shelston, a simple felloe that looks after an imployment [sic] (that was with me just upon my going to sea last).' (Diary 10th September 1660)

Presumably he had earlier been persuaded by Pepys to exhibit his wife for approval, in the hope that it might form the basis of a future employment contract. There is no sound evidence for this conjecture, other than it appears unlikely that a husband would behave in this way unless there were some financial inducement, and secondly, we know that Pepys later commonly used the bait of career advancement to secure sexual favours from the wives of his subordinates. Perhaps Mr Shelston was already aware of Pepys' growing predilection for other men's pretty wives.

On 14 May, Pepys and a small party landed on the sandy Dutch shore close to The Hague and he and John Creed (a fellow secretary in the Montagu household) contrived to take a coach into town in company with two Dutch couples:

> The rest of the company got a coach by themselves. Mr Creed and I went in the fore-part of a coach, wherein there were two very pretty ladies, very fashionable and with black patches, who very merrily sang all the way and that very well. And were very free to kiss the two blades that were with them. (Diary 14th May 1660)

Is there just a touch of envy in that last observation? Pepys was clearly impressed by the look of the Dutch women he saw on his first visit to town: 'The women, many of them very pretty and in good habitt, fashionable, and black spots.' (Diary 15th May 1660)

Throughout the diary Pepys often mentions when ladies are wearing patches. A dark mole that occurs naturally on the face was sometimes called a beauty mark. Throughout the seventeenth century, fashionable women imitated this natural mark by sticking black beauty patches, called *mouches* on their faces. These patches were eventually used to send flirtatious signals to members of the opposite sex, but they had a practical use as well. Carefully shaped black patches could be applied to hide blemishes and scars on the face, especially the deep round scars left on those who survived the frequent outbreaks of smallpox, or any common or garden skin blemishes as when Pepys catches sight of the Duchess of Newcastle; 'She had many black patches because of pimples about her mouth.' (Diary 1st May 1667)

Soon, the patches began to take on particular meanings and to send subtle signals to others at parties and other social events. A patch near the eye indicated passion, for example, and one by the mouth showed boldness. A black spot on the right cheek marked a married woman, while one on the left cheek indicated that she was engaged to be married. They were even used to indicate the political preferences of the wearer, right cheek for Whigs, left cheek for Tories.

It is possible to sense the frustration of the young Pepys. Attracted to pretty women, he has not yet developed the confidence to approach them, like an awkward teenager who cannot summon a persuasive chat up line: 'Back by water, where a pretty sober Dutch lass sat reading all the way, and I could not fasten any discourse upon her.' (Diary 18th May 1660)

He had commented previously on the use of patches to be what he obviously thought to be an attractive trait: 'But my wife, standing near her [the Queen] with two or three black patches on and well dressed, did seem to me much handsomer than she.' (Diary 22nd November 1660)

Pepys may have approved of the fashion, but not everyone of the period approved:

> Ladies turn conjurers, and can impart
> The hidden mystery of the black art,
> Black artificial patches do betray;
> They more affect the works of night than day.
> The creature strives the Creator to disgrace,
> By patching that which is a perfect face:
> A little stain upon the purest dye
> Is both offensive to the heart and eye.
> Defile not then with spots that face of snow,

> Where the wise God His workmanship doth show,
> The light of nature and the light of grace
> Is the complexion for a lady's face.
>
> (*Flamma Sine Fumo*, by R. Watkyns, 1662)

On the 19th May, after a tourist visit to the village of Lausdune, Pepys and his party return to The Hague, where he comes across an old university chum named Anderson and his friend named Wright, now both physicians. They are obviously familiar with the lie of the land, for they take Pepys out with them…

> … to a Dutch house where there was an exceedingly pretty lass and right for the sport; but it being Saturday, we could not have much of her company; but however, I stayed with them. … till 12 at night; by that time Charles was almost drunk; and then broke up, he resolving to go thither again (after he had seen me at my lodgings) and lie with the girl, which he told me he had done in the morning.' (Diary 19th May 1660)

It seems clear that the 'Dutch house' is in fact a brothel, and it being a Saturday night, the 'exceedingly pretty lass' is unsurprisingly fully booked! Pepys, being a stranger in town, has to be seen home before his drinking partners can get down to the serious business of the evening. Pepys' frustration and envy are almost palpable.

Thus far on this journey, Pepys has had occasion only to gaze upon attractive women. Then on the 20th May, a real opportunity for some illicit sexual activity presents itself. In the seventeenth century, rooms at inns were often furnished with several beds, and these could and often were occupied by complete strangers of either sex. Whilst waiting for his transport, Pepys goes to the bedchamber for a bit of a rest:

> … I went to lie down in a chamber in the house, where in another bed there was a pretty Dutch woman in bed all alone; but though I had a month's-mind to her [i.e. to have a strong expectation or anticipation], I had not the boldness to go to her. So there I slept an hour or two. (Diary 20th May 1660)

The woman wakes up and Pepys paces about as he watches her dress, but then his courage fails him and he chickens out:

> At last she rise; and then I rise and walked up and down the chamber and saw her dress herself after the Dutch dress, and talked to her as much as I could; and took occasion, from her ring which she wore on her first finger, to kiss her hand; but had not the face to offer anything more. So at last I left her there and went to my company. (Diary 20th May 1660)

Strange as it may now seem to share a hotel room with a stranger of either gender, both that and the act of dressing in the presence of a member of the opposite sex (even though only the outer clothes would have been removed to go to bed) were not unusual in seventeenth century Europe:

> … and so to the King's house: and there, going in, met with Knepp, and she took us up into the tireing-rooms: and to the women's shift, where Nell was dressing herself, and was all unready, and is very pretty, prettier than I thought. (Diary 5th October 1667)

Likewise on a private social call:

> Thence to my Lady Peterborough, she desiring to speak with me; she loves to be taken dressing herself, as I always find her; and there, after a little talk to please her about her husband's pension…I away thence home. (Diary 27th January 1668)

How interesting that upon the occasion of his visits, Pepys should 'always find her' in the act of dressing herself – was Lady Peterborough herself titillated by his presence whilst engaged upon an intimate activity, or was she perhaps aware that such an overtly erotic distraction might work in her favour? Perhaps Pepys knew her habits and timed his visits accordingly – we will never know.

Later on in April, he visits the King's playhouse and …

> After the play done, I down to Knipp [sic] and did stay her undressing herself and there saw the several players, men and women, go by; and pretty, to see how strange they are all one to another after the play is done. Here I saw a wonderful pretty maid of her own, that come to undress her, and one so pretty that she says she intends not to keep her, for fear of her being undone in her service … (Diary 7th April 1668)

'Wonderful pretty maids' will figure large in Pepys' life. In the meantime, no further opportunities for dalliance appear to have presented themselves in Holland and on June 10th, Whit Sunday, Pepys is reunited with his wife Elizabeth. The entry for that day closes with 'to bed with my wife'. One hopes that she was in the right frame of mind and did not have a headache!

Chapter 7

Sunday Recreations

Church going and religious observance of Sunday was a serious matter in Pepys' day and infringements could be severely punished. For example, on Sunday, 30th April 1690, a married Durham woman named Eleanor Wilson was found to be intoxicated in church and as a result, was publicly stripped to the waist and whipped at the post on the following market day between the hours of 11.00 and 12.00 noon.

Pepys and his wife were of their time; religious and as a rule regular church goers by any standards, attending both morning and afternoon services on Sundays and holy days, as well as saying prayers at home in the evening. However, these habits were broken when other matters intervened and sometimes weeks might pass between church attendances. For example, during the period of the Great Fire of London in 1666, neither attended church at all between the 9th and 30th of September and again in 1668, when Pepys was heavily involved in the matter of the Tangier colony and the Committee for Accounts with regard to prize-goods, he failed to attend at all between the 26th January and the 29th March. On occasion however, this preoccupation with work did not prevent him from spending a good part of one Sunday reading a newly-acquired obscene book, *L'escholle des Filles* (Girls' School) by one Michel Millot:

> … and I to my chamber, where I did read through *L'escholle des Filles*; a lewd book, but what doth me no wrong to read for information sake but it did hazer [make] my prick to stand all the while, and una vez to decharger [made me have an orgasm]; and after I had done it, I burned it, that it might not be among my books to my shame. … (Diary 9th February 1668)

The Navy Office had a pair of private pews in St Olave's Church in the City of London and it was here that Samuel and Elizabeth most regularly attended, although sometimes, the prospect of an especially good sermon might attract them to worship elsewhere.

These attendances might have been of greater merit had Pepys not usually seen them as an opportunity to ogle pretty women, even on occasion through a small telescope, an experience which invariably made him randy:

… but I did entertain myself with my perspective glass up and down the church, by which I had the great pleasure of seeing and gazing (upon) a great many very fine women; and what with that and sleeping, I passed away the time till sermon was done; and then to Mrs. Martin and stayed with her an hour or two, and there did what I would with her. (Diary Sunday, 26th May 1667)

… my wife telling me that there was a pretty lady come to church with Peg Pen to-day, I against my intention had a mind to go to church to see her, and did so, and she is pretty handsome. (Diary 24th May 1663)

Sometimes, Pepys would become obsessed with watching one particular woman, even to the extent of engaging in what would now be regarded as stalking. These obsessions often lasted for years, for example, his fixation with a well-known beauty of the time: 'And just by the window that I stood at, there sat Mrs. Butler, the great beauty.' (Diary Sunday, 17th June 1660)

This obsession was to last throughout most of the diary period, without achieving any sort of consummation: 'In the afternoon to Henry the 7ths chapel – where I heard a sermon and spent (God forgive me) most of my time in looking upon Mrs. Butler.' (Diary Sunday, 17th June 1660)

'… but above all, the ladies that I then saw, or ever did see, Mrs. Frances Butler (Monsieur L'impertinent's sister) is the greatest beauty.'

'To our own church in the forenoon, and in the afternoon to Clerkenwell church [St James the Less] only to see the two fayre Botelers [i.e. Mrs. Butler and her sister]; and I happened to be placed in the pew where they afterwards came to sit. But the pew by their coming being too full, I went out into the next and there sat and had my full view of them.'

'… and thence to Clerkenwell church, and there (as I wished) sat next pew to the fair Butler, who endeed is a most perfect beauty still. And one I do very much admire myself for my choice of her for a beauty – she having the best lower part of her face that ever I saw all the days of my life.'

'… and so walked out to St. Jones's Church, thinking to have seen fair Mrs. Butler; but could not, she not being there – nor, I believe, lives thereabouts now.'

Pepys is still stalking the lovely Frances Butler eight years after the first diary entry referencing her: '… and so over the fields to Clerkenwell to see whether I could find that the fair Botelers do live there still, I seeing Frances the other day in a coach with Cary Dillon, her old servant, but know not where she lives.' (Diary 20th September 1668)

A similar obsession gripped Pepys when he visited his barber Richard Jervas in July 1664 and set eyes upon the maid Jane Walsh. He pursued her throughout the remainder of that year and throughout January 1665. He made several assignations with her, upon which she regularly stood him up: 'Left my wife to go to church alone; and I walked in haste, being late, to the Abbey at Westminster according to promise to meet Jane Walsh; and there wearily walked, expecting her till 6 a-clock from 3. But no Jane came, which vexed me.' (Diary Sunday, 11th September 1664)

Despite his disappointment, Pepys tried again the following week:

'After dinner walked to Westminster…and there spent all the afternoon in the Cloyster, as I had agreed with Jane Walsh; but she came not, which vexed me, staying till 5 a-clock.' (Diary Sunday, 18th September 1664)

> … into the New Year, he is still trying to meet the elusive Jane:
>
> … as I had appointed, to the Trumpett, there expecting when Jane Walsh should come; but anon comes a maid of the house to tell me that her mistress and maister would not let her go forth, not knowing of my being here but to keep her from her sweetheart. (Diary Sunday, 22nd January 1665)

Pepys never manages to obtain his wicked way with the lovely Jane and she eventually takes off with the wastrel of a boyfriend, who later turns out to be already married with a child. Interestingly, at no time does Pepys ever record any comments from his wife, regarding the fact that he often disappears for many hours at a time on Sunday afternoons with apparently no explanation of where he is going or with whom he is meeting.

Despite some rejections, Pepys enjoyed much more success with several other women whom he added to his ménage. On one occasion he was told a drunken story about a man who persuaded a gullible pretty woman to let him handle her private parts by pretending to be a doctor. The story made a deep impression on Pepys, so much so that he went looking for the woman concerned, no doubt hoping to repeat the trick. Whether she was the woman in the story or not, Pepys met Betty Lane, who worked in Westminster Hall, where she ran a draper's stall from which he sometimes bought his linen. During their long intimate relationship she married a Mr Martin, a change which did not seem to affect her relationship with Pepys one iota: '… and thence, going out of the hall, was called to by Mrs. Martin. So I went to her, and bought two bands and so parted, and by and by met at her chamber and there did what I would; and so away home …' (Diary Ash Wednesday, 28th February 1666)

> I to St. Margaret's Westminster, and there saw at church my pretty Betty Michell. And thence to the Abbey, and so to Mrs. Martin and there did what je voudrais avec her [did what I would with her], both devante [forward] and backward, which is also muy bon plazer [my great pleasure]. (Diary Sunday, 3rd June 1666)

And here I went to Mrs. Martin's to thank her for her oysters and there yo did hazer tout ce que je would con her, [did all that I would with her] and she grown la plus bold moher of the orbis (very bold woman of the world) so that I was almost defessus of the pleasure que ego was used para tener with ella [tired of the pleasure that I used to have with her]. (Diary 16th February 1666)

The diary contains 112 references to Mrs. Martin (b. Lane), more often than not along the lines of 'I did what I would with her'. Despite alleging that he is almost tired of her company, Pepys is still seeing her just before the diary period ends in May 1669: '… and so to Mrs. Martin's lodging, who come to town last night, and there je did hazer her, [I did have her] she having been a month, I think, at Portsmouth with her husband, newly come home from the Streights.' (Diary 12th May 1669)

Betty had a sister, the widow Doll Powell, who was as compliant and willing to be subjected to Pepys' lust as her sister. Although there are only twenty-eight references to her in the diary, the entry in July 1667 makes it clear that she and Pepys have had sexual commerce more than a hundred times:

… and after dinner to Mrs. Martin's, and there find Mrs. Burroughs, and by and by comes a pretty widow, one Mrs. Eastwood, and one Mrs. Fenton, a maid; and here merry kissing and looking on their breasts, and all the innocent pleasure in the world. But, Lord! to see the dissembling of this widow, how upon the singing of a certain jigg by Doll, Mrs. Martin's sister, she *seemed* to be sick and fainted and God knows what, because the jigg, which her husband (who died this last sickness) loved. But by and by I made her as merry as is possible, and towzed and tumbled her as I pleased, and then carried her and her sober pretty kinswoman Mrs. Fenton home to their lodgings … (Diary 1st August 1666)

But here happened the best instance of a woman's falseness in the world, that her sister Doll, who went for a bottle of wine, did come home all blubbering and swearing against one Captain Vandener, a Dutchman of the Rhenish Wine House, that pulled her into a stable by the Dog tavern, and there did tumble her and toss her, calling him all the rogues and toads in the world, when she knows that elle hath suffered me to do anything with her a hundred times. (Diary 6th July 1667)

This diary entry speaks volumes about the position and rights of women in Pepys' time. Doll clearly had no possibility of redress against the Dutch captain who effectively raped her and even her relationship with Pepys seems to be that of a submissive and subjugated nature. However, some women had learned to protect themselves from gropers and lechers, as did this lady that Pepys stood close to in a crowded church:

I walked towards White Hall, but, being wearied, turned into St. Dunstan's Church, where I heard an able sermon by the minister of the place; and stood by a pretty, modest maid, whom I did labour to take by the hand and the body; but she would not, but got further and further from me; and, at last, I could perceive her to take pins out of her pocket to prick me if I should touch her again – which seeing I did forbear, and was glad I did spy her design. And then I fell to gaze upon another pretty maid in a pew close to me, and she on me; and I did go about to take her hand, which she suffered a little and then withdrew. So the sermon ended, and the church broke up, and my amours ended also, and so took coach and home, and there took my wife, and to Islington with her. (Diary Sunday, 18th August 1667)

Some women who Pepys had not managed to grope in church were stalked in order to discover who they were, presumably with a view to seeking them out at some later date:

Thence, it being time enough, to our own church; and there stood privately at the great doore to gaze upon a pretty lady and from church dogged her home, whither she went to a house near Tower Hill; and I think her to be one of the prettiest women I ever saw. (Diary Sunday, 9th October 1664)

This day is kept strictly as a holy day, being the King's Coronacion [sic] … and in my way did take two turns forward and backward through the Fleete ally to see a couple of pretty whores that stood off the doors there; and God forgive me, I could scarce stay myself from going into their homes with them, so apt is my nature to evil, after once, as I have these two days, set upon pleasure again. (Diary 29th May 1663)

When not actually groping or stalking women in church, Pepys contented himself with simply ogling them through the service: '… in the afternoon, I to the French church – where much pleased with the three sisters of the parson, very handsome; especially in their noses – and sing prettily.' (Diary Sunday, 11th December 1664)

To church; where God forgive me, I spent most of my time in looking at my new Morena at the other side of the church … (Diary Sunday, 18th December 1664)

… I returned to Mr. Rawlinson's church, where I heard a good sermon. … And very great store of fine women there is in this church, more then I know anywhere else about us. (Diary Sunday, 25th December 1664)

... and so at church all the afternoon. Several handsome ladies at church ...
(Diary Sunday, 16th July 1665)

Pepys' lascivious appetite in places of worship found expression on occasions other than on the Sabbath. One Christmas Eve he took himself off to the Queen's Chapel in St James's to watch the ceremonies taking place there and where he stayed as part of a great crowd from 9.00pm until 2.00am:

The Queen was there, and some ladies. But, Lord! what an odde thing it was for me to be in a crowd of people, here a footman, there a beggar, here a fine lady, there a zealous poor papist, and here a Protestant, two or three together, come to see the shew ...

... we broke up, and nothing like it done: and there I left people receiving the Sacrament: and the Queen gone, and ladies; only my Lady Castlemayne [Barbara Palmer, a great beauty and one of the king's mistresses, with whom Pepys was particularly besotted] who looked prettily in her night-clothes ... 'But here I did make myself to do la cosa [do the thing, i.e. ejaculate] by mere imagination, mirando a jolie mosa [looking at the jolly mass] and with my eyes open, which I never did before – and God forgive me for it, it being in the Chapel. ...' (Diary 24th December 1667)

Not all Pepys' Sunday groping went on in church. Sometimes opportunities presented themselves elsewhere on the Sabbath:

And so to Captain Cocke's, but he I found had sent for me to come to Mrs. Pennington's; and there I went and we were very merry and supped. And Cocke being sleepy, he went away betimes. I stayed alone talking and playing with her till past midnight – she suffering me a hazer whatever ego voulus avec ses mamelles [to do whatever I wanted with her breasts] – and I had almost led her by discourse to make her tocar mi cosa naked, [touch my bare penis] which ella [she] did presque [almost] and did not refuse. (Diary Sunday 26th November 1665)

One wonders what Pepys had to say to Elizabeth when he returned home well after midnight in the small hours of Monday morning, with a damp patch in his breeches and smelling of Mrs. Judith Pennington? Perhaps she had gone to bed in her own chamber and did not hear him come in.

Chapter 8

Servant Girls

'The virtue of Pepys' female servants, if good-looking, was usually attacked by him.' (Henry B. Wheatly: *Pepysiana* 1899)

In the nearly ten years of the diary period, thirty-two women come and go in the Pepys household. Their duties range from those of a humble under-cook maid through to the elevated status of a companion for the lady of the house. A few are mere ghosts, without even a name to identify them to posterity. Most are simply recorded by their given name and only a very few have a full identity, making it possible to place them accurately in an historical context. Some are in Pepys' employment for only a matter of days:

'… and there Mrs. Harper sent for a maid for me to come and live with my wife; I like the maid's looks well enough and I believe may do well, she looking very modestly and speaking so too.' (Diary 4th September 1663)

Pepys' confidence is misplaced however, for a few days later: 'This day our cook-mayde (we having no luck in maids nowadays), which was likely to prove a good servant, though none of the best cooks, fell sick and is gone to her friend, having been with me but four days.' (Diary 10th September 1663)

Some did not even last that long: 'My wife. … is to look out again for another little girl, the last we had being also gone home, the very same day she came.' (Diary 28th April 1666)

Given what we know about Pepys' treatment of some of his maids, one could be forgiven for wondering why she ran out on the same day! Elizabeth Pepys obviously had her own set of criteria when hiring female servants:

This morning came the maid that my wife hath lately hired for a chamber maid. She is very ugly, so that I cannot care for her, but otherwise she seems very good. But however she do come about three weeks hence, when my wife comes back from Brampton, if she go with my father.' (Diary 10th August 1661)

Once again, Pepys' optimism about the new maid's abilities is misplaced: '… coming home again found our new maid Doll asleep, that she could not hear to let us in, so that we were fain to send the boy in at a window to open the door to us'. (Diary 8th September 1661)

… and finally – although little did Pepys know exactly how much trouble keeping servants would bring a few years later:

> At my coming home I am sorry to find my wife displeased with her maid Doll, whose fault is that she cannot keep her peace, but will always be talking in an angry manner, though it be without any reason and to no purpose, which I am sorry for and do see the inconvenience that do attend the increase of a man's fortune by being forced to keep more servants, which brings trouble.

The most successful of Pepys' maids, and the one who appears in the very first diary entry, is Jane Birch, who was 15 years old at that time. Pepys shows her to have been an affectionate, emotional, brave, stubborn, humorous, high-spirited and hard working girl, all of which was rewarded with a wage of just three pounds a year and an occasional whipping. She stayed with the Pepys' for three years, in spite of the fact that she was not always treated well: 'This morning, observing some things to be laid up not as they should be by the girl, I took a broom [i.e. a birch] and basted [i.e. thrashed] her till she cried extremely, which made me vexed, but before I went out I left her appeased.' (Diary 1st December 1660)

It is often said that coming events cast their shadows before them and the diary reveals that Pepys is beginning to notice his maids in a different light (on this occasion in spite of being unwell):

> 'About the middle of the night I was very ill — I think with eating and drinking too much — and so I was forced to call the maid, who pleased my wife and I in her running up and down so innocently in her smock …' (Diary 27th December 1660)

Nevertheless, their relationship remained a cordial one – Jane married his clerk, Tom Edwards, in March 1669 and Pepys was later to become godfather to their son, Sam, born in 1673. They kept in touch with one another throughout most of Pepys' life and in 1690 he settled a £15 annuity on the by then twice-widowed ex-maid. Many however come and go for a variety of reasons:

> … and in the evening our maid Mary (who was with us upon trial for a month) did take leave of us, going as we suppose to be married, for the maid liked us and we her, but all she said was that she had a mind to live in a tradesman's house where there was but one maid.' (Diary 16th October 1661)
>
> … my wife and I had another falling out about Sarah, against whom she has a deadly hate, I know not for what, nor can I see but she is a very good servant. (Diary 2nd December 1662)
>
> Up betimes, and my wife up and about the house, Susan beginning to have her drunken tricks, and put us in mind of her old faults and folly and distractednesse [sic], which we had forgot, so that I became mightily troubled

with her……So home and there found my wife almost mad with Susan's tricks, so as she is forced to let her go and leave the house all in dirt and the clothes all wet, and gets Goody Taylour to do the business for her till another comes.' (Diary 19th August 1663)

In 1667, the Pepys household acquired a new cook-maid, and the diary entries relating to her relationship with her employers over the subsequent twelve months illustrate what was most probably a common progression of events; Pepys chats up girl, Pepys touches up girl, Pepys progresses to serious groping, Pepys tries to get girl somewhere where he can have sex with her. Mrs Pepys probably guesses something is going on and finds a reason to get rid of the girl. Pepys subsequently meets up with girl and tries to take up where he left off. An exactly similar progression takes place with Deb Willett with much more serious consequences. (See Chapter 15 'A Pretty Companion')

Up and to the office, where sat all the morning. At noon dined at home with my wife and find a new girle, a good big girle come to us, got by Payne to be our girle; and his daughter Nell we make our cook. (Diary 21st May 1667)

I staid at home busy, and did show some dalliance to my maid Nell, speaking to her of her sweetheart which she had, silly girle. (Diary 16th June 1667)

I have lately played the fool much with our Nell, in playing with her breasts. (Diary 17th June 1667)

Up, and did this morning dally with Nell and touch her thing, which I was afterward troubled for. (Diary 18th June 1667)

I into my closet and there slept a little, as I do now almost every day after dinner; and then, after dallying a little with Nell, which I am ashamed to think of, away to the office. (Diary 20th June 1667)

I to my chamber, and there dallied a little with my maid Nell to touch her thing, but nothing more. (Diary 2nd July 1667)

Toying with the private parts of the cook-maid seems to have become a daily habit – in fact the diary shows that it was nothing new, as neither was Pepys' alleged shame at his behaviour:

Dressed and had my head combed by my little girle, to whom I confess que je sum demasiado kind, nuper ponendo mes mains in su des choses de son breast, mais il faut que je leave it lest it bring me to alcun major inconvenience.

[Dressed and had my head combed by my little girl to whom I confess that I am too friendly, recently often putting my hands in the two things of her breast; but I had to stop it lest it bring me to some major inconvenience.] (Diary 6th August 1665)

For 'major inconvenience' read either 'spending in his breeches' or the failure of his marriage – or quite possibly both! It wasn't just the maids who found themselves being touched up. He had also done much the same with Mary Mercer, Elizabeth Pepys' companion for two years, who was 17 years of age when she was hired in 1664: '… away home and to bed – apres ayant tocado les mamelles de Mercer, que eran ouverts, con grand plaisir' [after having touched Mercer's breasts, which were uncovered, with great pleasure]. (Diary 18th April 1666)

Given Pepys' inclination to grope the female staff at any opportunity, one wonders why Mary Mercer had her breasts uncovered in his presence? There is nothing in Pepys' note to indicate that she was in any way unwilling to be touched. The Pepys household employed a number of 'Mary's' throughout the diary period, none of whom lasted more than a few months, or in some cases, only weeks. Several reasons are offered for their departure, but whatever the truth, Elizabeth was well aware of the danger to her marriage that would ensue from the employment of attractive young maids:

> … with content with my wife, and so to bed, she pleasing me, though I dare not own it, that she hath hired a chambermaid; but she, after many commendations, told me that she had one great fault, and that was, that she was very handsome, at which I made nothing, but let her go on; but many times to-night she took occasion to discourse of her handsomeness, and the danger she was in by taking her, and that she did doubt yet whether it would be fit for her, to take her. But I did assure her of my resolutions to have nothing to do with her maids, but in myself I was glad to have the content to have a handsome one to look on. (Diary 11th March 1669)

Given what we know of his track record, Pepys' assurances are worthless. The third Mary to be employed, in March 1665, is hired by Elizabeth who had described her to Pepys as handsome, but described by him as being a 'disappointment' as she turned out to be 'a very ordinary wench'. However, that fact does not stop him from subjecting her to the usual assault:

> But broke up before the dinner half over and by water to the Harp and Ball, and thence had Mary meet me at the New Exchange, and there took coach and I with great pleasure took the ayre to Highgate, and thence to Hampstead, much pleased with her company, pretty and innocent, and had what pleasure almost I would with her, and so at night, weary and sweaty, it being very hot beyond bearing, we back again, and I set her down in St. Martin's Lane. (Diary 11th July 1665)

This Mary left in December of the same year, perhaps weary of being groped by her employer. The very first Mary entered the Pepys' household in September

1661 and left of her own volition the following month. The second Mary came in February 1663 and was dismissed two months later by Elizabeth for 'being too high for her'. Mary number four came in May 1666 and left in June, as the diary records that 'she was not able to do my work'. We might be forgiven for reading that as 'un-cooperative'! The fifth Mary came in May 1667 and left two months later, claiming she wanted to be employed on a day to day basis, in order that she might have time to herself when she wanted it. In the meantime, as we have already seen, things had escalated with Nell, Pepys no longer being satisfied with touching only her breasts: 'Up, and did this morning dally with Nell and did touch her thing, which I was afterward troubled for.' (Diary 18th June 1667)

Troubled he may have been, but it has obviously put him in the mood for another dalliance, as he tries to set up another woman for a groping:

> To the office, and there all the morning. Peg Pen come to see me, and I was glad of it, and did resolve to have tried her this afternoon, but that there was company with elle [her] at my home, whither I got her. Dined at home, W. Hewer with me, and then to the office, and to my Lady Pen's, and did find occasion for Peg to go home with me to my chamber, but there being an idle gentleman with them, he went with us, and I lost my hope. (Diary 18th June 1667)
>
> I into my closet and there slept a little, as I do now almost every day after dinner; and then, after dallying a little with Nell, which I am ashamed to think of, away to the office. (Diary 20th June 1667)
>
> Up, and in dressing myself in my dressing chamber comes up Nell, and I did play with her and touch her belly and thing, but did not kiss her. (Diary 26th June 1667)
>
> They gone, I to my chamber, and there dallied a little with my maid Nell to touch her thing, but nothing more. (Diary 2nd July 1667)
>
> My wife mighty angry with Nell, who is turned a very gossip, and gads abroad as soon as our backs are turned, and will put her away tomorrow, which I am not sorry for. (Diary 5th August 1667)
>
> My wife, as she said last night, hath put away Nell to-day, for her gossiping abroad and telling of stories. (Diary 6th August 1667)

It was fortunate for Pepys that Nell did not tell Elizabeth where Pepys had had his hand every morning. Even though she is no longer employed, she is still fair game for a grope from her ex-employer: 'This evening, coming home in the dusk, I saw and spoke to our Nell, Pain's daughter, and had I not been very cold I should have taken her to Tower Hill para together et toker her.' (Diary 30th April 1668)

> … then I did see our Nell, Payne's daughter, and her yo did desear venga after migo [I desired her to come after me] and so ella did seque me [she did follow me] to Tower Hill to our back entry there that comes upon the degres entrant

into nostra [back entrance into our] garden; and there ponendo [placing] the key in the door, yo tocar sus mamelles con mi mano and su cosa with mi cosa et yo did dar-la a shilling [touched her breasts with my hand and her thing with my thing and did give her a shilling] and so parted, and yo [I] home to put up things against to-morrow's carrier for my wife… (Diary 6th May 1668)

Some ten months later, Pepys comes across Nell again by accident, in the company of Mrs Bagwell, one of his long term mistresses. What she is doing there is never made clear. Perhaps they have been comparing notes:

This done, they took barge, and I with Sir J. Smith to Captain Cox's; and there to talk, and left them and other company to drink; while I slunk out to Bagwell's; and there saw her, and her mother, and our late maid Nell, who cried for joy to see me, but I had no time for pleasure then nor could stay, but after drinking I back to the yard, having a month's mind para have had a bout with Nell, which I believe I could have had, and may another time. (Diary 4th March 1669)

Mrs Pepys senses that something is going on again, although she is not sure exactly what …

So to Cox's, and thence walked with Sir J. Smith back to Redriffe; and so, by water home, and there my wife mighty angry for my absence, and fell mightily out, but not being certain of any thing, but thinks only that Pierce or Knepp was there, and did ask me, and, I perceive, the boy, many questions. But I did answer her; and so, after much ado, did go to bed, and lie quiet all night; but [she] had another bout with me in the morning, but I did make shift to quiet her, but yet she was not fully satisfied, poor wretch! in her mind, and thinks much of my taking so much pleasure from her; which, indeed, is a fault, though I did not design or foresee it when I went. (Diary 4th March 1669)

Perhaps Elizabeth should have ensured that all her maids were like Luce – 'very ugly and plaine, but may be a good servant for all that' and a cook maid from 26th June 1666 until May the following year, when she was dismissed for persistent drunkenness. Strangely, Luce threatens Elizabeth with something that she will tell Pepys that he won't like to hear. As it never happens, we will never know what, if anything, it was:

… by and by home and there find our Luce drunk, and when her mistress told her of it would be gone, and so put up some of her things and did go away of her accord, nobody pressing her to it, and the truth is, though she be the dirtiest, homeliest servant that ever I kept, yet I was sorry to have her go, partly through my love to my servants, and partly because she was a very drudging, working wench, only she would be drunk. But that which did a little trouble me was that I did hear her tell her mistress that she would tell her master something before she was aware of her that she would be sorry to have him know; but did it in such a silly, drunken manner, that though it trouble me a little, yet not knowing what to suspect she should know, and not knowing well whether she said it to her mistress or Jane, I did not much think of it. (Diary 18th May 1667)

A few for whatever reason did manage to escape Pepys' lustful intentions and roving hands, on this occasion in his office:

'Up betimes and to my office, where I find Griffins girl making it clean; but God forgive me, what a mind I have to her, but did not meddle with her.' (Diary 30th June 1662)

… God forgive me, I was sorry to hear that Sir W Pens maid Betty was gone away yesterday, for I was in hopes to have had a bout with her before she had gone, she being very pretty. I have also a mind to my own wench, but I dare not, for fear she should prove honest and refuse and then tell my wife. (Diary 1st August 1662)

However, Pepys did not always miss his chance with the servants of other men – never one to pass up an opportunity, he seizes the chance (both literally and figuratively):

Thence to my Lord's, where nobody at home but a woman that let me in, and Sarah above; whither I went up to her and played and talked with her and, God forgive me, did feel her; which I am much ashamed of, but I did no more, though I had so much a mind to it that I spent in my breeches. (Diary Sunday, 7th September 1662)

Or when he visits the actress Mrs Knipp, but finding her not at home: '… and here yo did besar her ancilla [kiss her maid], which is so mighty belle.' (Diary 16th May 1668)

The thirty-two female servants that are employed by the Pepys' household during the diary period have no independent voice in the historical record, indeed some have not even left us a name. A few remained in his employment for many years; Jane Birch for the whole of the diary period, despite being severely thrashed on occasion by her master. For whatever reason, others lasted only a few weeks or even days. The diary gives us enough evidence to conclude that Pepys would have 'tried it on' with any of them that he found sufficiently attractive and no doubt many considered it worthwhile to acquiesce in the best interests of their continued employment. A very few even found him attractive enough to enter into a full sexual affair, and one of those affairs was serious enough to come within a hair's breadth of wrecking his marriage.

Chapter 9

A Pretty, Conceited Woman

Throughout the entire diary period, Pepys records the whole gamut of his sexual activity, from his marital relationship with his wife, to his attempts – successful or otherwise – on the virtue of other women. These forays range from kissing to casual groping; through seduction to full sexual intimacy and even to what would now be regarded as rape and sexual violence. The women who are the objects of the Pepysian lust fall into three broad categories. First are those of a lower social order than himself, i.e. the maids and servants of his friends and acquaintances, as well as those of his own household. Secondly, the wives of men inferior in rank to himself, who were prepared to sacrifice their virtue to secure advancement for their spouses. Thirdly, women who might be regarded as being of more or less equal social standing; successful business women, or actresses of repute. At no time does he make any attempt upon the virtue of women of superior rank and social class, even though – as in the case of the king's mistress, Lady Castlemaine, he buys three portraits of her and even letches over the sight of her underwear on the washing-line: 'And in the Privy-garden saw the finest smocks and linnen petticoats of my Lady Castlemaine's, laced with rich lace at the bottom, that ever I saw; and did me good to look upon them.' (Diary 21st May 1662)

Pepys' avoidance of any dalliance with the upper classes is hardly surprising, even though as his career advances, he came into daily contact with them. Contemporary moralists recommended that married couples should be of similar age, background, financial circumstances and religious beliefs, and Pepys clearly believed that these criteria should also apply in casual sexual relationships.

Apart from beggars, maids and female servants probably represented the lowest social order in seventeenth century England. For the most part, they were the uneducated daughters of uneducated parents, with no social standing or wealth. Exceptions might be made in the case of female companions to the wife of the household, who were generally quite well educated (as was Deb Willett) but even these were still employees who could be hired and fired at will, and whose services could be bought for little more than their board and lodging. They had little or no legal protection from physical abuse – apart from sexually interfering with the maids, Pepys thrashed both his male and female servants as and when he thought they warranted it:

… hearing from my wife and the maids' complaints made of the boy, I called him up, and with my whip did whip him till I was not able to stir. (Diary 21st June 1662)

Thence to my brother's, and there told him how my girl has served us which he sent me, and directed him to get my clothes again, and get the girl whipped. (Diary 21st August 1663)

Sexual advances by their employers were to be tolerated by servants if they cared for their jobs, a situation that pertained right through to and including Victorian England. In 1693 the London newspaper *The Athenian Mercury* carried the story of a manservant who, with his employer's active encouragement, married a maidservant in the same household only to discover that she was already pregnant with the master's child. The employer said he was grateful to have 'such cracked ware [taken] off his hands' and gave financial compensation to the couple. Most maids made pregnant by their employers were not so fortunate.

Actresses were considered to be women of easy virtue and therefore became easy sexual prey, as the contemporary satirist and pamphleteer Tom Brown tells us: 'Tis as hard a matter for a pretty woman to keep herself honest in a theatre as 'tis for an apothecary to keep his treacle from the flies in hot weather.'

The new plays that Pepys was so fond of watching (sometimes two or three in a day) invariably cast women – newly allowed to act upon the stage – as sexual objects, usually 'discovered' as the curtain went up, in a distressed state of undress, having been recently violated. There was no restriction of male visitors to the 'tiring house' where the actresses changed, and Pepys availed himself of this facility on many occasions, at times observing both Mrs Knepp and Nell Gwyn in states of undress.

Leaving aside the maids and servants, Pepys appears to confine his attentions almost exclusively to married women. Presumably this is because their marital status, in an age that regarded adultery as a mortal sin, meant that they were much more likely to be discreet, whatever the outcome of his advances. By the same token, they would be unable to demand that he make 'a respectable woman' of them after the event. However, it should be noted that 'Mrs' as used in the diary is a contraction of 'mistress' – a term applied to both married and unmarried women of the period, so unless further corroboration of their marital status is available, they could be in either state. With the attractive wives of his subordinates, sexual compliance was the price of his patronage – blackmail of the oldest kind, and most of his victims decided that at least some compliance was a price worth paying if it resulted in their husband's promotion.

By 1665, Pepys was appointed surveyor-general of victualling for the navy, and was beginning to move in more exalted circles:

Thence to my lodging, where I find my Lord Rutherford, of which I was glad. We supped together and sat up late, he being a mighty wanton man with a daughter-in-law of my landlady's, a pretty conceited woman, big with child; and he would be handling her breasts, which she coyly refused. (Diary 23rd October 1665)

The lady is Mrs Daniel, daughter of Mrs Clerke, Pepys' landlady during his stay during the plague at her home in Greenwich and the wife of a navy lieutenant who lived next door to her mother. More will be heard of her in due course.

Mrs Judith Penington is the daughter of Sir Isaac Pennington, previously Lord Mayor of London, and Pepys regularly comes across her at Captain Cocke's – a Baltic merchant and navy contractor with whom he did much business, and she is often a member of the party when they dine, Pepys having on at least one occasion sent her a barrel of oysters as a gift. On an evening in early December however, he records beginning to see the lady in a different light:

So I to the office and among other business prepared a deed for him to sign and seale to me about our agreement, which at night I got him to come and sign and seale, and so he and I to Glanville's, and there he and I sat talking and playing with Mrs. Penington, whom we found undrest in her smocke and petticoats by the fireside, and there we drank and laughed, and she willingly suffered me to put my hand in her bosom very wantonly, and keep it there long. Which methought was very strange, and I looked upon myself as a man mightily deceived in a lady, for I could not have thought she could have suffered it, by her former discourse with me; so modest she seemed and I know not what. (Diary 4th December 1665)

This conclusion is rather odd, as previous month Pepys had encountered this lady at Captain Cocke's and a similar scenario has ensued:

… and so to Captain Cocke's to dinner……but here his brother Solomon was, and, for guests, myself, Sir G. Smith, and a very fine lady, one Mrs. Penington, and two more gentlemen. But, both [before] and after dinner, most witty discourse with this lady, who is a very fine witty lady, one of the best I ever heard speake, and indifferent handsome… and Cocke being sleepy, he went away betime. I stayed alone talking and playing with her till past midnight -- she suffering me a hazer whatever ego voulus avec ses mamelles [to do whatever I wanted with her breasts] – and I had almost led her by discourse to make her tocar mi cosa naked, [touch my bare penis] which ella [she] did presque [almost] and did not refuse. (Diary 26th November 1665)

The following month, Pepys fancies another bout with the lady and visits her at home:

… and thence I to Mrs. Penington, and had a supper from the King's Head for her, and there mighty merry and free as I used to be with her, and at last, late, I did pray her to undress herself into her nightgowne, that I might see how to have her picture drawne carelessly (for she is mighty proud of that conceit), and I would walk without in the streete till she had done. So I did walk forth, and whether I made too many turns or no in the darke cold frosty night between the two walls up to the Parke gate I know not, but she was gone to bed when I come again to the house, upon pretence of leaving some papers there, which I did on purpose by her consent. So I away home, and was there sat up for to be spoken with my young Mrs. Daniel, to pray me to speake for her husband to be a Lieutenant. I had the opportunity here of kissing her again and again, and did answer that I would be very willing to do him any kindnesse, and so parted, and I to bed … (Diary 20th December 1665)

It is not clear why Pepys had to go outside into the street whilst she undressed – it appears that she had no intention of waiting up for him, so perhaps it was simply a ruse to get rid of him. Having failed to get Mrs Penington into her nightdress, Pepys consoles himself with the very pregnant lieutenant's wife, Mrs Daniel. Pepys is clearly not put off by the fact that she is heavily pregnant and she obviously thinks she is onto a good thing, as the very next day:

Coming home and going to bed, the boy tells me his sister [Mrs] Daniel has provided me a supper of little birds killed by her husband, and I made her sup with me, and after supper were alone a great while, and I had the pleasure of her lips, she being a pretty woman, and one whom a great belly becomes as well as ever I saw any. She gone, I to bed.

As an afterthought, the diary reveals that Pepys had already interviewed a third lady earlier in the day, the widow of another navy lieutenant killed in action earlier in the year: 'This day I was come to by Mrs. Burrows, of Westminster, Lieutenant Burrows (lately dead) his wife, a most pretty woman and my old acquaintance; I had a kiss or two of her, and a most modest woman she is.' (Diary 21st December 1665)

Thus in a little over two months, Pepys has added three ladies; Mrs Daniel, Mrs Burrows and Mrs Penington to his 'little black book'. However, either Pepys has gone off the boil for Mrs Penington, or she has grown tired of his groping, as there is no further mention of her in the remaining four years of the diary and it seems possible that Pepys never saw her again.

On 7 January in the New Year of 1666, the plague having greatly diminished, Pepys moves out of Mrs Clerke's house in Greenwich, complaining that he had 'paid dear for the time I have spent there' – he had paid five pounds, ten shillings a month since 11th October 1665, a massive rent in the period. In May the diary records that Mrs Daniel had been delivered of a son, and although his wife goes to visit, it is 2nd June before Pepys renews his acquaintance with her – and as her husband is serving on board the *Royal Charles* deliberately avoids telling her that the English fleet is in action; in fact, John Daniel returned safely to London two days later.

In July, Pepys finds himself working late at Greenwich, so stays the night at his old lodging house with Mrs Clerke, whose daughter is unsurprisingly in attendance:

> … away and on shore at Greenwich, the night being late and the tide against us; so, having sent before, to Mrs. Clerke's and there I had a good bed, and well received, the whole people rising to see me, and among the rest young Mrs. Daniel, whom I kissed again and again alone, and so by and by to bed and slept pretty well … (Diary 11th July 1666)

Mrs Daniel becomes a regular guest at the Pepys' residence, coming to dine with them on 20 July and again on 25 October. Although he has added new names to his list of 'gropees', Pepys still keeps up with his old favourites: 'I out to the Bell Taverne, and thither comes Doll to me and yo [I] did tocar la cosa [I did touch the thing] of her as I pleased … (Diary 14th December 1666)
…although not always with the greatest success…

> Thence to the Swan, and there I sent for Sarah and mighty merry we were, but contra [against] my will were very far from hazer algo [doing something]. (Diary 17th December 1666)

A few days later, Mrs Clerke arrives with her daughter, Mrs Daniel, and this time they want to do another deal:

> Lay long, and when up find Mrs. Clerk of Greenwich and her daughter Daniel, their business among other things was a request her daughter was to make, so I took her into my chamber, and there it was to help her husband to the command of a little new pleasure boat building, which I promised to assist in. And here I had opportunity para baiser elle, and toucher ses mamailles [kiss her and touch her breasts] so as to make mi mismo espender [make myself come] with great pleasure. (Diary 21st December 1666)

In the New Year, Mrs Daniel obviously feels it is worth gritting her teeth and putting up with Pepys' groping, as she needs another favour for her husband:

> After dinner, I to my chamber and my wife and father to talk; and by and by they tell Mrs. Daniel would speak with me, so I down to the parlour to her and sat down together and talked about getting her husband a place; and here I did adventure etsi the porta etait operta para put my mano abajo su

jupes two or three temps et touch her cosa con great pleasure, ella resisting pretty much, sed never the minus submitted. I do promise, and mean to do what kindness I can to her husband; and after having been there hasta yo was ashamed, de peur that my people pensaient to pragma de it, or lest they might espy nous through some trees, we parted, and I to the office and presently back home again, and there was asked by my wife, I know not whether simply or with design, how I came to look as I did, car yo was in much calor et de body and of animi; which I put off the heat of the season, and so to other business, and I had some fear hung upon me lest algo had sido decouvert …

[After dinner, I to my chamber and my wife and father to talk; and by and by they tell Mrs. Daniel would speak with me, so I down to the parlour to her and sat down together and talked about getting her husband a place; and here I did risk – despite the door being open – to put my hand under her skirts two or three times and touch her thing with much pleasure, she resisting pretty much, but never the less submitted. I do promise, and mean to do what kindness I can to her husband …']

Although the diary does not explain, Pepys obviously takes the lady outside to continue his assault and returns home out of breath:

['… and after having been doing it till I was ashamed, scared what my people thought I was doing, or lest they might espy us through some trees, we parted, and I to the office and presently back home again, and there was asked by my wife, I know not whether simply or with design, how I came to look as I did, because I was in much heat of body and breath; which I put off the heat of the season, and so to other business, and I had some fear hung upon me lest something had been found out.']

Although Pepys does not explain the circumstances, and in spite of having taken a huge risk of discovery and has aroused Elizabeth's suspicions, a last minute addition to the diary mentions another opportunity for a further grope later the same day: ' This afternoon I had opportunity para jouer with Mrs. Pen, tocando her mamelles and besando ella being sola in the casa of her pater and she fort willing.'

[This afternoon I had opportunity to sport [play] with Mrs. Pen, touching her breasts and kissing her being alone in the house of her father and she very willing.] (Diary 23rd May 1667)

Ironically, even though he was far from averse to using force to get his wicked way with women, Pepys professes himself troubled to see women pestered by men in the park, and confesses himself to being a coward when it comes to offering protection to ladies in distress:

Among others, there were two pretty women alone, that walked a great while, which being discovered by some idle gentlemen, they would needs take them up; but to see the poor ladies how they were put to it to run from them, and they after them, and sometimes the ladies put themselves along with other company, then the other drew back; at last, the last did get off out of the house, and took boat and away. I was troubled to see them abused so; and could have found in my heart, as little desire of fighting as I have, to have protected the ladies. (Diary 28th May 1667)

A couple of days later, Mrs Daniel is back, still trying to influence Pepys to get her husband some advantage:

Up, and there came young Mrs. Daniel in the morning as I expected about business of her husband's. I took her into the office to discourse with her about getting some employment for him And there I did put my hand to her belly, so as to make myself do, but she is so lean that I had no great pleasure with her. (Diary 31st May 1667)

In addition to his routine groping of his maids, Pepys still has a mind to try it on with Mrs Margaret Lowther:

Up, and did this morning dally with Nell and touch her thing, which I was afterward troubled for. To the office, and there all the morning. Peg Pen came to see me, and I was glad of it; and did resolve to have tried her this afternoon, but that there was company with ella [her] at my house, whither I got her… (Diary 18th June 1667)

Mrs Daniel is still trying to get help for husband: 'Up, and to my office, where busy, and there comes Mrs. Daniel; and it is strange how the merely putting my hand to her belly through her coats do make me do …'

[here the shorthand is garbled but presumably makes reference to making Pepys orgasm]. (Diary 22nd June 1667)

One wonders if Mr Daniel knew what was going on with his wife when he visits Pepys in company with his wife a week later, seeking help in finding a position, but Pepys' mind is grappling with what to do with several members of the victualling business that are shortly to be discharged. She obviously gives it up as a bad job, as she makes no appearance again in the diary until March of the following year, when Pepys comes upon her by accident:

… in Seething Lane met young Mrs. Daniel, and I stopped; and she had been at my house but found nobody within, and tells me that she drew me for her Valentine this year; so I took her into the coach, and was going to the other end of the town, thinking to have taken her abroad; but remembering that I was to go out with my wife this afternoon, I only did hazer her para tocar my prick con her hand which did hazer me hazer [make her touch my penis with her hand which did make me come] and so to a milliner at the corner shop. … (Diary 25th March 1668)

Finally, Mrs Daniel makes three cursory appearances in the diary. The shorthand is garbled and blotted and unusually includes some German, the overall carelessness of the entry perhaps reflecting Pepys' impatience with the lady who has failed to live up to his expectations:

… and after dinner comes Creed, whom I hate, to speak with me, and before him comes Mrs. Daniel about business and yo did tocar su cosa with mi mano [touch her thing with my hand]. She gone, Creed and I to the King's playhouse. … (Diary 22nd June 1668)

Up, and to the office, where Mrs. Daniel comes and I could not tocar su cosa, she having ellos sobre her [I could not touch her thing, she having her period]. (Diary 20th July 1668)

… and so home to the Office, where Mrs. Daniel come and staid talking to little purpose with me to borrow money, but I did not lend her any, having not opportunity para hater allo thing mit her.[to do anything with her] (Diary 15th September 1668)

Chapter 10

Haberdasherie & Hanky-Panky

Westminster Hall was, and still is, the oldest building on the Parliamentary Estate, and indeed in the country, it having been built in 1097 under the rule of William II and over the successive centuries the scene of many great public events – including the trial of King Charles I in January 1649. In common with many large public spaces, it attracted traders very early in its history – merchandise being sold inside the Hall by the 1290s. Due to the presence of the law courts, the Hall also became a covered market for legal paraphernalia and various shops and stalls jostled with each other along the walls selling wigs, pens and other stationery. In the sixteenth century, the scholars of Westminster School were permitted to erect stalls to sell their books; by Pepys' time, drapers and ribbon sellers had joined the throng and were trading next to them. In 1666, the year of the Great Fire, there were forty-eight shops in the Hall, and it remained what might now be termed a shopping centre until they were removed in 1780.

Sometime prior to or during 1660, Pepys heard a drunken story about a man who persuaded a gullible pretty woman to let him handle her private parts by pretending to be a doctor. This made such an impression on Pepys that he went looking for the woman in question, who allegedly resided in Westminster Hall. He failed to find her, but did come across a real woman named Betty Lane. Betty was a Nottinghamshire girl who had come to London in order to set up her own business as a draper in the Hall and Pepys subsequently patronised her for ribbons, gloves and linens for the women in his life. She had a willing and permissive attitude to sex, she got on with Pepys, and he was (at least, initially) fascinated by her.

Her first appearance in the diary is soon after the beginning in January 1660, when he refers to her simply as 'Mrs Lane'. She does not appear again until 4 August that year, when '...I went and bespoke some linen of Betty Lane in the hall'. He clearly knows her better by this time, as she has become 'Betty'. Furthermore, he obviously makes good progress in the intended seduction, as on 12 August: 'I took her to my Lord's and gave her a bottle of wine in the garden, where Mr. Fairbrother of Cambridge did come and find us and drank with us.' (Diary 12th July 1660)

Pepys obviously feels secure that both Lord Montagu and his old friend from Cambridge will be discreet in not revealing his illicit assignation. When he moved to Seething Lane in June, into the house that went with his new job, he vacated the little property in Axe Yard, which was still vacant at this point, although one assumes, unfurnished. Now it was to come in very handy. The wine did its work and … '… after that I took her to my house where I was extremely free in dallying with her, and she not unfree to take it.' (Diary 12th August 1660)

Earlier reviewers of the diary invariably took the view that any lapse in moral behaviour was the fault of the woman in the case. This was noted by Henry Wheatley writing in 1899 in his work, *Pepysiana*, who then goes on to follow the same path:

> It seems hard that the women with whom Pepys associated should have their characters destroyed in the nineteenth century, but as few of them are known outside the diary perhaps not much harm is done. Mrs Betty Lane, afterwards Mrs Martin, who figures so largely in Pepys's pages, is the most objectionable of all. There is no evidence that she ever had any virtue to lose, and her conduct throughout is revolting. It even seems to have disgusted Pepys himself, and he was by no means fastidious.

Pepys' 'disgust' does not seem to have inhibited his interest in the lady. On 25 August, he buys a 'half-shirt' from her and on 3rd November, together with a friend and colleague Tom Doling, they collect her from the Hall and take her to an ale house, where Betty falls out with Pepys over his adverse comments about her new sweetheart. On 10 January the following year Pepys meets up with John Hawley, an ex-neighbour from Axe Yard and colleague, who, over a drink, talks of how *he* is wooing Mrs Lane. She is obviously an attractive and compliant lady in great demand. Then strangely and inexplicably she disappears from the diary for two and a half years. On Monday, 29 June 1663, at least as far as the diary is concerned, Pepys renews his acquaintanceship with her. She at first affirms that she has turned over a new leaf and mended her wicked ways, but he obviously knows how to charm the lady:

> … then came again to the Hall and fell to talk with Mrs. Lane, and after great talk that she never went abroad with any man as she used heretofore to do, I with one word got her to go with me and to meet me at the further Rhenish wine-house, where I did give her a Lobster' … (Diary 29th June 1663)

As on the previous occasion, the bottle of wine and the expensive dinner do their job, and Pepys' hands go to work: '… and do so touse her and feel her all over, making her believe how fair and good a skin she has, and indeed she has a very white thigh and leg, but monstrous fat.' (Diary 29th June 1663)

Depending upon which dictionary one consults, 'touse' means to pull; to haul; to tear; to worry; 'tousle' means to ruffle or untidy someone's hair. One suspects that both are true in this case; Pepys obviously gets carried away with his frenetic groping and at very least has the lady's skirts up high enough to observe her thighs, no mean feat with such voluminous clothes. It is likely that the inn must have been divided up into 'snugs' (small drinking cubicles) which would have afforded some privacy. However, whatever the arrangement, the subsequent occurrence makes it sound as though the pair are actually sitting in a window seat, as Pepys outrageous behaviour appears to have been observed by a passer-by:

> When weary I did give over and somebody, having seen some of our dalliance, called aloud in the street, 'Sir! why do you kiss the gentlewoman so?' and flung a stone at the window, which vexed me, but I believe they could not see my touzing her, and so we broke up and I went out the back way, without being observed I think, and so she towards the Hall and I to White Hall …
> (Diary 29th June 1663)

On the 14th, Pepys is apparently once more in a randy mood:

> and so home to supper and to bed – before I sleep, fancying myself to sport with Mrs. Steward with great pleasure.' (Diary 14th July 1663)

On the 15th July, Pepys is again in a 'hot humour', and fancies a return bout with Mrs Lane, but circumstances frustrate his plan, so he contents himself with imagining a similar assignation with the Queen:

> Thence by water to Westminster, and there spent a good deal of time walking in the Hall, which is going to be repaired, and, God forgive me, had a mind to have got Mrs. Lane abroad, or fallen in with any woman else (in that hot humour). But it so happened she could not go out, nor I meet with anybody else, and so I walked homeward, and in my way did many and great businesses of my own at the Temple among my lawyers and others to my great content, thanking God that I did not fall into any company to occasion spending time and money. To supper, and then to a little viall and to bed, sporting in my fancy with the Queen.' (Diary 15th July 1663)

By the 18th, the itch is still in need of scratching; whilst waiting for Mrs Lane he fancies the Howlett's daughter, but Betty returns and off they go for a chicken dinner, affording Pepys the opportunity for some more heavy petting, although stopping short of full sexual intercourse:

> So to the Temple, Wardrobe, and lastly to Westminster Hall, where I expected some bands made me by Mrs. Lane, and while she went to the starchers for them, I staid [sic] at Mrs. Howlett's, who with her husband were abroad, and only their daughter (which I call my wife) was in the shop, and I took occasion to buy a pair of gloves to talk to her, and I find her a pretty spoken girl, and

will prove a mighty handsome wench. I could love her very well. By and by Mrs. Lane comes, and my bands not being done she and I posted and met at the Crown in the Palace Yard, where we eat a chicken I sent for, and drank, and were mighty merry, and I had my full liberty of towzing her and doing what I would, but the last thing of all … for I felt as much as I would and made her feel my thing also, and put the end of it to her breast and by and by to her very belly -- of which I am heartily ashamed, but I do resolve never to do more so. (Diary 18th July 1663)

Presumably the Crown was an ale house in which the tables must have been divided up into 'snugs' otherwise how could they have behaved so outrageously in a public place? Betty is obviously on the lookout for a husband, and one wonders whether she is testing Pepys out, as he drops a little clue that perhaps he has not told her that he is already married:

I know she would have me.… But, Lord! to see what a mind she has to a husband, and how she showed me her hands to tell her fortune, and everything that she asked ended always whom and when she was to marry. And I pleased her so well, saying as. I know she would have me, and then she would say that she had been with all the artists in town, and they always told her the same things, as that she should live long, and rich, and have a good husband, but few children, and a great fit of sickness, and 20 other things, which she says she has always been told by others. Here I staid [sic] late before my bands were done, and then they came, and so I by water to the Temple, and thence walked home, all in a sweat with my tumbling of her and walking, and so a little supper and to bed, fearful of having taken cold. (Diary 18th July 1663)

After failing to find her in on 4 August, Pepys tries again the next day with better luck, but this time he is observed by Lord Sandwich's daughter Jemimah which causes him some concern that he might be betrayed. Notwithstanding, he is soon at it yet again, although she still holds out against full sexual intercourse:

… in the afternoon to Westminster Hall, and there found Mrs. Lane, and by and by agreement we met at the Parliament stairs (in my way down to the boat who should meet us but my lady Jemimah, who saw me lead her but said nothing to me of her, though I ought to speak to her to see whether she would take notice of it or no) and off to Stangate and so to the King's Head at Lambeth marsh, and had variety of meats and drinks, but I did so towse her and handled her, but could get nothing more from her though I was very near it; but as wanton and bucksome as she is she dares not adventure upon the business, in which I very much commend and like her. Staid pretty late,

> and so over with her by water, and being in a great sweat with my towsing of her durst not go home by water, but took coach … (Diary 5th August 1663)

Pepys' obviously neglects her for a month as Betty enquires after him on the 4th September and he tries and fails to see her on the 9th; it is the 23rd before they meet up again. Once again, Betty denies him full consummation, but goes far enough to make him ejaculate:

> In the afternoon telling my wife that I go to Deptford, I went, by water to Westminster Hall, and there finding Mrs. Lane, took her over to Lambeth, where we were lately, and there, did what I would with her, but only the main thing, which she would not consent to, for which God be praised … . . and yet I came so near, that I was provoked to spend. But, trust in the Lord, I shall never do so again while I live. After being tired with her company I landed her at White Hall, and so home and at my office writing letters till 12 at night almost, and then home to supper and bed, and there found my poor wife hard at work, which grieved my heart to see that I should abuse so good a wretch, and that is just with God to make her bad with me for my wrongin [sic] of her, but I do resolve never to do the like again. So to bed.' (Diary 23rd September 1663)

Pepys is either jaded with her company, or fears he is getting in over his head, but in any event, as we shall see, he has other fish to fry. He clearly wants to get her off his hands as she does not appear again in the diary in 1663, other than a note on 22 December, when he tries to get one of the clerks of George Downing (after whom Downing Street in London is named) to be interested in her: 'I did go to Westminster Hall, and there met Hawley, and walked a great while with him. Among other discourse encouraging him to pursue his love to Mrs. Lane, while God knows I had a roguish meaning in it. (Diary 22nd December 1663)

In the New Year, Pepys tries and fails to see her on the 4 January, but makes an appointment to meet up on the 9th, which he does – first getting his wife and her maid out of the way:

> After dinner by coach I carried my wife and Jane to Westminster, leaving her at Mr. Hunt's, and I to Westminster Hall, and there visited Mrs. Lane, and by appointment went out and met her at the Trumpet, Mrs. Hare's, but the room being damp we went to the Bell tavern, and there I had her company, but could not do as I used to do (yet nothing but what was honest) for that she told me she had those [i.e. she had her period]. (Diary 9th January 1664)

His plan to palm her off on Mr Hawley appears to be a non-starter, as is his plan to meet the attractive girl he came across in the shop back in July:

…So I to talk about her having Hawley, she told me flatly no, she could not love him. I took occasion to enquire of Howlett's daughter, with whom I have a mind to meet a little to see what mettle the young wench is made of, being very pretty, but she tells me she is already betrothed to Mrs. Michell's son.… (Diary 9th January 1664)

He sends her three bottles of wine on the 11th (something he apparently promised to do) and then sees her again on the 16th, when he clearly has an appetite for much more than just the usual groping:

He being gone, I by water to Westminster-hall and there did see Mrs. Lane, and de la, elle and I to a cabaret at the Cloche in the street du roy; and there, after some caresses, je l'ay foutee sous de la chaise deux times [I fucked her twice under the chair], and the last to my great pleasure: mais j'ai grand peur que je l'ay fait faire aussi elle meme [but I greatly fear that I made her do it herself it as well] Mais after I had done, elle commencait parler [but after I had done, she began talking] as before and I did perceive that je n'avais fait rein de danger a elle [I had done her nothing which might be dangerous]. Et avec ca, [with that] I came away; and though I did make grand promises a la contraire, nonobstant je ne la verrai pas long time [although I did make great promises to the contrary, nonetheless I will not see her for a long time].… So home to bed-with my mind un peu trouble pour ce que j'ai fait today [my mind a little troubled by what I've done today]. But I hope it will be la derniere de toute ma vie' [the last time in my whole life]. (Diary 16th January 1664)

Pepys fears that he 'made her do it herself it as well' i.e. brought her to orgasm, presumably because he is afraid that she might become pregnant – it was commonly thought that a woman's orgasm was in some way linked to conception. By 'done her nothing that might be dangerous' he presumably means that this was unlikely as a result of their encounter.

In February, not being a man to take no for an answer, Pepys has not given up on the Hawley idea, and is still lusting after the Howlett girl:

I went and talked with Mrs. Lane about persuading her to Hawly, and think she will come on, which I wish were done, and so to Mr. Howlett and his wife, and talked about the same, and they are mightily for it, and I bid them promote it, for I think it will be for both their goods and my content. But I was much pleased to look upon their pretty daughter, which is grown a pretty mayd, and will make a fine modest woman. (Diary 8th February 1664)

However, by 29 February, it seems certain that the Hawley plan is a dead duck and Betty is becoming irritated by Pepys' nagging: '…and so to Westminster Hall, and there talked with Mrs. Lane and Howlett, but the match with Hawly I perceive

will not take, and so I am resolved wholly to avoid occasion of further ill with her.'
(Diary 29th February 1664)

There is no mention of Betty during March, but in April, Pepys is still trying to
persuade her to Hawley, which succeeds only in angering her further, easily done
as she is apparently having her period:

> I to Westminster Hall, and by and by by agreement to Mrs. Lane's lodging,
> whither I sent for a lobster, and with Mr. Swayne and his wife eat it, and
> argued before them mightily for Hawly, but all would not do, although I made
> her angry by calling her old, and making her know what herself is. Her body
> was out of temper for any dalliance… (Diary 5th April 1664)

Later the same day, Pepys goes home and in a fit of pique physically assaults his
wife, thereby adding wife-beating to the catalogue of wrongs he has done her:

> …home myself, where I find my wife dressed as if she had been abroad, but I
> think she was not, but she answering me some way that I did not like I pulled
> her by the nose, indeed to offend her, though afterwards to appease her I
> denied it, but only it was done in haste. The poor wretch took it mighty ill,
> and I believe besides wringing her nose she did feel pain, and so cried a great
> while, but by and by I made her friends, and so after supper to my office a
> while, and then home to bed. (Diary 5th April 1664)

On Monday 18th April, Pepys intends to collect Betty and take her off for another
'tousing', but she is not to be found at her premises and his plan is frustrated. Two
days later on the 20th he is more successful, but this time seems more intent on
establishing an alibi:

> I went also out of the Hall with Mrs. Lane to the Swan at Mrs. Herbert's in
> the Palace Yard to try a couple of bands, and did (though I had a mind to be
> playing the fool with her) purposely stay but a little while, and kept the door
> open, and called the master and mistress of the house one after another to
> drink and talk with me, and showed them both my old and new bands. So
> that as I did nothing so they are able to bear witness that I had no opportunity
> there to do anything. (Diary 20th April 1664)

Betty disappears from the narrative for three months, but then Pepys hears what
for him is good news:

> But being at Westminster Hall I met with great news that Mrs. Lane is
> married to one Martin, one that serves Captain Marsh. She is gone abroad
> with him to-day, very fine. I must have a bout with her very shortly to see how
> she finds marriage. (Diary 20th July 1664)

Having a married mistress lets Pepys off the hook and he can do what he likes with her. He quickly takes advantage of his new status and does not delay in 'having a bout' with her – the very next day he pays her a visit and as luck would have it, finds her new husband not at home:

> Thence to Westminster and to Mrs. Lane's lodgings, to give her joy, and there suffered me to deal with her as I hoped to do, and by and by her husband comes, a sorry, simple fellow, and his letter to her which she proudly showed me a simple, nonsensical thing. A man of no discourse, and I fear married her to make a prize of, which he is mistaken in, and a sad wife I believe she will prove to him, for she urged me to appoint a time as soon as he is gone out of town to give her a meeting next week. (Diary 21st July 1664)

Mr Martin obviously goes out of town sooner than expected, for two days later, Pepys is planning to cuckold him:

> … away to Westminster Hall, and there light of Mrs. Lane, and plotted with her to go over the water. So met at White's stairs in Chanel Row, and over to the old house at Lambeth Marsh, and there eat and drank, and had my pleasure of her twice, she being the strangest woman in talk of love to her husband sometimes, and sometimes again she do not care for him, and yet willing enough to allow me a liberty of doing what I would with her. So spending 5s. or 6s. [25–30 pence] upon her, I could do what I would, and after an hour's stay and more back again and set her ashore there again… (Diary 23rd July 1664)

Having dropped her off after more than an hour of sexual congress, Pepys incredibly heads off to a brothel, but loses his nerve for fear of catching some venereal disease:

> …I forward to Fleet Street, and called at Fleet Alley, [disappeared in the Great Fire and its location is not precisely known, but conjecture places it close to the Fleet Prison – a likely setting for a red light district containing a 'wicked house'] not knowing how to command myself, and went in and there saw what formerly I have been acquainted with, the wickedness of these houses, and the forcing a man to present expense. The woman indeed is a most lovely woman, but I had no courage to meddle with her for fear of her not being wholesome, and so counterfeiting that I had not money enough, it was pretty to see how cunning she was, would not suffer me to have to do in any manner with her after she saw I had no money, but told me then I would not come again, but she now was sure I would come again, but I hope in God I shall not, for though she be one of the prettiest women I ever saw, yet I fear her abusing me. So desiring God to forgive me for this vanity, I went home,

taking some books from my bookseller, and taking his lad home with me, to whom I paid 10l. [£10] for books I have laid up money for, and laid out within these three weeks, and shall do no more a great while I hope. So to my office writing letters, and then home and to bed, weary of the pleasure I have had to-day, and ashamed to think of it. (Diary 23rd July 1664)

A month later, Pepys' suppositions about Betty's husband prove to be well-founded and the new husband is apparently penniless. However, Betty sees an opportunity:

...and thence to the Trumpett, [inn located in King Street, Westminster] whither came Mrs. Lane, and there begins a sad story how her husband, as I feared, proves not worth a farthing, and that she is with child and undone, if I do not get him a place. I had my pleasure here of her, and she, like an impudent jade, depends upon my kindness to her husband, but I will have no more to do with her, let her brew as she has baked, seeing she would not take my counsel about Hawly. After drinking we parted... (Diary 15th August 1664)

By September, Betty has found an ally:

...and so home and to dinner, and thither came W. Bowyer and dined with us. ... he tells us how Mrs. Lane is undone, by her marrying so bad, and desires to speak with me, which I know is wholly to get me to do something for her to get her husband a place, which he is in no wise fit for. (Diary 5th September 1664)

Pepys still does nothing for Mr Martin, so Betty tries yet again:

This morning Mrs. Lane [now Martin] like a foolish woman, came to the Horseshoe hard by [not known for certain which of three inns of this name within walking distance of the Navy Office] , and sent for me while I was at the office; to come to speak with her by a note sealed up, I know to get me to do something for her husband, but I sent her an answer that I would see her at Westminster, and so I did not go, and she went away, poor soul...' (Diary 1st October 1664)

On Sunday, the Pepyses go to church, but his wife is not so blind to his escapades as he might think, and dark domestic clouds begin to gather: '...and so after church walked all over the fields home, and there my wife was angry with me for not coming home, and for gadding abroad to look after beauties, she told me plainly, so I made all peace, and to supper.' (Diary 2nd October 1664)

Elizabeth Pepys is obviously not as vacuous as she looks in her portraits. With unfortunate timing, the same evening brings visitors:

This evening came Mrs. Lane [now Martin] with her husband to desire my help about a place for him. It seems poor Mr. Daniel is dead of the Victualling Office, a place too good for this puppy to follow him in. But I did give him the best words I could, and so after drinking a glasse of wine sent them going, but with great kindnesse. Go to supper, prayers, and to bed. (Diary 2nd October 1664)

Nearly two months later, Pepys has still made no effort to find Mr Martin a place. Having parked his wife, he drops into Westminster Hall:

…and by and by in the evening took my wife out by coach, leaving her at Unthanke's [John Unthanke was Elizabeth Pepys' tailor, and he had a large shop at Charing Cross. It also served as a sort of ad hoc ladies club] while I to White Hall and to Westminster Hall, where I have not been to talk a great while, and there hear that Mrs. Lane and her husband live a sad life together, and he is gone to be a paymaster to a company to Portsmouth to serve at sea. She big with child. (Diary 25th November 1664)

Pepys has other fish to fry. In November, Mrs. Bagwell had at last given into him, on the usual promise that he would do something to further her husband's career. However, less than two weeks later, Pepys is again in Westminster Hall, where, unsurprisingly, Mrs. Lane takes the opportunity to lobby him yet again. Under the ploy of a purchase, Pepys induces her to return home, whence he follows, and in spite of the fact that she is heavily six months pregnant, sexually abuses her in her own house:

I to Westminster Hall, and there spent much time till towards noon to and fro with people. So by and by Mrs. Lane comes and plucks me by the cloak to speak to me, and I was fain to go to her shop, and pretending to buy some bands made her go home, and by and by followed her, and there did what I would with her, and so after many discourses and her intreating [sic] me to do something for her husband, which I promised to do, and buying a little band of her, which I intend to keep to, I took leave, there coming a couple of footboys to her with a coach to fetch her abroad I know not to whom. She is great with child, and she says I must be godfather, but I do not intend it. (Diary 6th December 1664)

Betty has obviously found other benefactors, as a coach with footmen has arrived to take her off somewhere. In the New Year, Pepys again takes her out to supper and then back to her place, where as usual he 'does what he would with her':

Then to the Hall, and there agreed with Mrs. Martin, and to her lodgings which she has now taken to lie in, in Bow Streete, pitiful poor things, yet she thinks them pretty, and so they are for her condition I believe good enough. Here I did 'ce que je voudrais avec' [everything I wanted with] her most freely, and it having cost 2s. [10 pence] in wine and cake upon her, I away sick of her impudence… (Diary 6th December 1664)

Back home, the storm clouds that began to gather over his marriage the previous September have not gone away:

So back again home, where thinking to be merry was vexed with my wife's having looked out a letter in Sir Philip Sidney about jealousy for me to read, which she industriously and maliciously caused me to do, and the truth is my conscience told me it was most proper for me, and therefore was touched at it, but tooke no notice of it, but read it out most frankly, but it stucke in my stomach… (Diary 6th December 1664)

As if the liaisons with Mrs. Martin and Mrs. Bagwell were not sufficient, Pepys also makes a pass at his barbers' maid, Jane. He writes in the diary: 'je avait grande envie envers elle avec vrai amour et passion' [I longed for her with great love and passion] but he is rebuffed. Three months apparently passes before Pepys returns to Westminster Hall:

…where I hear Mrs. Martin is brought to bed of a boy and christened Charles, which I am very glad of, for I was fearful of being called to be a godfather to it. But it seems it was to be done suddenly, and so I escaped. It is strange to see how a liberty and going abroad without purpose of doing anything do lead a man to what is bad, for I was just upon going to her, where I must of necessity [have] broken my oath or made a forfeit. But I did not, company being (I heard by my porter) with her, and so I home again… (Diary 9th March 1665)

In spite of sexually abusing her both before and after her marriage, as well as during her advanced pregnancy, and despite his promises to obtain a place for her cuckolded husband, Pepys has done nothing:

…so I home, and there meeting a letter from Mrs. Martin desiring to speak with me, I (though against my promise of visiting her) did go, and there found her in her childbed dress desiring my favour to get her husband a place. I staid not long… (Diary 13th March 1665)

Two weeks later, Pepys is up to his old tricks again, leaving his wife somewhere else whilst he goes off in search of compliant female company, this time a barmaid at The Swan, before calling briefly at Mrs. Martin's:

Thence abroad, carried my wife to Westminster by coach, I to the Swan, Herbert's, and there had much of the good company of Sarah and to my wish, and then to see Mrs. Martin, who was very kind, three weeks of her month of lying in is over. So took up my wife and home… (Diary 23rd March 1665)

And he is back to his old abusive ways with her only four days later: 'Thence to Mrs. Martin, who, though her husband is gone away, as he writes, like a fool into France, yet is as simple and wanton as ever she was, with much I made myself merry and away.' (Diary 27th March 1665)

Apparently, Mr Martin has learned that what is sauce for the goose is sauce for the gander:

Thence to see Mrs. Martin, whose husband being it seems gone away, and as she is informed he hath another woman whom he uses, and has long done, as a wife, she is mighty reserved and resolved to keep herself so till the return of her husband, which a pleasant thing to think of her. (Diary 30th March 1665)

In June, probably to his great relief, Betty drops out of Pepys' life for some eight months:

Here I hear Mrs. Martin is gone out of town, and that her husband, an idle fellow, is since come out of France, as he pretends, but I believe not that he hath been. I was fearful of going to any house, but I did to the Swan, and thence to White Hall… (Diary 28th June 1665)

Mrs Lane (Pepys refers to her by her former name) makes no further appearance in the diary until some eight months later:

I away to Westminster Hall, and there hear that Mrs. Lane is come to town. So I staid loitering up and down till anon she comes and agreed to meet at Swayn's, and there I went anon, and she come, but staid but little, the place not being private. I have not seen her since before the plague. So thence parted and 'rencontrais a' her last 'logis', [met her at her last lodgings] and in the place did what I 'tenais a mind pour ferais con her' [did what I had a mind to do with her]. At last she desired to borrow money of me, 5l. [five pounds] and would pawn gold with me for it, which I accepted and promised in a day or two to supply her. (Diary 20th February 1666)

It has not taken long for Pepys to get up to his old tricks with the lady and far from having nothing more to do with her as he resolved, he is even lending her money:

…and thence going out of the Hall was called to by Mrs. Martin, so I went to her and bought two bands, and so parted, and by and by met at her chamber, and there did what I would……. Thence to the Palace Yard, to the Swan, and there staid till it was dark, and then to Mrs. Lane's, and there lent her 5l. upon 4l. 01s. in gold. And then did what I would with her, and I perceive she is come to be very bad, and offers anything, that it is dangerous to have to do with her, nor will I see [her] any more a good while. (Diary 28th February 1666)

The only way to interpret the strange transaction is that Pepys is acting as a pawnbroker, and advancing cash against a security – presumably he offered a better rate than a bona fide dealer. The following month, Pepys is at a loose end after Sunday dinner, so goes out for a stroll, hoping to set eyes on Frances Butler, the renowned beauty who occasionally pops up in the diary from 1660 onwards:

(Lord's day). Up and my cold better, so to church, and then home to dinner, and so walked out to St. James's Church, thinking to have seen faire Mrs. Butler, but could not, she not being there, nor, I believe, lives thereabouts now. (Diary 18th March 1666)

In spite of his resolve not to see Mrs Lane [aka Mrs Martin] for a good while, he can't resist the temptation. Being Sunday, the lady's husband is at home, but this does not cause the resourceful Mr Pepys too much of a problem, sending Mr Martin out on a shopping errand to buy wine for them while he has his wicked way with his wife:

So walked to Westminster, very fine fair dry weather, but all cry out for lack of rain. To Herbert's and drank, and thence to Mrs. Martin's, and did what I would with her; her husband going for some wine for us. The poor man I do think would take pains if I can get him a purser's place, which I will endeavour. (Diary 18th March 1660)

Back in January 1663, Pepys had mentioned the daughter of a bookseller in Westminster Hall that he had a fancy to: 'I took occasion to enquire of Howlett's daughter, with whom I have a mind to meet a little to see what mettle the young wench is made of, being very pretty, but she tells me she is already betrothed to Mrs. Michell's son …' (Diary 9th January 1663)

In spite of his referring to her as 'my second wife', this Betty seems to be one that got away:

… She tells me as a secret that Betty Howlet of the Hall, my little sweetheart, that I used to call my second wife, is married to a younger son of Mr. Michell's (his elder brother, who should have had her, being dead this plague), at which I am glad, and that they are to live nearer me in Thames Streete, by the Old Swan. (Diary 18th March 1666)

On the 16th April, Pepys looks for Mrs Lane in Westminster Hall, but on the way calls in at his stationers 'for my ruled papers, and they are done, and I am much more taken with her black maid Nan'. He fails to find her, but later in the week has more luck:

> Up, and after an houre or two's talke with my poor wife, who gives me more and more content every day than other, I abroad by coach to Westminster, and there met with Mrs. Martin, and she and I over the water to Stangold, and after a walke in the fields to the King's Head, and there spent an houre or two with pleasure with her, and eat a tansy and so parted. (Diary 20th April 1666)

As is often the case, Pepys is at a loose end on Sunday afternoon, so takes a stroll in search of his usual amusement, although on this occasion, without success: '… I to and again up and down Westminster, thinking to have spent a little time with Sarah at the Swan, or Mrs. Martin, but was disappointed in both.' (Diary 13th May 1666)

The Sarah to whom he refers is Sarah Udall, who with her sister Frances, are serving maids at the Swan Inn in New Palace Yard adjacent to Westminster Hall. The former married John Harmond in 1666, although that did not stop Pepys, as is recorded elsewhere. On the following Sunday, he is at it yet again with Betty Martin: '… I out to Westminster, and straight to Mrs. Martin's, and there did what I would with her, she staying at home all the day for me; and not being well pleased with her over free and loose company, I away to Westminster Abbey …' (Diary 20th May 1666)

The Sunday excursion is becoming a habit, but this week she has company: '… I by water to Westminster to Mrs. Martin's, and there sat with her and her husband and Mrs. Burrows, the pretty, an hour or two, then to the Swan a while, and so home by water, and with my wife by and by …' (Diary 27th May 1666)

The following week he is more fortunate: '… and thence to the Abbey, and so to Mrs. Martin, and there did what 'je voudrais avec her [what I would with her] …' (Diary 3rd June 1666)

Through the rest of the month and into July, Pepys calls on her but seems to confine himself to conversation:

> Thence to the Hall and with Mrs. Martin home and staid with her a while, and then away to the Swan and sent for a bit of meat and dined there … (Diary 20th June 1666);
>
> Thence parted and to Mrs. Martin's lodgings, and sat with her a while, and then by water home. (Diary 31st July 1666)

However, visiting her on the 25th, the pregnant Mrs Martin is greatly concerned over the safety of her husband, whom she thinks has sailed away to war. For whatever reason, Pepys does not tell her that Mr Martin is still in port:

> … I away to Mrs. Martin's new lodgings, where I find her, and was with her close, but, Lord! how big she is already. She is, at least seems, in mighty trouble for her husband at sea, when I am sure she cares not for him, and I would not undeceive her, though I know his ship is one of those that is not gone, but left behind without men. (Diary 25th July 1666)

Having left her, Pepys calls upon another lady of his acquaintance, the widow of a naval lieutenant who had died the previous year, and with whom he had several dalliances: 'Thence to White Hall again to hear news, but found none; so back toward Westminster, and there met Mrs. Burroughs, whom I had a mind to meet, but being undressed [i.e. not wearing foundation garments or formal gown] did appear a mighty ordinary woman.' (Diary 25th July 1666)

On Wednesday, 1st August, Pepys calls on Mrs Martin again and this time strikes gold, for she has a house full of amiable lady visitors, who are apparently more than willing to take part in a rough and tumble:

> And I to Mrs. Martin's, but she abroad, so I sauntered to or again to the Abbey, and then to the parish church, fearfull of being seen to do so, and so after the parish church was ended, I to the Swan and there dined upon a rabbit, and after dinner to Mrs. Martin's, and there find Mrs. Burroughs, and by and by comes a pretty widow, one Mrs. Eastwood, and one Mrs. Fenton, a maid; and here merry kissing and looking on their breasts, and all the innocent pleasure in the world' But, Lord! to see the dissembling of this widow, how upon the singing of a certain jigg by Doll, Mrs. Martin's sister, she seemed to be sick and fainted and God knows what, because the jigg, which her husband (who died this last sickness) loved. But by and by I made her as merry as is possible, and towzed and tumbled her as I pleased, and then carried her and her sober pretty kinswoman Mrs. Fenton home to their lodgings in the new market of my Lord Treasurer's, and there left them. Mightily pleased with this afternoon's mirth, but in great pain to ride in a coach with them, for fear of being seen. (Diary 1st August 1666)

Wednesday afternoons seemed to have temporarily replaced Sundays as an occasion for erotic entertainments – on a Wednesday in September Pepys goes: '… Thence to Martin, and there did 'tout ce que je voudrais avec' [everything I wanted with] her, and drank, and away by water home and to dinner. …' (Diary 12th September 1666)

This might have been sufficient unto the day for most men, but Pepys still has an appetite for more and is not shy in recording the details; indeed, one has to admire his energy:

So we back home, and then I found occasion to return in the dark and to [Mrs] Bagwell, and there nudo in lecto con ella [naked in bed with her] did do all that I desired; but though I did intend para aver demorado con ella toda la night [intended to stay with her all night], yet when I had done ce que je voudrais [what I wanted], I did hate both ella and la cosa [hated both her and the thing, i.e.sex]; and taking occasion from the occasion of 'su marido's return ... did me lever', [uncertain of her husband's return that night, did get up] and so away home late. ... (Diary 12th September 1666)

One wonders what he told Elizabeth when he got home in the early hours? The diary is silent on this point. A month later on the 12th October, Pepys gets himself sexually aroused by toying with the serving maid in The Swan and then pops round for a bout with the heavily pregnant Betty;

So to the Swan, and there sent for a piece of meat and dined alone and played with Sarah, and so to the Hall a while, and thence to Mrs. Martin's lodging and did what I would with her. She is very big, and resolves I must be godfather. (Diary 12th October 1666)

A couple of days later he calls again on Sunday afternoon, but this time trying to meet up with the beautiful Mrs Burrows, but without success. Another week goes by, and after taking his wife to church in the morning, calls again on Betty in the afternoon. This time, her sister Doll (who was amongst the group with whom he romped in August) is also visiting, and he adds another score to his growing tally: 'This afternoon I went to see and sat a good while with Mrs. Martin, and there was her sister Doll, with whom, contrary to all expectation, I did what I would, and might have done anything else.' (Diary 21st October 1666)

One wonders what Mrs Betty Martin was doing whilst her erstwhile lover was enjoying himself with her sister. The following Sunday, a similar pattern occurs of church followed by a visit to Betty – this time for a double header:

I presently to Mrs. Martin's, and there met widow Burroughes and Doll, and did tumble them all the afternoon as I pleased, and having given them a bottle of wine I parted and home by boat (my brother going by land), and thence with my wife to sit and sup with my uncle and aunt Wight, and see Woolly's wife, who is a pretty woman, and after supper, being very merry, in abusing my aunt with Dr. Venner, we home. ... (Diary 28th October 1666)

The reference to his brother is interesting – it sounds as though he was also present, although the diary does not say so. On 19 November, Pepys sends Mrs Martin six bottles of wine as he had earlier promised. On Saturday, Mr Martin comes round to tell him that Betty has been delivered of a baby girl. On Monday,

Pepys meets Mrs Burrows (or Burroughs as she has now become in the diary) after which he retires to the usual inn:

> Thence to the Swan, having sent for some burnt claret, and there by and by comes Doll Lane, and she and I sat and drank and talked a great while, among other things about her sister's being brought to bed, and I to be godfather to the girle. I did tumble Doll, and do almost what I would with her, and so parted, and I took coach, and to the New Exchange, buying a neat's [calf's] tongue by the way, thinking to eat it out of town … (Diary 26th November 1666)

The insatiable Pepys is still game for more when he chances upon Mrs Burroughs for a second time, but she is unable to accompany him: '… but there I find Burroughs in company of an old woman, an aunt of hers, whom she could not leave for half an hour. So after buying a few baubles to while away time, I down to Westminster …' (Diary 26th November 1666)

Later in December, Pepys pops round to the Martin's on Sunday afternoon, but they have visitors and her husband is home:

> Then after dinner by water to Westminster to see Mrs. Martin, whom I found up in her chamber and ready to go abroad. I sat there with her and her husband and others a pretty while, and then away to White Hall, and there walked up and down to the Queen's side, and there saw my dear Lady Castlemayne, who continues admirable, methinks, and I do not hear but that the King is the same to her still as ever. (Diary 16th December 1666)

Two days later, it sounds as though Betty is telling him that he is the father of the child, as the timing fits exactly:

> So to Westminster Hall, where the Lords are sitting still, I to see Mrs. Martin, who is very well, and intends to go abroad to-morrow after her childbed. She do tell me that this child did come is 'meme jour that it ought to hazer after my avoir ete con elle before her marid did venir home … [the same day that it ought to have been after my being with her before her husband came home].

As Mrs Martin is clearly not up for it on this occasion, Pepys goes off to find Sarah Udall, usually a sure bet for a kiss and a grope: 'Thence to the Swan, and there I sent for Sarah, and mighty merry we were …' (Diary 18th December 1666)

On the last day of the year, he meets another lady with a business in Westminster Hall, who is no doubt filed away for future reference: '… so going back again I met Doll Lane [Mrs. Martin's sister], with another young woman of the Hall, one Scott, and took them to the Half Moon Taverne and there drank some burnt wine with them, without more pleasure …' (Diary 31st December 1666)

On the 1st February, Pepys pays a visit to Mrs Bagwell (whom we shall meet elsewhere) and has an energetic afternoon. Following this, he away to Westminster Hall, where he comes across Betty's sister Doll, who he takes to the Bell Tavern although she puts up some little resistance, affords him much pleasure. On the 5th February, he complains of a bruise on his right testicle, but does not know how he came by it (the reader is permitted one guess). This provides an excellent excuse for some more hanky-panky with Betty:

> Thence by coach to the New Exchange and there laid out money, and I did give Betty Mitchell two pair of gloves and a dressing-box. And so home in the dark over the ruins with a link. I was troubled with my pain, having got a bruise on my right testicle, I know not how. But this I did make good use of to make my wife shift sides with me, and I did come to sit avec Betty Mitchell and there I had her mano [hand], which ella [she] did give me very frankly now, and did hazer whatever I voudrais avec la [wanted with her] – which did plazer me grandement [give me great pleasure]. (Diary 5th February 1667)

Astonishingly, Pepys swops seats with his wife in the coach in order to be able to sit next to Mrs Mitchell thereby making it possible for her to wank him off during the journey! How is this possible with his wife seated opposite them? In the world as we now experience it, we are rarely without artificial light. However, the interior of Pepys' coach would have been in pitch darkness, there being no street lights or even lights from the surrounding buildings, they having been destroyed in the fire. Pepys mention of a 'link' implies that there was a torch, although whether on or carried ahead of the coach is not clear.

Pepys is clearly not a subscriber to a feminist school of thought and obviously liked his women to be rather more submissive than Betty had become, as he complains about her worldly attitude:

> … and thence to the Temple to walk a little only, and then to Westminster to pass away time till noon, and here I went to Mrs. Martin's to thank her for her oysters and there did hazer tout ce que je would con her, [did everything that I would with her] and she grown la plus bold moher of the orbis [very bold woman of the world] – so that I was almost defessus [tired] of the pleasure que ego was used para tener with ella [that I used to have with her]. (Diary 16th February 1667)

On Wednesday, 13th March, Pepys gets rid of his wife for a while and goes off to the Martins in search of female company. Mrs Burroughs is also there on a visit, but Mr Martin is also at home, so he draws a blank. Off Pepys goes in search of Betty's sister, Doll, and finds her at Westminster Hall and arranges to meet her at The Rose inn (one of three in the diary – probably the one located in King Street, close to Westminster Hall). However, in spite of the fact that he waits around for two hours, she fails to show up:

> ... sent my wife to the New Exchange. I staid not here, but to Westminster Hall, and thence to Martin's, where he and she both within, and with them the little widow [Mrs. Burroughs] that was once there with her when I was there, that dissembled so well to be grieved at hearing a tune that her, late husband liked, but there being so much company, I had no pleasure here, and so away to the Hall again, and there met Doll Lane coming out, and 'par contrat did hazer bargain para aller to the cabaret de vin', [by arrangement did go to the tavern] called the Rose, and 'ibi' [there] I staid two hours, 'sed' she did not 'venir', 'lequel' [but she did not come] troubled me, and so away by coach and took up my wife, and away home ... (Diary 13th March 1667)

Next Wednesday is a very busy day for our lothario ...

> Thence to Westminster Hall and drank at the Swan, and besado the petite moza; [kissed the little miss – Sarah Udall] and so to Mrs. Martins who I find in opposante and su hermana [her sister] rising. So here I had opportunity para tocar tout sobra su [to play with her] body as I would, and did traher su pernos out of the lecto [broke the springs of the bed] and do hazer myself hazer [make myself do the thing, i.e. orgasm]. I sent for some burnt wine, and drank and then away, not pleased with my folly, and so to the Hall again, and there staid a little, and so home by water again ... (Diary 20th March 1667)

The following Sunday, far from being a day of rest, is an extremely busy one for Pepys. After discussing the fortifications on the Medway with the king and the Duke of York, he then goes to church before returning home to dinner with his brother. Then off to Whitehall with Balty, walking in the park whilst giving him employment advice, before going ...

> I to Martin's, where I find her within, and su hermano [her sister] and la veuve [the widow] Burroughs. Here I did demeurer toda [stayed all the afternoon] bezando las [kissing her] and drank; and among other things, did by a trick arrive at tocando el poilde la thing de the veuve [touching the hair of the thing of the widow] above said. By and by come up the mistress of the house, Crags, a pleasant jolly woman. I staid all but a little ... (Diary Sunday, 24th March 1667)

Pepys tries to see her again on one or two occasions, and succeeds on the 23rd April, but his relationship with her seems to have become routine and hardly worth noting: '... and so to Mrs. Martin's, and there did hazer [all] what I would con [with] her ...' (Diary 23rd April 1667)

He does not see Betty again until nearly a month later, but on the same day records as an afterthought that he has also partially stripped a young girl in the Swan (presumably in order to touch her breasts) and was caught in the act by the girl's uncle:

> … and so away to Mrs. Martin's lodging, who was gone before, expecting me, and there je hazer what je vellem cum [did what I would with] her and drank, and so by coach home (but I have forgot that I did in the morning go to the Swan, and there tumbling of la little fille [little girl], son uncle did trouver her cum su [find her with her] neckcloth off, which I was ashamed of, but made no great matter of it, but let it pass with a laugh … (Diary 20th May 1667)

A week on finds him titillating himself by observing women in church through his telescope, after which he is no doubt in the right mood for his usual after church tryst:

> … so I to the church, and seeing her return did go out again myself, but met with Mr. Howlett, who, offering me a pew in the gallery, I had no excuse but up with him I must go, and then much against my will staid out the whole church in pain while she expected me at home, but I did entertain myself with my perspective glass up and down the church, by which I had the great pleasure of seeing and gazing at a great many very fine women; and what with that, and sleeping, I passed away the time till sermon was done, and then to Mrs. Martin, and there staid with her an hour or two, and there did what I would with her … (Diary 26th May 1667)
>
> … So away thence, and after church time to Mrs. Martin's, and then hazer what I would with her. (Diary 9th June 1667)

However, Pepys is in for a shock. …

> … I to Mrs. Martin's, and there she was gone in before, but when I come, contrary to my expectation, I find her all in trouble, and what was it for but that I have got her with child … and is in exceeding grief, and swears that the child is mine, which I do not believe, but yet do comfort her that either it cannot be so, or if it be that I will take care to send for her husband, though I do hardly see how I can be sure of that, the ship being at sea, and as far as Scotland, but however I must do it, and shall find some way or other of doing it, though it do trouble me not a little. (Diary 3rd July 1667)

Luckily for him, the panic is short lived, for three days later Pepys discovers that it has all been a false alarm:

… and then to Mrs. Martin's, where I met with the good news que elle ne est con child, [she is not with child] the fear of which she did give me the other day, had troubled me much. My joy in this made me send for wine, and thither come her sister and Mrs. Cragg, and I staid a good while there.

Betty's sister Doll goes out for the wine, and on the way gets more than she bargained for:

But here happened the best instance of a woman's falseness in the world, that her sister Doll, who went for a bottle of wine, did come home all blubbering and swearing against one Captain Vandener, a Dutchman of the Rhenish Wine House, that pulled her into a stable by the Dog tavern, and there did tumble her and toss her, calling him all the rogues and toads in the world, when she knows that elle hath suffered me to do anything with her a hundred times. (Diary 6th July 1667)

As if to prove his point, Pepys goes in for a three-in-a-bed romp: 'So to Westminster Hall and there staid a while, and thence to Mrs. Martin's, and there did take a little pleasure both with her and her sister.' (Diary 21st August 1667)

For whatever reason, Doll is a lot cooler towards him when they next have an encounter:

… and there called at Michell's, and there had opportunity para kiss su moher, [kiss her sister] but elle [she] did receive it with a great deal of seeming regret, which did vex me. But however I do not doubt overcoming her as I did the moher of the monsieur at Deptford.

Unfazed by this experience, Pepys continues with his regular visits to Betty:

Thence to the Hall, and there talked a little with Mrs. Michell, and so to Mrs. Martin's to pay for my cuffs and drink with her and did hazer la cosa [have my way] with her. (Diary 17th September 1667)

… and away to the Hall, and thence to Mrs. Martin's, to bespeak some linen, and there je did avoir [I did have] all with her, and drank, and away … (Diary 30th September 1667)

… to Mrs. Martin's lodging, whither I sent for her, and there hear that her husband is come from sea, which is sooner than I expected; and here I staid and drank, and so did toucher elle [feel her] and away … (Diary 4th October 1667)

After dinner with my wife and girl to Unthanke's, and there left her, and I to Westminster, and there to Mrs. Martin's, and did hazer con elle [did everything with her] what I desired, and there did drink with her … (Diary 31st December 1667)

In the new year, Pepys has other fish to fry and Betty Martin is neglected for some time. It is March before he picks up where he left off, and in spite of other company being present on the next two occasions still manages to slake his lust. Whether the others present sat and watched, participated in the activities, or retired discreetly to another room, sadly we will never know:

> Thence to Mrs. Martin's, where I have not been also a good while, and with great difficulty, company being there, did get an opportunity to hazer what I would con her … [do what I would with her]. (Diary 1st March 1668)
>
> After dinner, away hence, and I to Mrs. Martin's, and there spent the afternoon, and did hazer con elle, [and did it with her] and here was her sister and Mrs. Burrows, and so in the evening got a coach and home … (Diary 15th March 1668)
>
> … but then to Westminster Hall and took a turn, and so to Mrs. Martin's, and there did sit a little and talk and drink, and did hazer con her, and so took coach and called my wife at Unthanke's … (Diary 27th March 1668)
>
> … and thence to Mrs. Martin's, and, there did what I would, she troubled for want of employ for her husband, spent on her 1s [1 shilling = 5 pence] (Diary 16th April 1668)
>
> … and so to walk towards Michell's to see her, but could not, and so to Martin's, and her husband was at home, and so took coach and to the Park, and thence home and to bed betimes. (Diary 19th April 1668)

Then comes some sad news: 'Thence to walk in the Hall, and there hear that Mrs. Martin's child, my god-daughter, is dead …' (Diary 5th May 1668)

This was not unusual in Pepys' day – a cumulative total of 36 per cent of children died before the age of 6, and another 24 per cent between the ages of 7 and 16. In all, of 100 live births, 60 would die before the age of 16.

This is the child that Mrs Martin had tried to persuade Pepys was his, but he would only acknowledge it in so far as he was prepared to become its godfather, and had from time to time bought the little girl clothes: 'She doth tell me that this child did come la meme jour [the same day] that it ought to hazer after my avoir ete con elle [having been with her] before her marido [husband] did venir [did come] home …' (Diary 18th December 1666)

However, with child mortality being common the grief did not last long, for two weeks later, Pepys was back to his old habits: '… and so to Mrs. Martin's, and there did hazer cet que je voudrai mit her [what I would like to with her] and drank and sat most of the afternoon with her and her sister …' (Diary 21st May 1668)

On the 1st June, Pepys on his regular visit, not only does what he wants with Betty, but even manages to grope her landlady!

> … hence I to Westminster and to Mrs. Martin's, and did hazer what je would con her, and did once toker la thigh de su landlady. …

Now in the mood for a little voyeuristic titivation, Pepys next takes himself off to Fox Hall. Located on the south side of the Thames across from Whitehall, it was an area of avenues, gardens, covered walks and booths in which one could obtain a drink. It provided a place to take the air, and also for providing discreet, amatory meetings. By the early eighteenth century it was notorious for its quantity of prostitutes. Here he spies on two couples for upwards of an hour before tiring of the sport and returning home:

> … and thence all alone to Fox Hall, and walked and saw young Newport, and two more rogues of the town, seize on two ladies, who walked with them an hour with their masks on; perhaps civil ladies; and there I left them, and so home … (Diary 1st June 1668)
>
> So to the Fair, [a Charter Fair held within the precincts of the priory of St. Bartholomew's in West Smithfield] and there saw several sights; among others, the mare that tells money, and many things to admiration; and, among others, come to me, when she was bid to go to him of the company that most loved a pretty wench in a corner. And this did cost me 12d. [i.e. 1 shilling = 5 pence] to the horse, which I had flung him before, and did give me occasion to baiser a mighty belle fille [kiss a mighty pretty girl] that was in the house that was exceeding plain, but fort belle. (Diary 1st September 1668)

Betty and her sister Doll are not mentioned again for more than six months. It is the following spring before Pepys records visiting them again:

> Thence to Westminster by water and to the Hall, where Mrs. Michell do surprize me with the news that Doll Lane is suddenly brought to bed at her sister's lodging, and gives it out that she is married, but there is no such thing certainly, she never mentioning it before, but I have cause to rejoice that I have not seen her a great while, she having several times desired my company, but I doubt to an evil end. (Diary 17th March 1669)

Pepys makes one or two further calls in April and May, but Betty has gone off with her husband to Portsmouth:

> Thence out, and slipped out by water to Westminster Hall and there thought to have spoke with Mrs. Martin, but she was not there, nor at home. So back again … (Diary 9th April 1669)
>
> … thence by water to Westminster Hall, and there did beckon to Doll Lane, now Mrs. Powell, as she would have herself called, and went to her sister Martin's lodgings, the first time I have been there these eight or ten

months, I think, and her sister being gone to Portsmouth to her husband, I did stay and talk and drink with Doll ... So away ... (Diary 19th April 1669)

Thence I to White Hall, and there took boat to Westminster, and to Mrs. Martin's, who is not come to town from her husband at Portsmouth. So drank only at Cragg's with Doll, and so to the Swan, and there baiser [kiss] a new maid that is there, and so to White Hall again ... (Diary 10th May 1669)

Finally on the 12th May, Mrs Martin returns from Portsmouth and Pepys has sex with her for what may or may not have been the last time, as from the tone of this final entry his attraction to her has clearly turned sour:

... and so to Mrs. Martin's lodging, who come to town last night, and there je did hazer her, she having been a month, I think, at Portsmouth with her husband, newly come home from the Streights. But, Lord! how silly the woman talks of her great entertainment there, and how all the gentry come to visit her, and that she believes her husband is worth 6 or 700l., which nevertheless I am glad of, but I doubt they will spend it as fast. (Diary 12th May 1669)

The diary comes to an end on the 31st May, as Pepys thought he was going blind, so whether or not he ever met Betty again we shall probably never know, although Samuel Martin was corresponding with him between 1672 and 1674. Without the diary, she disappears from history at this point, although we know a little about her husband's subsequent career. Her claim that he was worth six or seven hundred pounds in 1669 seems unlikely. Pepys described him as being 'not worth a farthing', although when he married Mrs Lane in 1664, he was gainfully employed in the Ordnance Office of the Tower of London. He later became a purser in at least five ships until 1672 when he was appointed to the prestigious position of Consul in Algiers. He corresponded with Pepys in that capacity, in tones of great respect, and showed himself to be a man of some ability.[3] In 1674 he sent Pepys a tame lion, which Pepys found 'good company' although how and where he kept it remains a mystery.

---

3. Samuel Martin's story (and by inference that of Betty) does not have a happy ending. In 1677 he found himself in debtor's prison through having engaged in some unsuccessful trading ventures, and he died a year later in 1678, most probably leaving an impoverished widow. If this were the case, it seems highly unlikely that, given their long association, Betty did not approach Pepys for financial assistance. Whether or not he gave it we will almost certainly never know.

Chapter 11

A Most Modest Woman

Elizabeth Burrows was the attractive young widow of Anthony Burrows, a naval lieutenant who had been killed in action in 1665. Her mother was Mrs Crofts who kept a shop in Westminster where Elizabeth seems to have worked. She first appears in the diary in June 1665, when she is obviously already known to Pepys:

> … to Westminster Hall, where I visited 'the flowers' in each place, and so met with Mr. Creed, and he and I to Mrs. Croft's to drink and did, but saw not her daughter Borroughes. (Diary 2nd June 1665)
>
> … and so to Mrs. Croft's, where I found and saluted Mrs. Burrows, who is a very pretty woman for a mother of so many children. (Diary 20th July 1665)

Later in the year, she turns up needing Pepys' help, probably with getting her late husband's unpaid salary. Naval seamen during the Dutch wars were paid by 'ticket', effectively an IOU which, due to the difficulty in obtaining payment, were often encashed at a discount. Pepys is not slow to turn her predicament to his lecherous advantage: 'This day I was come to by Mrs. Burrows, of Westminster, Lieutenant Burrows (lately dead) his wife, a most pretty woman and my old acquaintance; I had a kiss or two of her, and a most modest woman she is.' (Diary 21st December 1665)

She is clearly too modest for Pepys' taste, as she disappears from the diary until the following spring, when she makes a re-appearance: 'After dinner we broke up and I by water to Westminster to Mrs. Martin's, and there sat with her and her husband and Mrs. Burrows, the pretty, an hour or two, then to the Swan a while, and so home by water …' (Diary 27th May 1666)

On 15 June, Mrs Burrows turns up at Pepys' office, seeking his assistance in getting her late husband's ticket paid for his service. There would, as usual, be a price to pay for Pepys' assistance:

> So to the office, and thither came my pretty widow Mrs. Burrows, poor woman, to get her ticket paid for her husband's service which I did pay her myself, and did bezar her muchas vezes [kiss her many times] and I do hope may hereafter have mas de su [more of her] company. (Diary 15th June 1666)

… thence to the office, where Mrs. Burroughs, my pretty widow, was and so I did her business and sent her away by agreement, and presently I by coach after and took her up in Fenchurch Streete and away through the City, hiding my face as much as I could, but she being mighty pretty and well enough clad, I was not afeard, but only lest somebody should see me and think me idle. I quite through with her, and so into the fields Uxbridge way, a mile or two beyond Tyburne, and then back and then to Paddington, and then back to Lyssen green, a place the coachman led me to (I never knew in my life) and there we eat and drank and so back to Charing Crosse, and there I set her down. All the way most excellent pretty company. I had her lips as much as I would, and a mighty pretty woman she is and very modest and yet kinde in all fair ways. All this time I passed with mighty pleasure, it being what I have for a long time wished for, and did pay this day 5s. [25 pence] forfeite for her company. (Diary 12th July 1666)

… so back toward Westminster, and there met Mrs. Burroughs, whom I had a mind to meet, but being undressed did appear a mighty ordinary woman. ['Undress' in the seventeenth century referred to informal everyday clothes without stays or corsets] (Diary 25th July 1666)

Pepys has better luck the following month, although one wonders if his wife would agree with his definition of his kissing other women and looking on their breasts as 'innocent pleasure':

… after dinner to Mrs. Martin's, and there find Mrs. Burroughs, and by and by comes a pretty widow, one Mrs. Eastwood, and one Mrs. Fenton, a maid; and here merry kissing and looking on their breasts, and all the innocent pleasure in the world.(Diary 1st August 1666)

A week later, and Mrs Burrows needs Pepys' help once more, so another assignation in a coach with dinner thrown in, in return for a couple of hours of 'honest' pleasure:

… I into the Park, and there I met with Mrs. Burroughs by appointment, and did agree (after discoursing of some business of her's) for her to meet me at New Exchange, while I by coach to my Lord Treasurer's, and then called at the New Exchange, and thence carried her by water to Parliament stayres, and I to the Exchequer about my Tangier quarter tallys, and that done I took coach and to the west door of the Abby, where she come to me, and I with her by coach to Lissen-greene where we were last, and staid an hour or two before dinner could be got for us, I in the meantime having much pleasure with her, but all honest. And by and by dinner come up, and then to my sport again, but still honest; and then took coach and up and down in the country toward Acton, and then toward Chelsy, and so to Westminster, and there set her down where I took her up, with mighty pleasure in her company, and so I by coach home … (Diary 8th August 1666)

Having failed to meet up with the widow on one or two occasions, on a Sunday in late October, Pepys has better luck and enjoys a threesome:

I presently to Mrs. Martin's, and there met widow Burroughes and Doll, and did tumble them all the afternoon as I pleased, and having given them a bottle of wine I parted and home by boat (my brother going by land), and thence with my wife to sit and sup with my uncle and aunt Wight, and see Woolly's wife, who is a pretty woman, and after supper, being very merry, in abusing my aunt with Dr. Venner, we home, and I to do something in my accounts, and so to bed. (Diary 28th August 1666)

One wonders what he told his wife he had been doing all afternoon. He enjoys 'looking on' the breasts of other women, but when Elizabeth tries to show off hers, he flies into a fit of righteous indignation: 'At noon home to dinner, where my wife and I fell out, I being displeased with her cutting away a lace handkercher sewed about the neck down to her breasts almost, out of a belief, but without reason, that it is the fashion.' (Diary 22nd November 1666)

In the meantime, Pepys has his women almost forming a queue … 'This noon Bagwell's wife was with me at the office, and I did what I would, and at night comes Mrs. Burroughs, and appointed to meet upon the next holyday and go abroad together.' (Diary 22nd November 1666)

He tries to meet up with Mrs Burrows, but either she is busy with elderly relatives or she does not show up. Still, there is always her mother:

Thence to Westminster Hall and the Abbey, thinking as I had appointed to have met Mrs. Burroughs there, but not meeting her I home … only, I did go drink at the Swan, and there did meet with Sarah, who is now newly married; [Sarah Udall, now Mrs. Harmond] and there I did lay the beginnings of a future amor con ella [affair with her], which in time may come para laisser me hazer alguna cosa con elle [let me play something with her]. Thence, it being late, away; called at Mrs. Burroughs mother's door, and she came out to me and I did hazer whatever I would con su mano tocando mi cosa [do whatever I would with her hand touching my thing] ; and then parted and home; and after some playing at cards with my wife, we to supper and to bed. (Diary 30th November 1666)

It is difficult to imagine the conversation when Pepys knocks at the door and enquires after Mrs Burroughs. If Pepys is to be believed, it must have gone something like this: 'Good evening, is your daughter at home? No, well never mind, you'll do. Would you like to put your hand in my breeches and jerk me off?'

The first day of December sees Pepys still trying to meet up with Mrs Burrows. She is at the christening of Betty Martin's daughter on Sunday 2nd, but we hear of no explanation for her failing to meet with Pepys, but he apparently makes yet another appointment for the following day, this time with more success:

> After sitting long, till the church was done, the Parson comes, and then we to christen the child. I was Godfather, and Mrs. Holder (her husband, a good man, I know well), and a pretty lady, that waits, it seems, on my Lady Bath, at White Hall, her name, Mrs. Noble, were Godmothers. After the christening comes in the wine and the sweetmeats, and then to prate and tattle, and then very good company they were, and I among them. Here was old Mrs. Michell and Howlett, and several married women of the Hall, whom I knew mayds. Here was also Mrs. Burroughs and Mrs. Bales, the young widow, whom I led home, and having staid till the moon was up, I took my pretty gossip to White Hall with us, and I saw her in her lodging, and then my owne company again took coach … (Diary 2nd December 1666)
>
> I left her (Mrs. Kate Joyce, wife of a Clerkenwell innkeeper) with my wife, and away myself to Westminster-hall by appointment, and there found out Burroughs; and I took her by coach as far as my Lord Treasurers, and called at the Cake-house by Hale's, and there in the coach eat and drank, and then carried her home with much ado making her to tocar mi cosa [touch my thing], she being endeed very averse a alguna cosa [to something] of that kind. However, time can hazer-la [do it] the same as it hath hecho [made] others. So having set her down in the palace, I to the Swan, and there did the first time bezar [kiss] the little sister of Sarah, [Frances Udall] this is come into her place; and so away by coach home … (Diary 3rd December 1666)

Obviously, Elizabeth has no idea what her husband has been up to all evening. Pepys does not record what excuses he made for where he had been. In the New Year, the widow has become a sure thing for a wank … however, she will go thus far and no further:

> This noon Mrs. Burroughs came to me about busi[ness], whom I did besar and haza ella tocar mi chose [kiss and made her touch my thing]. (Diary 10th January 1667)
>
> At noon dined with my wife and were pleasant; and then to the office, where I got Mrs. Burroughs sola cum ego and did tocar su mamelles so as to hazer me hazer. She gone, I to my business …' [got Mrs.Burroughs alone with me and did touch her breasts so as to make me come]. (Diary 15th January 1667)

So home and to dinner; and after dinner to the office, where yo had Mrs. Burrows all sola a my closet, and there did besar and tocar su mamelles as much as yo quisere hasta a hazer me hazer, but ella would not suffer that yo should poner mi mano abaxo ses jupes, which yo endeavoured [kiss and touch her breasts as much as I wanted to, but she wouldn't allow me to put my hand under her skirts, which I tried to do]. (Diary 18th February 1667)

However, Mrs Burrows is no match for the wiles of Mr Pepys:

.... So he and I parted, and I to Martin's, where I find her within, and su hermano [her brother] and la veuve [the widow] Burroughs. Here I did demorar toda [take all] the afternoon bezando las [kissing her] and drank; and among other things, did by trick arrive at tocando el poil la thing the veuve abovesaid [did by trick arrive at touching the pubic hair of the widow]. (Diary 24th March 1667)

Either Pepys has decided that he has got all he is going to get, or Mrs Burrows thinks things have gone far enough, as she disappears from the diary for some four months, and even then only appears by chance: 'Thence I to White Hall, and in the street I spied Mrs. Borroughs, and took a means to meet and salute her and talk a little, and then parted, and I home by coach, taking up my wife at the Exchange ...' (Diary 13th July 1667)

A month later she turns up at the office, although we are not told why and Pepys is too afraid of discovery to try anything:

I to the Office, only met at the door with Mrs. Martin and Mrs. Burroughs, who I took in and drank with, but was afraid my wife should see them, they being, especially the first, a prattling gossip, and so after drinking with them parted, and I to the Office ... (Diary 6th August 1667)

... and so I to Mrs. Martin, where was Mrs. Burroughs, and also fine Mrs. Noble, my partner in the christening of Martin's child, did come to see it, and there we sat and talked an hour, and then all broke up and I by coach home ... (Diary 8th September 1667)

And thence only walked to Mrs. Martin's and there sat with her and and there drank her sister and Borroughs and did tocar la prima [touch the first] and talked and away by water home. ... (Diary 13th October 1667)

A couple of months later Pepys comes across the lady again and makes a half-hearted attempt to make her accompany him, but she is obviously having none of it:

... and thence towards White Hall by coach, and spying Mrs. Burroughs in a shop did stop and 'light and speak to her' and so to White Hall, where I light and went and met her coming towards White Hall, but was upon business, and I could not get her to go any whither and so parted, and I home with my wife … (Diary 4th December 1667)

In March of the new year, Pepys tries once or twice to meet up with the lady, but she is either not about or is busy in her mother's shop. Finally, in April, Mrs Burrows makes her last appearance…

… I to the New Exchange, there to meet Mrs. Burroughs; and did tomar [drink] her in a carosse [closed coach] and carry ella [her] towards the Park, kissing her and tocanda su breast, [touching her breast] so as to make myself do [i.e.orgasm] but did not go into any house [i.e. tavern] …' (Diary 9th April 1667)

As her mother had a shop in Westminster Hall, one of Pepys' principal stomping grounds, he must have come across her again on a regular basis, either by accident or design, in the remainder of the diary period. Whether he did or not, he obviously did not think it worth mentioning and the 'most pretty' Mrs Burrows fades into oblivion.

Chapter 12

My Dear Mrs. Knipp

When the theatres in London reopened for business in 1660 after being closed for eighteen years by Cromwell and the Puritans, Pepys was one of the first playgoers. Despite his regular resolutions to avoid too many visits to the theatre, he records attending performances on no fewer than 351 occasions during the nine years and five months of the diary period, sometimes going twice in the same day. He greatly admired Ben Jonson's work upon which he invariably showered much praise but was markedly less enthusiastic about Shakespeare – he thought *Romeo and Juliet* 'a play of itself the worst that ever I heard in my life' (Diary 1st March 1662). *A Midsummer Night's Dream* he described as a play 'which I had never seen before, nor shall ever again, for it is the most insipid ridiculous play that ever I saw in my life.' (Diary 29th September 1662). *Twelfth Night* he thought to be 'a silly play, and not related at all to the name or day.' (Diary 6th January 1663).

On a visit to the theatre on the 3 January 1661 Pepys was witness to a revolutionary change in playacting. He wrote in his diary, 'to the Theatre, where was acted Beggars bush – it being very well done; and here the first time that ever I saw Women come upon the stage.' Until that point female roles were played by boys or youths, who would appear on stage dressed in women's clothing. King Charles had seen women act whilst in exile in France but they mainly played the roles of boys, dressed in breeches to show off their shapely legs, which in an age of full length voluminous skirts, undoubtedly proved a titillating experience for the audience.

Pepys clearly appreciated seeing women on stage. In March 1667 he wrote, 'to the Theatre, and there saw The Scornfull Lady, now done by a woman, which makes the play appear much better than ever it did to me'. It was not only their acting qualities he admired. He took to visiting the actresses in their dressing rooms, delighting in coming upon them in various states of undress. Some he began meeting socially away from the theatres and the diary makes mention of several of their number; the king's mistress Nell Gwynne; Hester Davenport, Mary 'Moll' Davis, Mary Saunderson and last but far from least, Elizabeth Knepp.

Elizabeth Knipp (she appears in the diary as Knipp, Knip and Knepp) was an actress, a singer and a dancer in the King's Company between 1664 and 1678. The dramatist and theatre manager Tom Killigrew told Pepys that she was '… like to make the best actor that ever come upon the stage.' Born Elizabeth Carpenter, she married a horse dealer named Christopher Knepp at Knightsbridge in 1659. He is described by Pepys as 'an ill, melancholy, jealous-looking fellow' (Diary 8th December 1665) who treated his wife badly. Nevertheless, it seems she was a spirited and flirtatious lady with something of a reputation as a hell-raiser; in 1668 she was twice arrested for otherwise unidentified 'misdemeanors' at the Theatre Royal. She created the role of Lady Fidget, spokeswoman for 'the virtuous gang' of sex-hungry wives, in Wycherley's play *The Country Wife* at Drury Lane in 1675. Pepys became besotted by her and she appears in the diary no less than 106 times between 1665 and 1669 when the diary closes, although they never seem to have become full lovers.

Pepys first becomes acquainted with Mrs Knipp in December 1665 with whom he is clearly taken, as by January 2nd he is describing her as 'my dear Mrs. Knipp, with whom I sang; and in perfect pleasure I was to hear her sing, and especially her little Scotch song of Barbary Allen.'

Later that evening, Pepys has an itch that he must scratch. …

… before I came to my office, longing for more of her company, returned and met them coming home in coaches; so I got into the coach where Mrs.Knipp was, and got her upon my knee (the coach being full) and played with her breasts and sung; and at last set her at her house, and so goodnight. (Diary 2nd January 1666)

The lady appears in the diary again and again – daily between 3 and 7 January. On the fifth, Pepys tries to arrange an assignation with her, but she is otherwise engaged and sends him an apology, signing herself 'Barbary Allen'. He tries again the next day, inviting her by letter and signing himself 'Dapper Dicky'. The boy who delivers the letter returns with a further apology and tells Pepys that he found the lady in tears, leading him to believe that she is being badly treated by her husband. This is confirmed by Mrs Knipp herself when she visits Pepys to explain why she has not been able to take up his invitations: '…complaining how like a devil her husband treats her, but will be with us in town a week hence.' (Diary 7th January 1666)

Sure enough, the following week Pepys attends a party where he is disappointed to find that Mrs Knipp has failed to turn up, although her husband is there alone. She arrives very late, supper being finished, in a state of 'undress' (i.e. informally, without stays). However, a couple of days later, she goes to dinner at Captain Cockes, where Pepys has a good evening and is greatly cheered up: '… where mighty merry, and sing and dance with great pleasure.' (Diary 18th January 1666)

There is much of the same throughout February and March – Mrs Knipp and Pepys singing together and making merry. On the 10th March, Pepys buys her a gift of six pairs of gloves and has taken to calling her 'Bab Allen': '… Bab and I sang, and were mighty merry as we could be there, where the rest of the company did not overplease.' (Diary 7th April 1666)

A month on and Pepys is still seeing Mrs Knipp socially on a regular basis. However, Mrs Pepys is beginning to smell a rat:

> … and so home, where my wife in mighty pain, [she had severe cholic] and mightily vexed at my being abroad with these women – and when they were gone, called them "whores" and I know not what; which vexed me, having been so innocent with them. (Diary 9th May 1666)

As with most of Elizabeth's gripes, justified or otherwise, they tend to rumble on and on: '… but she doth find, with reason, that in the company of Pierce – Knipp – or other women that I love, I do not value her, or mind her as I ought.'(Diary 12th May 1666)

Nevertheless, this did not stop Elizabeth seeing Mrs Knipp (who is now heavily pregnant) socially: 'Thence home, and there find Knipp at dinner with my wife, now very big and within a fortnight of lying down.' (Diary 25th May 1666)

Mrs Knipp gives birth to a boy and invites Pepys to be godfather, to which he agrees, the baby being named Samuel in his honour. The Pepys' continue to see Mrs Knipp socially throughout the rest of the year, despite Elizabeth occasionally calling her unflattering names, such as 'wench' and 'whore' in private. They are all dancing and singing together at a party when they receive news of a bad fire in Whitehall, which throws them into a panic, one woman falling into a fit. In November, Pepys calls at the Knipps' home to collect her and take her to dinner, giving us a clue as to what is at the back of his mind: '… and then to Knipp again and there stayed, reading of Wallers verses while she finished her dressing – her husband being by, I had no other pastime.' (Diary 14th November 1666)

In the New Year, Pepys gives a party in the office, which goes on with much dancing and merry making until almost three in the morning. Mrs Knipp becomes a little sick, and Mrs Pepys takes her home with her to put her to bed. It presents Pepys with an opportunity he can't pass up:

> The company all being gone to their homes, I up with Mrs. Pierce to Knipp, who was in bed; and we waked her and there I handled her breasts and did baiser la [kiss her] and sing a song, lying by her on the bed. … and so to bed myself – my mind mightily satisfied with all this evening's work … (Diary 24th January 1667)

In February, she challenges Pepys to be her valentine, which he does, laying out thirty-two shillings [£1.60] in gifts for her. In April he goes to see *The Taming of the Shrew* which he thinks is 'but a mean play':

Samuel Pepys (probably after John Closterman). Painted in the 1690s when Pepys was in or approaching his 60s. (*Copyright: National Portrait Gallery*)

John Evelyn (Engraving by Thom. Bragg after Sir. Godfrey Kneller 1818). The 'other' 17th century diarist and Pepys' friend for forty years. (*Copyright: National Portrait Gallery*)

Elizabeth Pepys (Engraving by James Thomson after John Hayls 1828). The original oil of this 1666 portrait was destroyed in the 19th century by a nun who was offended by the revealing nature of the gown. (*Copyright: National Portrait Gallery*)

Barbara Palmer – Lady Castlemaine, Duchess of Cleveland. Mistress of King Charles ll of whom Pepys entertained erotic fantasies. (*Copyright: National Portrait Gallery*)

Eleanor (Nell) Gwynn (after Sir Peter Lely 1670s). Orange seller turned actress and mistress of King Charles II. Pepys called her 'pretty, witty Nell' and used to visit her in her theatre dressing room to watch her dress. Her son by King Charles became the first Duke of St. Albans. (*Copyright: National Portrait Gallery*)

William Hewer (Engraving after Sir Godfrey Kneller 1825). Pepys' clerk and lifelong friend who was by his deathbed and became executor of his will. (*Copyright: National Portrait Gallery*)

Paul Lorrain's dedication to Pepys from 'Rites of Funeral' 1683. Pepys' secretary, translator and copyist for 22 years, Lorrain translated Paul Muret's work from the French and dedicated it effusively to Pepys. The words of dedication shows Pepys' public persona to be very different from his private behaviour. (*Copyright: Author*)

To the Honourable

SAMUEL PEPYS Esq;

SIR,

TO *apologize* for this *Dedication* under the worn pretence of a desire of *Protection*, were at once to do violence, both to the Character of my *Author* (whose Fame has rais'd him above the need of any) and my own *Modesty*, who am too conscious of what the best performances of this kind amount to, not to know, That *Pardon* only

A 2   (with-

The Epistle Dedicatory.
(without *Protection*) is Indulgence sufficient to the frailties of a *Translation.*

THAT then which alone emboldens me to the inscribing this to *YOUR REVER'D NAME,* is a belief I have, that the *Copy* cannot be disagreeable to *YOU* of an *Original,* in whose diversities of Entertainment and Reading, You have been sometimes pleas'd to own so much satisfaction, especially upon a Subject of such singularity as this, touching the different *Rites* of *Funeral* in practice with Mankind.

OF which *Rites,* however entitled *YOUR VIRTUES* have long since rendred YOU to those of the most Solemn, or YOUR severer *PHILOSOPHY* may nevertheless make YOU partial to others

The Epistle Dedicatory.
others of the less studied Methods mention'd in this *Treatise* ; *GOD* grant Your arrival at either may be as late for the benefit of *Others,* as *YOUR KNOWN INTEGRITY* and *FORTITUDE* render impossible its coming too soon with regard to *YOUR SELF.* Which is the most fervent Prayer of,

HONOUR'D SIR,

Your most Faithful and

most Obedient Servant,

PAUL LORRAIN.

Novemb. 6.
1682.   A 3

Title page and illustrations from 'School of Venus' 1680. The English version of the French work *L'Escholle des Filles* 1668, the only known surviving copy of which is in the Bayerische Straatsbiblioteck – Munich. Pepys burned his copy of the *School of Venus*, describing it as '*the most bawdy, lewd book that ever I saw*'. (*Copyright: Public Domain*)

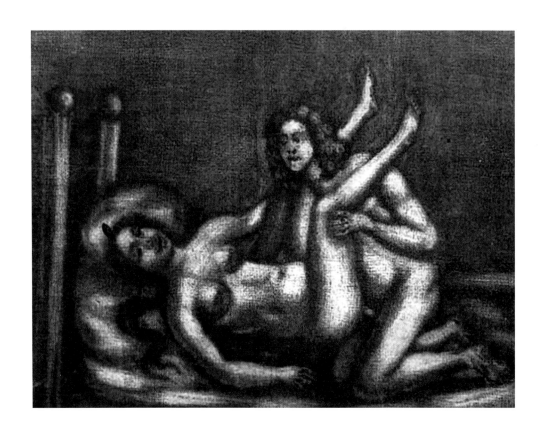

St. Olaves Church. Mr. & Mrs. Pepys regular place of worship and where Pepys habitually spied on pretty women with his '*perspective glass*'. The church is a very rare architectural gem from 17th century London, having survived both the great fire of 1666 and the bombing blitz of the Second World War. (*Copyright* (*appears in multiple websites with no owner identification*))

Westminster Hall.
Although a somewhat later picture, this shows the view of the inside of Westminster Hall with market stalls, much as it would have appeared in Pepys' time and where many of his assignations took place. (*Copyright: The Trustees of the British Museum*)

Elizabeth Pepys' memorial by Benjamin Till. Situated on the wall of St. Olaves Church, near the high altar where Pepys had it placed after her death from what is now thought to have been typhoid in November 1669. (*Copyright (appears in multiple websites with no owner identification*))

The George Inn, Southwark. Rebuilt in 1677 after a fire, it is one of only two 17th century coaching inns to survive in Greater London, and is the only galleried example. This inn is not named in the diary, but he did however patronise another very similar coaching inn, also called the George in Holborn, which is probably the inn from where Elizabeth Pepys took the coach; '*Up early, and by six o'clock, after my wife was ready, I walked with her to the George, at Holborn Conduit, where the coach stood ready to carry her and her maid to Bugden.*' (Diary 28th July 1662) (*Copyright: No known owner*)

17th Century Wine Bottle. In Pepys day, wine was drunk young and unclarified. Corks did not come into use until the end of the 17th century, so wine was stored in casks and served at table in onion shaped bottles, in the manner of a decanter. Pepys often suffered from its' deleterious effects; "...*having drunk so much wine that my head was troubled and was not very well all night*..." Diary 8th December 1660. (*Copyright: No known owner*)

Shakespeare's 'Othello' London playbill 1630. Pepys saw *Othello* acted on three occasions; on 11th October 1660 he described it as being '*well done*'; on 20th August 1666 it '*seems a mean thing*' and finally on 6th February 1669 it was '*ill-acted in parts*'. (*Copyright: No known owner*)

THE
Tragœdy of Othello,
The Moore of Venice.

As it hath beene diverſe times acted at the Globe, and at the Black-Friers, by his Maiesties Servants.

Written by VVilliam Shakeſpeare.

LONDON,
Printed by *A. M.* for *Richard Hawkins,* and are to be ſold at his ſhoppe in Chancery-Lane, neere Sergeants-Inne.
1630.

Charles ll sixpence. Mary Meggs, a former prostitute nicknamed 'Orange Moll' held the licence to '*vend, utter and sell oranges, lemons, fruit, sweetmeats and all manner of fruiterers and confectioners wares*' within the King's House theatre. She hired Nell Gwyn and her older sister Rose as scantily clad 'orange-girls', to sell the small, sweet china oranges to theatre audiences for sixpence (2½ p) each. In 1649, a sailor in Pepys' navy earned fifteen shillings (equivalent to thirty sixpences) a month. (*Copyright: No known owner*)

Execution of Charles l and the Regicides. Pepys was a witness to the execution of both Charles l and later to that of Major-General Harrison, one of the signatories of Charles' death warrant, who was hanged, drawn and quartered as a traitor. Pepys recorded that: "…*he* [Harrison] *was presently cut down and his head and his heart shown to the people, at which there was (sic) great shouts of joy.*" (Diary 13th October 1660) (*Copyright: Public Domain*)

Hackney Carriage circa 1680. Pepys often records stealing a kiss (or something more) in the relative privacy of a Hackney. (*Copyright: No known owner*)

London Bridge much as it would have appeared in Pepys' day. (*Copyright: emailed 31st March 2017 via website no response received*)

The Fleet River was effectively London's main sewer in Pepys time. Today it is confined underground and flows into the Thames close to Blackfriars Bridge (in the centre of the picture in the shadow). (*Copyright: Public Domain*)

Mary Skinner. Pepys' companion for the last thirty years of his life and regarded by many as the de facto second Mrs. Pepys, although he never married her. (*Copyright: By permission of the Master and Fellows of Magdalene College Cambridge. Photography by Douglas Atfield*)

Pepys Library building at Magdalene College, Cambridge. (*Copyright: By permission of the Master and Fellows of Magdalene College Cambridge*)

Pepys library today. The 3,000 books collected by Pepys are today preserved in a purpose built building in Magdalene College, Cambridge, to whom they passed following the death of his nephew John Jackson. They are kept in the original bookcases made to Pepys' order for the purpose. (*Copyright: By permission of the Master and Fellows of Magdalene College Cambridge. Photography by Douglas Atfield*)

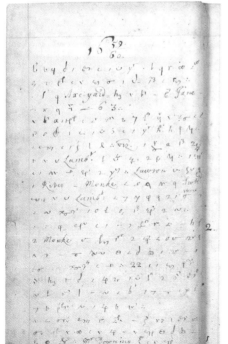

The first page of Pepys' diary, a preliminary note. The whole is in Shelton's shorthand learnt by Pepys whilst at Cambridge University. However, proper names, e.g. Axe Yard, Jane, etc. are given in full. (*Copyright: By permission of the Pepys Library, Magdalene College Cambridge*)

Fumifugium by John Evelyn. The extensive use of coal as fuel made for very poor air quality in London during Pepys' time and his long-term friend and fellow diarist John Evelyn led an abortive campaign to remedy the situation. Title page of a 1772 reprint of the 1661 original. (*Copyright: Author*)

FUMIFUGIUM:

O R,

The Inconvenience of the A E R,

A N D

SMOAKE of LONDON

DISSIPATED.

TOGETHER

With fome REMEDIES humbly propofed

By J. E. Efq;

To His Sacred MAJESTIE,

A N D

To the PARLIAMENT now Affembled.

Publifhed by His Majefties Command.

Lucret. l. 5.
Carbonumque gravis vis, atque odor infinuatur
Quam facile in cerebrum?——

L O N D O N:
Printed by W. GODBID, for GABRIEL BEDEL, and THOMAS
COLLINS; and are to be fold at their Shop at the Middle
Temple Gate, neer Temple Bar. M.DC.LXI.
Re-printed for B. WHITE, at Horace's Head, in Fleet-ftreet.
MDCCLXXII.

Portrait of an unknown woman 1653 (artist unknown). Pepys often records having toyed with women's breasts. The fashion of the day shows how easy this would have been. (*Copyright: Published in 'A Visual History of Costume – 17th Century'. 1984 Batsford Ltd. Attributed to V&A museum, who cannot trace this picture (by email 28th April 2017)*)

… and had a mind to have taken out Knepp to have taken the ayre with her, and to that end sent a porter in to her that she should take a coach and come to me in the piatza in Covent-garden; where I waited for her, but was doubtful I might have done ill in doing it if we should be visto ensemble [seen together]; sed ella [but she] was gone out, and so I was eased of that care. … (Diary 9th April 1667)

Foiled in his plans, Pepys heads off to where he knows he stands a good chance of venting his frustration:

… and therefore away to Westminster to the Swan, and there did bezar la little mosa [kissed Frances Udall] and hazer tocar mi thing through mi chemise con su mano [made her touch my thing through my chemise with her hand], at which she was enojado [angry]; but I did donat ella algo [give her something], and so all well and drank. (Diary 9th April 1667)

Sunday, 12th May begins calmly enough, Pepys sitting in his chamber settling some accounts, but Elizabeth is still festering over his relationship with Mrs Knipp, and she knows just how to paint her husband into a corner:

Up, and to my chamber, to settle some accounts there, and by and by down comes my wife to me in her night-gown, and we begun calmly, that upon having money to lace her gown for second mourning, [traditionally, the second period of mourning, during which black clothes are lightened or replaced by grey, white, or purple] she would promise to wear white locks no more in my sight, which I, like a severe fool, thinking not enough, begun to except against, and made her fly out to very high terms and cry, and in her heat told me of keeping company with Mrs. Knipp, saying, that if I would promise never to see her more — of whom she hath more reason to suspect than I had heretofore of Pembleton — she would never wear white locks more. This vexed me, but I restrained myself from saying anything, but do think never to see this woman — at least, to have her here more, but by and by I did give her money to buy lace, and she promised to wear no more white locks while I lived, and so all very good friends as ever, and I to my business, and she to dress herself. (Diary 12th May 1667)

Apart from a missed attendance at Mrs Pierce's party a week or two later (missed because Pepys has a tantrum about his wife's dress) at which Mrs Knipp was to be present, the lady disappears from the diary until 1st August, when the Pepys' join a party to see a play at the King's House theatre in which she is appearing. After the performance they all go off to Chelsea to eat, where the diary records 'my wife is out of humour, as she always is when this woman is by.' Hardly surprising, as the next day we discover that he had been 'leading her (Mrs Knipp) and sitting in the coach hand-in-hand and my arm about her middle …' (Diary 2nd August 1667)

Perhaps Pepys comes to realise that, while chasing other women, it is a good idea to also make love to your wife once in while:

> My wife waked betimes to call up her maids to washing, and so to bed again; whom I then hugged, it being cold now in the mornings, and then did la otra cosa con her [the other thing with her], which I had not done con ella [with her] for these tres meses [many months] past, which I do believe is a great matter towards the making of her of late so indifferent towards me, and with good reason; but now she had much pleasure, and so to sleep again. (Diary 12th August 1667)

For some weeks, Pepys only sees Mrs Knipp upon the stage, although often fails to tell Elizabeth that he has been to the theatre. In October, they visit the theatre together and Mrs Knipp takes them backstage, where Pepys observes Nell Gwynne dressing herself:

> … and so to the King's house: and there, going in, met with Knepp, and she took us up into the tireing-rooms: and to the women's shift, where Nell was dressing herself, and was all unready, and is very pretty, prettier than I thought. And so walked all up and down the house above, and then below into the scene-room, and there sat down, and she gave us fruit and here I read the questions to Knepp, while she answered me, through all her part of "Flora's Figary's," which was acted to-day.' (Diary 5th October 1667)

Mrs Knipp then disappears from the diary until the penultimate day of the year, when Pepys – having missed her at dinner, goes alone to the theatre to watch her act and then goes with her to Mrs Manuel's for a musical interlude:

> … and then with her to Mrs. Manuel's, where Mrs. Pierce was, and her boy and girl; and here I did hear Mrs. Manuel and one of the Italians, her gallant, sing well. … pleased to hear Knepp sing two or three little English things that I understood, though the composition of the other, and performance, was very fine. Thence, after sitting and talking a pretty while, I took leave and left them there, and so to my bookseller's, and paid for the books I had bought, and away home, where I told my wife where I had been. But she was as mad as a devil, and nothing but ill words between us all the evening while we sat at cards — W. Hewer and the girl by — even to gross ill words, which I was troubled for, but do see that I must use policy to keep her spirit down, and to give her no offence by my being with Knepp and Pierce, of which, though she will not own it, yet she is heartily jealous. At last it ended in few words and my silence (which for fear of growing higher between us I did forbear),

and so to supper and to bed without one word one to another. (Diary 30th December 1667)

In the new year, Pepys again has an opportunity to go backstage to watch the actresses disrobing, a privilege often accorded to close friends and relatives in the period:

… I by coach to the King's playhouse, and there saw 'The English Monsieur'; sitting for privacy sake in an upper box: the play hath much mirth in it as to that particular humour. After the play done, I down to Knipp, and did stay her undressing herself; and there saw the several players, men and women go by; and pretty to see how strange they are all, one to another, after the play is done. Here I saw a wonderful pretty maid of her own, that come to undress her, and one so pretty that she says she intends not to keep her, for fear of her being undone in her service, by coming to the playhouse. (Diary 7th April 1668)

Later in the month, Pepys' achieves a triumph he has long wished for over several years …

… it being quite night, home, and dark, about 9 a-clock or more and in my coming had the opportunity, the first time in my life, to be bold with Knepp by putting my hand abaxo de her coats [under her skirts] and tocar su thighs and venter [touch her thighs and ?]-- and a little of the other thing, ella [she] but a little opposing me; su skin very douce [her skin very soft] and I mightily pleased with this; and so left her at home, and so Mrs. Turner and I home to my letters and to bed. (Diary 21st April 1668)

Pepys has crossed the rubicon as far as Mrs Knipp is concerned, and only two days later he is at it again:

… then Knepp and I to the Temple again, and took boat, it being darkish, and to Fox Hall, it being now night, and a bonfire burning at Lambeth for the King's coronation-day. And there she and I drank; and yo did tocar her corps [I did touch her body] all over and besar sans fin her [kiss her endlessly], but did not offer algo mas [anything more]; and so back, and led her home, it being now ten at night … (Diary 23rd April 1668)

… and yet again (even though she is asleep):

… thence I back to the King's playhouse, and there saw "The Virgin Martyr," and heard the musick that I like so well, and intended to have seen Knepp, but I let her alone; and having there done, went to Mrs. Pierces back again, where she was, and there I found her on a pallet in the dark where yo did poner mi mano under her jupe and tocar su cosa [I did put my hand under her skirt and touch her thing] and waked her; that is, Knipp. (Diary 6th May 1668)

... and as Elizabeth is away, that same night Pepys is clearly in a state of arousal as he makes an even bolder move with a humble cookmaid:

And so to talk; and by and by did eat some curds and cream, and thence away home, and it being night, I did walk in the dusk up and down, round through our garden, over Tower Hill, and so through Crutched Friars, three or four times, and once did meet Mercer and another pretty lady, but being surprised I could say little to them, although I had an opportunity of pleasing myself with them, but left them, and then I did see our Nell, Payne's daughter, and her yo did desear venga after migo, and so ella did seque me to Tower Hill [I did desire her to come after me, and she did follow me to Tower Hill] to our back entry there that comes upon the degres entrant into nostra [our] garden; and there ponendo [placing] the key in the door, yo tocar sus mamelles con mi mano [I touched her breasts with my hand] and su cosa with mi cosa et yo did dar-la a shilling [her thing with my thing and I did give her a shilling]; and so parted, and yo [I] home to put up things against to-morrow's carrier for my wife. ... (Diary 6th May 1668)

The next day he goes off to the Duke of York's House theatre and there '... did kiss the pretty woman newly come, called Pegg, that was Sir Ch. Sidley's mistress – a mighty pretty woman, and seems, but is not, modest'. Then he collects Mrs Knipp in the coach and off they go to 'Marrowbone' (Marylebone?) to eat and drink until 9.00 o'clock:

... and so home by moonshine, I all the way having mi mano abaxo la jupe de Knepp con much placer and freedom [having my hand under Mrs. Knepp's skirt with much pleasure and freedom]; but endeavoring afterward to tocar her con mi cosa [touch her with my thing] , ella [she] did strive against that, but yet I do not think that she did find much fault with it, but I was a little moved at my offering it and not having it.' (Diary 7th May 1668)

The following Saturday, Pepys visits the King's playhouse to see Mrs Knipp act, and then waits at her house for her to come home, but she does not turn up. Never one to waste an opportunity, Pepys takes some consolation from: '... and here yo did besar her ancilla [kiss her maid], which is so mighty belle.' (Diary 16th May 1668)

On the 30th, Pepys meets Mrs Knipp at Mrs Pierce's, much afraid that she had taken offence at his recent groping of her in the coach. However, she is as friendly as ever, leading him to believe that 'she can bear with any such thing'.

In October, Elizabeth again insists that Pepys spends no more time with Mrs Knipp, which he accepts that there is some indiscretion in his relationship with her, but that 'there was no harm in it'. November sees their marriage come close to breaking point after Elizabeth catches him in flagrante with her companion Debs and in her rage, includes Mrs Pierce and Mrs Knipp in her accusations.

Until the end of the diary period in May 1669, Pepys often sees Mrs Knipp appear on stage, but despite the fact that he longs to see her, he dare not meet her for fear of his vows to Elizabeth. Whether or not he ever saw her again socially thereafter we have no way of knowing, but it seems certain that she never actually became his mistress. We do know that in the late 1670s she became mistress to the actor Joseph Haines, and sadly died in 1681 giving birth to his stillborn child.

Chapter 13

A Very Pretty Wench & Her Mother

In July 1663 Pepys does a round of shopping – a visit to his booksellers and then to his instrument makers to purchase a ruler and lastly to Westminster Hall …

… where I expected some bands made me by Mrs. Lane, and while she went to the starchers for them, I staid at Mrs. Howlett's, who with her husband were abroad, and only their daughter (which I call my wife) was in the shop, and I took occasion to buy a pair of gloves to talk to her, and I find her a pretty spoken girl, and will prove a mighty handsome wench. I could love her very well. (Diary 18th July 1663)

Pepys notices Betty Howlett because as well as being pretty, she apparently bears a close resemblance to his wife Elizabeth:

So to Westminster Hall, and there at Mrs. Michell's shop sent for beer and sugar and drink, and made great cheer with it among her and Mrs. Howlett, her neighbour, and their daughters, especially Mrs. Howlett's daughter, Betty, which is a pretty girl, and one I have long called wife, being, I formerly thought, like my own wife. (Diary 24th July 1663)

It is not long before he begins to stalk her; perhaps she saw him coming, as she obviously puts on some speed: '… to Westminster Hall, where, seeing Howlett's daughter going out of the other end of the Hall, I followed her if I would to have offered talk to her and dallied with her a little, but I could not overtake her.' (Diary 7th November 1663)

However, Betty is still a little young, even for Pepys, but he appears to be prepared to wait whilst anticipating what an attractive woman she will become: 'I was much pleased to look upon their pretty daughter, which is grown a pretty mayd, and will make a fine modest woman.' (Diary 8th February 1664)

Betty disappears from the pages of the diary for a while and it is nearly two years later when she next puts in an appearance, one of nearly a hundred entries in the diary detailing Pepys' obsession with her: '… there I did see Betty Howlet come after the sicknesse [i.e. the plague] to the Hall. Had not opportunity to salute her, as I desired, but was glad to see her and a very pretty wench she is.' (Diary 16th December 1665)

Betty has grown up and she is now definitely and firmly in Pepys' sights: '… walked to Westminster Hall, where I staid talking with Mrs. Michell and Howlett long and her daughter, which is become a mighty pretty woman …' (Diary 28th February1666)

It appears however that he may have missed the boat, for after another torrid session with Mrs Lane, she tells him …

> … that Betty Howlet of the Hall, my little sweetheart, that I used to call my second wife, is married to a younger son of Mr. Michell's (his elder brother, who should have had her, being dead this plague), at which I am glad, and that they are to live nearer me in Thames Streete … (Diary 18th March 1666)
>
> … where I may see Betty now and then, whom I from a girl did use to call my second wife, and mighty pretty she is. (Diary 23rd March 1666)

Throughout April Pepys chances upon Betty in Westminster Hall and passes a little time in conversation with her. On 1st May, Elizabeth having gone elsewhere, he takes the opportunity to find out where she is living in Thames Street. On the 13th, he chances upon the whole Mitchell family in St Margaret's church, and is invited to accompany them home, where: '… there had the opportunity to have salute[d] two or three times Betty, and make an acquaintance; which they are pleased with, though not so much as I am or they think I am.' (Diary 13th May 1666)

It is fortunate that the family do not know how pleased Pepys is or what his intentions are. Sunday, 3 June is Whitsunday, and Pepys does the two things he likes to do most on the Sabbath …

> I to St.Margaret's Westminster, and there saw at church my pretty Betty Mitchell. And thence to the Abbey, and so to Mrs.Martin and there did what je voudrais avec her [did what I would with her], both devante [forward] and backward, which is also muy bon plazer [my great pleasure]. (Diary 3rd June 1666)

Throughout the rest of June, Pepys occasionally comes across the Mitchells, even going into their shop for a drink of their 'strong waters'. On the 6th June, he calls in, and finding Mr Mitchell not at home, steals 'a kiss or two' from Betty. Pepys then embarks on what in modern times might be termed 'grooming'. He finds Mr Mitchell some business through the Navy Office, the two couples drive out to Hackney together to 'take the ayre' and the young couple are invited to dinner with the Pepys' household. Finding Betty alone at The Swan inn at dusk on the 31st, he steals another kiss or two. Likewise on Sunday the 5th August, he comes across husband and wife at The Swan, 'and had two or three long salutes from her out of sight of su marido [her husband], which pleased me mightily.'

On the 12th, the young couple are again dining with the Pepys. Two days later, he again finds Betty at The Swan, and tries to persuade her to go with him to Westminster, but she is obviously beginning to suspect that his intentions are less than honourable, as he finds her 'a little colder than she used to be methought.' Apart from a drink at The Swan a week later, Betty disappears from the narrative until Sunday, 2nd December, when Pepys, having attended a christening, takes a coach homeward round the city wall. The coach breaks down en route and there is a delay of an hour while it is fixed, however, who should be sitting next to him but Betty Mitchell, with whom he has clearly become a lot more familiar:

> Away round by the wall and Cowlane, for fear it should break again, and in pain about the coach all the way. But to ease myself therein, Betty Michell did sit at the same end with me, and there con su mano under my manteau, [with her hand under my coat] I did pull off her cheirotheca [glove] and did tocar mi cosa con su mano [touch my thing with her hand] through my chemise, but yet so as to hazer me hazer la grande cosa [to make me do the big thing] she did let me hazerle sin mucho trabaho [do this without much effort]. Being very much pleased with this, we at last came home; and so to supper, and then sent them by boat home, and we to bed. (Diary 2nd December 1666)

This is an astonishing entry – there are only four people in the coach: the Mitchells and the Pepys. Betty and Pepys are sitting on one side of the coach, while Elizabeth and Michael Mitchell are sitting on the other. The coach cannot have been very large and although it may have been very dark, Pepys gets a hand-job to the point of orgasm with his wife and the husband of the woman giving it to him seated facing them a couple of feet away! Admittedly, it was under a good deal of clothing, and 'without much effort', but the risk of discovery must have been enormous. Betty obviously did not mind too much, since she cooperated fully, any resistance on her part would have been quickly noticed by the two spouses opposite. One wonders whether this might not have been the first time this had occurred and it had simply been omitted from the diary? Unlikely, given Pepys' attention to the details of his private life, but equally, we seemed to have moved seamlessly from a cold reaction from Betty to accompanying Pepys in a coach in August, to wanking him off in front of her husband four months later!

On Sunday 23rd, the Mitchells are again dinner guests at the Pepys', and afterwards he gives them a lift to Westminster in the coach, as he goes for a musical appointment with Christopher Gibbon, the organist of Westminster Abbey. He tries to take Betty's hand as he had done previously, 'but she did in a manner withhold it'. By the time he wants to return home, it is a clear, cold, snowy night. On the way, he collects the Mitchells once again to bring them to supper; this time he is not taking no for an answer from Betty, even if it means using some force:

But this took me so much time, and it growing night, I was fearful of missing a coach; and therefore took a coach, and to rights to call Michell and his wife at their father Howletts; and so home, it being cold and the ground all snow, but the moon shining. In the way, I did prender su mano [did take her hand] with some little violence; and so in every motion she seemed para hazer contra su will,[to go against her will] but yet did hazer whatever I did hazerla tenerle et fregarle et tocar mi thigh [did whatever I wanted her to do by rubbing and touching my thigh] and so all the way home, and did doner ella us gans para put on encore [and did make her lust grow so that once again] – she making many little endeavours para oter su mano,[little endeavours with her hand] but yielded still. We came home, and there she did seem a little ill, but I did take several opportunities afterward para besar la [to kiss her], and so goodnight. (Diary 23rd December 1666)

With only the three of them in the coach, one wonders what Mr Mitchell is doing all this time – presumably staring out of the window whilst pretending not to notice that anything is going on – Pepys had been finding him business after all.

On the 6 January, the Mitchells are again invited to dinner and Pepys is worried that Betty may have taken offence at what he made her do in the coach and even worse, may have said something to her husband, but in the event all is well and the meal passes with 'a merry discourse' before Pepys and Mr Mitchell go for a stroll together! On Sunday 13th, Pepys has a mind to pursue his favourite Sabbath activity, but is frustrated in his design:

At noon sent for Mercer, who dined with us, and very merry; and so after dinner walked to the old Swan, thinking to have got a boat to White-hall; but could not, for was there anybody at home at Michells, where I thought to have sat with her et peut être obtain algo de her-which I did intend para essayer [and maybe obtain something from her which I did intend to try]. So home to church, a dull sermon; and then home at my chamber all the evening. So to supper and to bed. (Diary 13th January 1667)

Two weeks later, Pepys is determined to get his way with Betty, and at six in the evening, sends for the Mitchells to join him at The Swan in Palace Yard. Betty's parents also turn up and they all apparently drink too much, as when they get into the boat to return home, Betty is a little worse for wear with an aching head:

After walking up and down the Court with him, it being now dark and past 6 at night, I walked to the Swan in the Palace yard and there with much ado did get a waterman; and so I sent for the Michells and they came, and their father Howlett and his wife with them, and there we drank; and so into the boat – poor Betty's head akeing. We home by water, a fine moonshine and warm night, it having been also a very summer's day for warmth. I did get her hand to me under my cloak and did oter sa gans, but ella ne voudroit tocar mi cosa today, whatever the matter was, and I was loath to contrendre her to faire, de peur qu'ell faisait son mari prendre notice thereof [I did get her hand to me under my cloak and did remove her glove, but she didn't want to touch my thing today, whatever the matter was, and I was loath to force her to it, for fear that she would cause her husband to take notice thereof]. So there we parted at their house, and he walked almost home with me; and I to supper, and to read a little and to bed. (Diary 27th January 1667)

Not much more than a week later, Pepys is after Betty once again:

So down to the hall [Westminster] and there spied Betty Mitchell; so sent for burnt wine to Mrs. Mitchells and there did drink with the two mothers [i.e. Mrs. Howlett and Mrs. Mitchell senior] and by that means with Betty, poor girl, whom I love with all my heart. And God forgive me, it did make me stay longer and hover all the morning up and down the hall to buscar occasions para hablar con ella – but yo no podra' [to seek the chance to speak with her, but could not]. (Diary 6th February 1667)

The next morning Mrs Pepys has her husband's attention for a change as he records that he 'lay long with pleasure with my wife' before heading off to the office. On Sunday 10th, the Mitchells come to dinner, but leave without Pepys having any opportunity to grope Betty, who is now heavily pregnant. The very next day, he hatches an elaborate scheme to get Betty alone, which very nearly proves his undoing.

In the morning, Pepys calls at the Mitchells and gives Mr Mitchell 'a fair occasion' to send his wife to meet Mr And Mrs Pepys at the New Exchange at 5.00 pm. Betty duly arrives and is surprised not to find Elizabeth Pepys also meeting them – she is clearly still a little innocent of Pepys's wiles. However, Pepys 'makes an excuse good enough' and takes Betty to the cabinet makers where he buys her a dressing box, which will take an hour to customise to his requirements. He tries to persuade her to accompany him to a nearby inn (presumably where his hands will do their usual wandering) but she refuses and elects to wait in the shop while he visits the nearby shop of Drumbelby, a musical instrument maker. Returning to the cabinet makers, he and Betty watch the craftsmen working on the box, during which the mistress of the shop assumes them to be husband and pregnant wife, which Pepys does not deny. The whole process takes much longer than expected and it is quite late when they take a coach home. This accords Pepys the opportunity he has been waiting for and 'in the way tomando su mano [took her hand] and putting it where I used to do; which ella [she] did suffer but not avec tant [with such] freedom as heretofore, I perceiving plainly she had alguns apprehensions de me, [some apprehension of me] but I did offer natha [nothing] more then what I had often done'. (Diary 11th February 1667)

Preoccupied with his lustful intentions, Pepys only now perceives the risk he is taking – they should have been home hours ago, and Mr Mitchell will be becoming anxious:

> I did begin to fear that su marido [her husband] might go to my house to enquire por ella [after her], and there trovando mi moher [discovering my wife] at home, would not only think himself, but give my femme [wife] occasion to think strange things. This did trouble me mightily; so though ella [she] would not seem to have me trouble myself about it, yet did agree to stopping the coach at the street's end; and yo allais con ella home [accompanied her home] and there presently hear by him that he had newly sent her maid to my house to see for her mistress. This does much perplex me, and I did go presently home (Betty whispering me, behind tergo de her mari [behind her husband's back] that if I would say that we did come home by water, ella could make up la cosa well satis) [i.e. tell the same story].

Pepys is in a muck-sweat, wondering what explanation he can offer his wife. Luckily for him, the maid has either loitered on the way, or become lost, for no sooner has he arrived at his door than she comes up the steps enquiring as to which is Mr Pepys' house. Telling her that her mistress is already at home, she goes away without further question and Pepys is more than a little relieved: '… I did bless myself in my great good fortune in getting home before her … and so I in a-door and there find all well.' (Diary 11th February 1667)

Pepys' cause for concern is not entirely over, for two days later, he calls at the Mitchells and has a whispered conversation with Betty, who tells him all is well. However, she is prevented from telling him something she wanted to say due to her husband being within earshot 'which did trouble me' (Diary 13th February 1667). Perhaps her husband is becoming suspicious, for the following Sunday Pepys meets Betty and her husband, as well as the Mitchells senior at the Swan in Westminster. After a convivial evening he takes a boat homeward in company with the young Mitchells and is disturbed to find that Betty declines to sit near him and keeps as close to her husband as she can. When they land, Pepys sends Mitchell back to the boat on some excuse, and with the husband otherwise occupied he kisses Betty and tries to take her hand, but she pulls away. He asks 'shall I not touch you?' to which she replies that she does not love touching, and after a little while, they all go their separate ways, Pepys making one of his many meaningless resolutions: '… so I away home, troubled at this; but I think I will make good use of it and mind my business more.' (Diary 17th February 1667)

Having obtained no satisfaction from Betty, the very next day Pepys forgets his resolution and turns his attention elsewhere, this time to the comely shape of Elizabeth Burrows, the pretty widow of Lieutenant Anthony Burrows, killed in action two years earlier:

> So home and to dinner; and after dinner to the office, where yo had Mrs. Burrows all sola a my closet, and there did besar and tocar su mamelles as much as yo quisere hasta a hazer me hazer, but ella would not suffer that yo should poner mi mano abaxo ses jupes, which yo endeavoured. [… where I had Mrs. Burrows all alone in my closet, and there did touch her breasts as much as I wanted to do but she would not suffer that I put my hand under her skirts, which I tried.] (Diary 18th February 1667)

Betty is clearly no longer interested in satisfying Pepys' lust, and she is not mentioned again until April, when he sees her on several occasions, only to ask after her health – she is now nine months pregnant. On St George's Day she is delivered of a healthy daughter, Elizabeth Pepys assisting the midwife in the delivery. In May Pepys attends the child's christening, although Elizabeth remains at home, being 'not fit to be seen'. On the 15th of the month, Mrs Pepys receives word that the child – christened Elizabeth – is very sick and sadly dies three days later. A week later, the bereaved couple visit the Pepys and they sit quietly together in the garden until after dark, mourning the little girl.

In July, Pepys gets another shock when Mrs Martin (whose husband is away at sea) tells him that she is pregnant and that the child is his, which he does not believe. (See Haberdashery & Hanky-Panky). In October, Betty's mother, Mrs Howlett, makes an appointment to see Pepys, and he is fearful that she intends to complaint about his dalliances with her daughter. In fact, she has a serious complaint about her son-in-law and seeks Pepys' intercession:

> …to complain to me of her son-in-law, how he abuses and makes a slave of her, and his mother is one that encourages him in it, so that they are at this time upon very bad terms one with another; and desires that I would take a time to advise him and tell him what becomes him to do; which office I am very glad of, for some ends of my own also con su filia [with her daughter]; and there drank and parted, I mightily satisfied with this business. (Diary 14th October 1667)

Clearly the matter is high on Pepys' agenda, for although he often visits the Mitchell's shop through the remainder of the year and through the first six months of 1668, he rarely sees Betty and apparently never raises the matter of her treatment at the hands of her husband. On the 12th July, she is delivered of another daughter, again named Elizabeth: 'This last night Betty Michell about midnight cries out, and my wife goes to her, and she brings forth a girl, and this afternoon the child is christened, and my wife godmother again to a Betty.' (Diary 12th July 1668)

Although the Mitchells occasionally come to dinner, Pepys' ardour for Betty has cooled, and on Sunday, 9th May 1669, the last entry for her makes this plain:

> … and so to St. Margaret, Westminster, and there heard a sermon and did get places, the first time we have heard there these many years. And here at a distance I saw Betty Mitchell, but she is become much a plainer woman then she was a girl. (Diary 9th May 1669)

Quite a world away from an earlier view of Betty in church: '… anon to church, my wife and I and Betty Michell, her husband being gone to Westminster. Here at church (God forgive me), my mind did courir upon Betty Michell, so that I do hazer con mi cosa in la eglisa meme. [so that I do play with my thing even in the church] (Diary 11th November 1666)

The codicil to Pepys involvement with mother and daughter is recorded in the very last diary entry on the 31st May 1669. After dinner, he goes by water to Whitehall and calls at the Mitchell's establishment, where – finding Betty not at home, he makes a pass at her mother!

> … where I have not been many a day; and now I met her mother there and knew her husband to be out of town. And here yo did besar ella [I did kiss her] but have not opportunity para hazer mas with her [to do more with her] as I would have offered if yo [I] had had it.' (Diary 31st May 1669)

Without the diary, we have no way of knowing what relationship Pepys had with the Mitchells after the final entry, so Betty and her hapless husband fade into history.

Chapter 14

The Carpenter's Wife & Other Assignations

Sometime in 1662 or 1663, Pepys came across one William Bagwell, a 26-year-old navy carpenter with two characteristics – a burning ambition to further his career and an attractive and desirable young wife. It must have been apparent that Pepys found Mrs Bagwell sexually desirable, as either she unilaterally contrived to use this attraction to her husband's advantage, without his knowledge or consent, or her husband conceived the plan and one way or another, persuaded his wife to co-operate. The diary does not make it clear one way or the other, and indeed Pepys may not have known one way or the other, but given that their rather sordid affair continued on and off for the next six years, without any recorded suspicion on the part of her husband, the balance of probabilities seems to favour the latter. For example, the very first diary entry relates how Pepys 'luckily' meets up with them 'in the way'. Immediately one is drawn to the conclusion that 'luck' had very little to do with it:

> … thence I by water to Deptford, and there mustered the Yard, purposely, God forgive me, to find out Bagwell, a carpenter, whose wife is a pretty woman, that I might have some occasion of knowing him and forcing her to come to the office again, which I did so luckily that going thence he and his wife did of themselves meet me in the way to thank me for my old kindness, but I spoke little to her, but shall give occasion for her coming to me. (Diary 9th July 1663)

Only a few days later, they 'accidentally' meet up again, and take him home with them, where he finds they have already made preparations for his visit:

> Thence coming home I was saluted by Bagwell and his wife (the woman I have a kindness for), and they would have me into their little house, which I was willing enough to, and did salute his wife. They had got wine for me, and I perceive live prettily, and I believe the woman a virtuous modest woman. Her husband walked through to Redriffe with me, telling me things that I asked of in the yard. (Diary 17th July 1663)

Pepys obviously feels himself to be on a bit of a roll as far as women are concerned – only a couple of weeks earlier he had spent the afternoon with Mrs Betty Lane, with his hands up her skirts 'feeling her all over' and commenting on the whiteness of her legs.

On the 7th August, Pepys visits the dockyard at Deptford and on the way home bumps into Mr and Mrs Bagwell, whom he suspects have been waiting for him as they clearly have something on their minds:

> … and on my way young Bagwell and his wife waylayd me to desire my favour about getting him a better ship; which I shall pretend to be willing to do for them, but my mind is to know his wife a little better. (Diary 7th August 1663)

As we now know, Pepys intended to get to know Mrs Bagwell a whole lot better! However, for now there is no further mention of the Bagwells until February of the following year, so if they attempted to intercept Pepys in the intervening period, they appear to have been unsuccessful. Then Mrs Bagwell decides to take the bull by the horns:

> Up, but weary, and to the office, where we sat all the morning. Before I went to the office there came Bagwell's wife to me to speak for her husband. I liked the woman very well and stroked her under the chin, but could not find in my heart to offer anything uncivil to her, she being, I believe, a very modest woman. (Diary 27th February 1664)

Pepys may well be weary – a few days earlier he had once again spent the afternoon with Betty Lane when he tells us he 'did everything that I would with her.' He relates how Mrs Bagwell spoke to him *before* he went to the office. Did she come to his house? (in which case, she had previously taken the trouble to ascertain where he lived) or did she once again 'luckily' meet up with him on the road? Did her husband know that she was meeting Pepys to petition on his behalf? The diary is silent once again for a further three months until 31 May, when out of the blue, we find Pepys alone with Mrs Bagwell in his office, apparently at his invitation, so either he had established where the couple lived, or they have met in the meantime. Although nothing untoward transpires, he lets slip that his intentions had been otherwise when he arranged the assignation, but loses his nerve at the last minute:

> Dined at home, and so to the office, where a great while alone in my office, nobody near, with Bagwell's wife of Deptford, but the woman seems so modest that I durst not offer any courtship to her, though I had it in my mind when I brought her in to me. But I am resolved to do her husband a courtesy, for I think he is a man that deserves very well. (Diary 31st May 1664)

There follows another break in the Bagwell narrative for a further three months, when another assignation has been arranged, but this time, she stands him up: 'At noon home to dinner, then to my office and there waited, thinking to have had

Bagwell's wife come to me about business, that I might have talked with her, but she came not.' (Diary 6th September 1664)

One wonders what 'business' the secretary of the navy had to discuss with a carpenter's wife? It appears that the relationship with Mr and Mrs Bagwell has developed, but not been reported in the diary. The very next day's entry lets the cat out of the bag:

> So home and Creed with me, and to dinner, and after dinner I out to my office, taking in Bagwell's wife, who I knew waited for me, but company came to me so soon that I could have no discourse with her, as I intended, of pleasure. (Diary 7th September 1664)

It is difficult to see who is stringing along whom – Pepys promising advancement for her husband or Mrs Bagwell dangling the prospect of physical delights. A few weeks later, they take another step along the road. This time, Pepys is a little bolder, but the lady knows how to string him along with a little further teasing:

> But meeting Bagwell's wife at the office before I went home I took her into the office and there kissed her only. She rebuked me for doing it, saying that did I do so much to many bodies else it would be a stain to me. But I do not see but she takes it well enough, though in the main I believe she is very honest. So after some kind discourse we parted, and I home to dinner. (Diary 3rd October 1664)

Thus encouraged, Pepys tries something bolder. First a modest kiss in the office from which he feels encouraged. Then two weeks later he takes the lady to dinner and makes an indecent proposal, but his initial optimism is misplaced, for he subsequently receives a rebuff: 'Then I to my office, where I took in with me Bagwell's wife, and there I caressed her, and find her every day more and more coming with good words and promises of getting her husband a place, which I will do.' (Diary 20th October 1664)

> At noon to the 'Change, and thence by appointment was met with Bagwell's wife, and she followed me into Moorfields, and there into a drinking house, and all alone eat and drank together. I did there caress her, but though I did make some offer did not receive any compliance from her in what was bad, but very modestly she denied me, which I was glad to see and shall value her the better for it, and I hope never tempt her to any evil more. (Diary 3rd November 1664)

In spite of making one of his heartfelt, but usually short-lived resolutions, Pepys meets her again and makes a further appointment: 'I to my office, where Bagwell's wife staid for me, and together with her a good while, to meet again shortly.' (Diary 8th November 1664)

A date is set for a week later and Pepys obviously feeling himself to be, as the saying goes, 'on a promise':

That I might not be too fine for the business I intend this day, I did leave off my fine new cloth suit lined with plush and put on my poor black suit, and after office done (where much business, but little done), I to the 'Change, and thence Bagwell's wife with much ado followed me through Moorfields to a blind alehouse, and there I did caress her and eat and drink, and many hard looks and sooth the poor wretch did give me, and I think verily was troubled at what I did, but at last after many protestings by degrees I did arrive at what I would, with great pleasure, and then in the evening, it raining, walked into town to where she knew where she was, and then I took coach and to White Hall to a Committee of Tangier, where, and everywhere else, I thank God, I find myself growing in repute; and so home, and late, very late, at business, nobody minding it but myself, and so home to bed, weary and full of thoughts. (Diary 15th November 1664)

Although the language is ambivalent, it appears that Pepys has got what he is after, although how this is achieved in an alehouse and with seventeenth-century skirts is not clear. Perhaps there is a clue in the description 'blind alehouse'? This term has been variously described as being 'out of the way' or alternatively 'without windows'. Although such establishments in the seventeenth century were often furnished with high-backed settles and screened alcoves, full sexual intercourse in such a public place would seem unlikely, unless they hired a room. In Stuart England, many establishments provided private as well as public rooms, and as such, offered facilities for unescorted female customers or couples seeking privacy.

December begins in a busy fashion, as on the 6th he meets Mrs Lane and following her home 'did what I would with her'. The next day, no sooner has he risen than Mrs Bagwell comes calling, no doubt feeling that it is time to collect on the deal: 'Lay long, then up, and among others Bagwell's wife coming to speak with me put new thoughts of folly into me which I am troubled at.' (Diary 7th December 1664)

Another week goes by, and in the diary Mrs Bagwell has acquired a French appellation: 'Up, and by water to Deptford, thinking to have met "la femme de" Bagwell, but failed, and having done some business at the yard, I back again, it being a fine fresh morning to walk.' (Diary 16th December 1664)

Pepys' good mood does not last long and three days later harsh words with his wife over a domestic matter cause him to strike her in the face:

Going to bed betimes last night we waked betimes, and from our people's being forced to take the key to go out to light a candle, I was very angry and begun to find fault with my wife for not commanding her servants as she ought. Thereupon she giving me some cross answer I did strike her over her left eye such a blow as the poor wretch did cry out and was in great pain, but yet her spirit was such as to endeavour to bite and scratch me. But I coying (stroking or caressing) with her made her leave crying, and sent for butter and parsley, and friends presently one with another, and I up, vexed at my heart to think what I had done, for she was forced to lay a poultice or something to her eye all day, and is black ... (Diary 19th December 1664)

Having blacked his wife's eye in the morning, the afternoon finds him trying it on again with Mrs Bagwell, who on this occasion isn't having any of it:

Thence home, and not finding Bagwell's wife as I expected, I to the 'Change and there walked up and down, and then home, and she being come I bid her go and stay at Mooregate for me, and after going up to my wife (whose eye is very bad, but she is in very good temper to me), and after dinner I to the place and walked round the fields again and again, but not finding her I to the 'Change, and there found her waiting for me and took her away, and to an alehouse, and there I made much of her, and then away thence and to another and endeavoured to caress her, but 'elle ne voulait pas',[she would not let me] which did vex me, but I think it was chiefly not having a good easy place to do it upon. So we broke up and parted and I to the office... (Diary 19th December 1664)

The very next day, he has more success. It is worth noting that Mr Bagwell seems quite content to leave Pepys at home alone with his wife, whilst he goes out on a short errand craftily arranged by Pepys. He is either a very naïve and simple man, or is a willing party to the conspiracy. Given his later professional success (by 1696 he was Master Shipwright at Portsmouth) one might be lead into believing it was more than likely to be the latter:

Up and walked to Deptford, where after doing something at the yard I walked, without being observed, with Bagwell home to his house, and there was very kindly used, and the poor people did get a dinner for me in their fashion, of which I also eat very well. After dinner I found occasion of sending him abroad, and then alone 'avec elle je tentais a faire ce que je voudrais et contre sa force je le faisais biens que passe a mon contentment' [overcoming her resistance I did what I wanted to my contentment] By and by he coming back again I took leave and walked home, and then there to dinner... (Diary 20th December 1664)

Having practically raped Mrs Bagwell in her own home, he leaves her alone for a while whilst he renews his acquaintanceship with Betty Martin, on whom he spends two shillings on wine and cake, before taking her back to her lodging in Bow Street and 'doing what he wants with her'.

On Monday 23rd January he goes to Jervas's (home of Richard and Grace Jervas, his barber in Palace Yard) to renew his acquaintanceship with the maid Jane, whom he has tried several times to seduce without success. However, she is not there so after dinner, he returns to his office:

> … and finding Mrs. Bagwell waiting at the office after dinner, away she and I to a cabaret [inn] where she and I have ete before, and there I had her company 'toute l'apres-diner'and had 'mon plaisir' of 'elle'. [all after dinner and had my pleasure of her] But strange to see how a woman, notwithstanding her greatest pretences of love 'a son mari' [her husband] and religion, may be 'vaincue' [conquered]. (Diary 23rd January 1665)

Pepys' sexual appetite is insatiable and he returns to Jervas's again in the hope of finding Jane, but yet again 'mais elle n'etait pas dedans' [but she is not within]. Back in the office, he makes one of his many vows to leave off women, although this time for only a month. February 14th Saint Valentine's Day comes around, and Mrs Bagwell is bold enough to turn up unannounced at Pepys' own front door:

> I up about business, and, opening the door, there was Bagwell's wife, with whom I talked afterwards, and she had the confidence to say she came with a hope to be time enough to be my Valentine, and so indeed she did, but my oath preserved me from loosing any time with her, and so I and my boy abroad by coach to Westminster … (Diary 14th February 1665)

As Pepys has still not fulfilled his side of the bargain, Mrs Bagwell is beginning to make a nuisance of herself – it is almost possible to hear Pepys' irritation. However, having at last done as he had promised for so long, he wants to be suitably remunerated:

> Thence to the office, and there found Bagwell's wife, whom I directed to go home, and I would do her business, which was to write a letter to my Lord Sandwich for her husband's advance into a better ship as there should be occasion. Which I did, and by and by did go down by water to Deptford, and then down further, and so landed at the lower end of the town, and it being dark 'entrer en la maison de la femme de Bagwell' [entered the house of Bagwell's wife] and there had 'sa compagnie' [her company], though with a great deal of difficulty, 'neanmoins en fin j'avais ma volont d'elle' [nevertheless in the end I had my way with her] and being sated therewith, I walked home to Redriffe, it being now near nine o'clock, and there I did drink

some strong waters and eat some bread and cheese, and so home … (Diary 20th February 1665)

Elizabeth Pepys may not suspect what is going on with Mrs Bagwell, but she is clearly aware of the true nature of her husband…Pepys thinks she is only joking, but one wonders – or is it a case of many a true word being spoken in jest?

> … where at my office my wife comes and tells me that she hath hired a chamber mayde, one of the prettiest maydes that ever she saw in her life, and that she is really jealous of me for her, but hath ventured to hire her from month to month, but I think she means merrily. (Diary 20th February 1665)

Clearly Mrs Bagwell did not come quietly. The next morning Pepys gets up and finds that he has sustained a minor injury in struggling with the woman who inexplicably has become anonymous: 'Up, and to the office (having a mighty pain in my fore-finger of my left hand, from a strain that it received last night in struggling avec la femme que je mentioned yesterday [with the woman that I mentioned yesterday]. (Diary 21st February 1665)

Both sides having achieved their objectives, there seems to be a cessation of hostilities, and Mrs Bagwell does not get a mention for some five months, until he spots her as he is leaving the office. Before pursuing her however, Pepys cannot resist extracting a minor sexual token before signing a document for another lady:

> Up, and after all business done, though late, I to Deptford, but before I went out of the office saw there young Bagwell's wife returned, but could not stay to speak to her, though I had a great mind to it, and also another great lady, as to fine clothes, did attend there to have a ticket signed; which I did do, taking her through the garden to my office, where I signed it and had a salute [kiss] of her. (Diary 15th February 1665)
>
> Very late I went away, it raining, but I had a design pour aller a la femme de Bagwell [to go to Bagwell's wife] and did so, mais ne savais obtener algun cosa de ella como jo quisiere sino tocarla.[but did not know how to get anything I wanted from her other than touching her]. So away about 12; and it raining hard, I back to Sir G. Carteret, and there called up the page and to bed there – being all in a most violent sweat. (Diary 19th July 1665)

The final entry of 1665 relating to Mrs Bagwell has Pepys again making the journey to Deptford, sneaking in under cover of darkness:

> … I did leave him as soon as I could and by water to Deptford, and there did order my matters so, walking up and down the fields till it was dark night, that 'je allais a la maison [went to the house of] of my valentine, and there 'je faisais whatever je voudrais avec'[did whatever I would with] her, and,

about eight at night, did take water, being glad I was out of the towne; for the plague, it seems, rages there more than ever … (Diary 8th November 1665)

Mrs Bagwell then drops out of the diary narrative for some five months – she had been out of town accompanying her husband. Her next appearance in the diary is brief and uninformative: 'This noon Bagwell's wife come to me to the office, after her being long at Portsmouth.' (Diary 11th April 1666)

One might be forgiven for thinking that Pepys passion is cooling, but the next entry a month later shows this not to be the case:

… I going down to Deptford, and, Lord! to see with what itching desire I did endeavour to see Bagwell's wife, but failed, for which I am glad, only I observe the folly of my mind that cannot refrain from pleasure at a season above all others in my life requisite for me to shew my utmost care in. I walked both going and coming, spending my time reading of my Civill and Ecclesiastical Law book. (Diary 16th May 1666)

On the 12th June, naval business takes him again to Deptford, where he hopes to see Mrs Bagwell, but he is unsuccessful, although the diary next day seems to contradict this:

So we left the church and crowd, and I home (being set down on Tower Hill), and there did a little business and then in the evening went down by water to Deptford, it being very late, and there I staid out as much time as I could, and then took boat again homeward, but the officers being gone in, returned and walked to Mrs. Bagwell's house, and there (it being by this time pretty dark and past ten o'clock) went into her house and did what I would. But I was not a little fearfull of what she told me but now, which is, that her servant was dead of the plague, that her coming to me yesterday was the first day of her coming forth, and that she had new whitened the house all below stairs, but that above stairs they are not so fit for me to go up to, they being not so. (Diary 13th June 1666)

However, a couple of days later, a fresh opportunity presents itself when a poor wife comes to the Navy Office, trying to get her seaman husband's unpaid wages – an ongoing scandal at the time, due to the lack of available funds. Pepys pays the debt himself, but if one thinks that this is out of pity, then one is sadly mistaken. As more often than not, there is a price to pay:

So to the office, and thither came my pretty widow Mrs. Burrows, poor woman, to get her ticket paid for her husband's service – which I did pay her myself, and did bezar her muchas vezes (kiss her many times) – and I do hope may hereafter mas de su [much of her] company. (Diary 15th June 1666)

On Saturday, 30th June, Mr Bagwell returns to the fleet, so on Sunday, Pepys is off again to Deptford, but she is not there. The diary entry for the 1st July tells us that thus he 'missed what he went for'.

As September dawns, what we now know as the Great Fire of London raged for four days and nights, consuming more than thirteen-thousand houses, eighty-seven parish churches, St Paul's Cathedral and most of the buildings of the City authorities. Pepys is pre-occupied with saving his gold and goods. By the 8th the fire is out and the arguments and accusations have begun. Pepys returns to his office, where he finds '... the Bagwells wife and her husband come home. Agreed to come [to] their house tomorrow, I sending him away back to his ship today'. (Diary 8th September 1666)

Obviously excited by the fact that he has got rid of the husband, in fact, Pepys meant to say the day after tomorrow, which promise he keeps, but either Mrs Bagwell is not keen to see him, or she's gone shopping '... calling at Deptford, intending to see Bagwell, but did not 'ouvrir la porte comme je' [open the door as I] did expect. (Diary 10th September 1666)

The next day, Pepys has more luck and manages to arrange a liaison with the elusive lady for the following day. He is obviously in an insatiable mood, as he first visits Betty Martin for a bout with her:

.... thence to Martin, and there did tout ce que je voudrais avec her [all that I liked with her], and drank,. ... So we back home, and then I found occasion to return in the dark and to Bagwell, and there nudo in lecto con ella [naked in bed with her] did do all that I desired; but though I did intend para aver demorado con ella toda la night [to have stayed with her all night], yet when I had done ce que je voudrais [done what I wanted], I did hate both ella and la cosa [hate both her and the thing, i.e. sex]; and taking occasion from the uncertainty of su marido's return esta noche, did me levar [uncertainty of her husband's return that night, did get up]; and so away home late ... (Diary 12th September 1666)

There is no further mention of either Betty Mitchell or Mrs Bagwell in the diary for more than a month. On the 23 October, Pepys goes looking for the former in Westminster Hall, but she is not about. The next day he has a little more luck, with Betty, but in Deptford, a watchful Mrs Bagwell spots him and climbs over her fence to catch up with him!

Home to dinner, and after dinner, it being late, I down by water to Shadwell, to see Betty Michell, the first time I was ever at their new dwelling since the fire, and there find her in the house all alone. I find her mighty modest. But had her lips as much as I would, and indeed she is mighty pretty, that I love her exceedingly. I paid her 10l. 1s. that I received upon a ticket for her husband, which is a great kindness I have done them, and having kissed her as much as I would, I away, poor wretch, and down to Deptford to see Sir J. Minnes ordering of the pay of some ships there, which he do most miserably, and so home. Bagwell's wife, seeing me come the fields way, did get over her pales to come after and talk with me, which she did for a good way, and so parted, and I home, and to the office, very busy, and so to supper and to bed. (Diary 23rd October 1666)

Then another assignation at the office, where presumably a lack of suitable facilities means that Pepys has her bent over his desk? Perhaps he has a camp bed …

… I to my office, where I took in Mrs. Bagwell and did what I would with her, and so she went away, and I all the afternoon till almost night there, and then, my wife being come back, I took her and set her at her brother's … (Diary 1st November 1666)

On the 9th November, Pepys and his wife Elizabeth join with several other friends at Mrs Pierce's house for supper, dancing and music. With them goes Mary Mercer, Elizabeth's companion for several years from 1664. The party is interrupted by reports of a fire in Westminster, which gives Pepys concerns about the security of his house. After some difficulty, a coach is secured to take them all home, which they find to be safe, but not until Pepys has groped his wife's companion in the coach, with his wife sitting next to him. One cannot but admire his savoir-faire!

We got well home; and in the way I did con mi mano tocar la jambe de Mercer sa chair. Elle retirait sa jambe modestement, but I did tocar sa peau [touched Mercer's leg with my hand; she modestly withdrew her leg, but I did touch her skin] with my naked hand. And the truth is, la fille hath something that is assez jolie. …

Obviously Elizabeth did not see and Mary kept her mouth shut, as there do not seem to be any repercussions from this blatant assault.

On Sunday 11th November, Pepys and Elizabeth go to church, where his thoughts are neither on Mrs Bagwell, nor Mary Mercer, but on Betty Mitchell, to the extent that he has to have a surreptitious wank:

Anon to church, my wife and I and Betty Michell, her husband being gone to Westminster. Here at church (God forgive me), my mind did courir upon Betty Michell, so that I do hazer con mi cosa in la eglisa meme [so that I do play with my thing even in the church] … (Diary 11th November 1666)

This noon Bagwell's wife was with me at the office, and I did what I would, and at night comes Mrs. Burroughs, and appointed to meet upon the next holyday and go abroad together. (Diary 22nd November 1666)

The office assignations with Mrs Bagwell are becoming so much a matter of routine that Pepys hardly bothers to record them any longer. Mrs Elizabeth Burroughs, with whom Pepys is making an assignation, was an apparently pretty widow of a naval lieutenant, Anthony Burrows, who was killed in action in 1665. Her mother, Mrs Crofts, kept a shop in Westminster where Elizabeth seems to have worked.

Into the new year, and Pepys continues to employ his hands on ladies' bodies at any opportunity that presents itself. On the 15th January 1667 he went to the office '… where I got Mrs. Burroughs sola cum ego – and did tocar su mamelles [on her own with me and did touch her breasts].

On the 24 January he throws a party at the office for a number of people, including the actress in the King's Company, Elizabeth Knipp. During the evening, she feels unwell and retires to bed in Pepys' house, which presents an opportunity not to be missed:

The company being all gone to their homes, I up with Mrs. Pierce to Knipp, who was in bed; and we waked her, and there I handled her breasts and did baiser la [kiss her] and sing a song, lying by her on the bed, and then left my wife to see Mrs. Pierce in bed to her, in our best chamber, and so to bed myself, my mind mightily satisfied with all this evening's work, and thinking it to be one of the merriest enjoyment I must look for in the world, and did content myself therefore with the thoughts of it, and so to bed. (Diary 24th January 1667)

Up and to the office, where I was all the morning doing business. At noon home to dinner; and after dinner down by the water, though it was a thick misty and raining day, and walked to Depford from Redriffe and there to Bagwells by appointment – where the moher erat within expecting mi venida [the mother was expecting me to arrive]. And did sensa alguna difficulty monter los degrees and lie, comme jo desired it, upon lo lectum; and there I did la cosa con much voluptas. Je besa also her venter and cons and saw the poyle thereof. She would seem alguns veces very religious, but yet did permit me to hazer todo esto et quicquid amplius volebam. By and by su marido came in, and there, without any notice taken by him, we discoursed of our business of getting him the new ship building by Mr. Deane, which I shall do for him [and did climb the stairs and lie in the way I desired it upon the bed and did the thing with much sexual pleasure, I kiss also her belly and cunt and saw the hair thereof; she would seem sometimes very religious but yet did permit me to do all this and whatever else I wanted. By and by her husband came in. . . .].

So Mrs Bagwell's mother seems to be in on the arrangements as well…and later that same day …

Thence by water to Billinsgate and thence to the Old Swan and there took boat, it now being night, to Westminster; there to the Hall and find Doll Lane, and con ella I went to the Bell tavern, and ibi jo did do what I would con ella as well as I could, she sedento sobra una chair and making some little resistance – but all with much content and jo tena much plazer cum ista. There parted, and I by coach home and to the office, where pretty late doing business; and then home and merry with my wife, and to supper.

[and with her I went to the Bell Taverne, and there I did do what I would with her as well as I could, she lying under the chair [?] and making some little resistance. But all with much content, and I had much pleasure with her].

… and later still. . . .

I by coach home, and to the office, where pretty late doing business, and then home, and merry with my wife, and to supper. My brother and I did play with the base, and I upon my viallin, which I have not seen out of the case now I think these three years, or more, having lost the key, and now forced to find an expedient to open it. Then to bed.

Whatever one's opinion of Pepys morality, it is impossible not to admire his energy. Morning at work in the office, sex with two different women in the same afternoon, more business in the office, and then an evening playing music with his wife and brother!

The Bagwells drop out of the narrative for a month or so as Pepys pursues other quarry. On the 5th he takes his wife and Betty Michell to the theatre and then shopping:

Thence by coach to the New Exchange, and there laid out money, and I did give Betty Michell two pair of gloves and a dressing-box; and so home in the dark, over the ruins, with a link.

I was troubled with my pain, having got a bruise on my right testicle, I know not how. But this I did make good use of to make my wife shift sides with me, and I did come to sit 'avec' [with] Betty Michell, and there had her 'main'[hand] which 'elle'[she] did give me very frankly now, and did hazer [do] whatever I 'voudrais avec la'[I wanted with it] which did 'plaisir' me 'grandement [pleasure me greatly]' and so set her at home with my mind mighty glad of what I have prevailed for so far; and so home, and to the office, and did my business there, and then home to supper, and after to set some things right in my chamber, and so to bed. (Diary 5th February 1667)

Amazingly, he gets his wife to swop places with him in the coach in order that he might be next to Betty, and then gets her to wank him off during the journey, presumably without his wife noticing that anything is going on!

Perhaps for the next few days his wife fulfilled his extraordinary sexual needs, as he reports on the 7th February that upon awaking he 'lay long with pleasure with my wife.' Then on the 11th whilst engaged in the further seduction of Betty (who incidentally is heavily pregnant) he gets a real fright. First, he persuades Betty's husband to send his wife to meet himself and Mrs Pepys. Then, Pepys turns up without Elizabeth and tries to get Betty alone, but she isn't having any of it. Due to a delay in Betty's gift being ready, they have been out so long that Pepys is afraid Mr Michell may make enquiry of his wife at Pepys' home, and thereby both Elizabeth and Betty's husband will suspect that something is going on; here is the whole sordid episode in Pepys' own words:

> I home by water, calling at Michell's and giving him a fair occasion to send his wife to the New Exchange to meet my wife and me this afternoon. So home to dinner …

and later that day …

> … my Lord carried me and set me down at the New Exchange, where I staid at Pottle's shop till Betty Michell come, which she did about five o'clock, and was surprised not to 'trouver my muger' [find my wife] I there; but I did make an excuse good enough, and so I took 'elle'[her] down, and over the water to the cabinet-maker's, and there bought a dressing-box for her for 20s., but would require an hour's time to make fit. This I was glad of, thinking to have got 'elle' to enter to a 'casa de biber',[ale-house?] but 'elle' would not, so I did not much press it, but suffered 'elle' to enter 'a la casa de uno de sus hermanos', [the house of one of her brothers] and so I past my time walking up and down, and among other places, to one Drumbleby, a maker of flageolets, the best in towne. He not within, my design to bespeak a pair of flageolets of the same tune, ordered him to come to me in a day or two, and so I back to the cabinet-maker's and there staid; and by and by Betty comes, and here we staid in the shop and above seeing the workmen work, which was pretty, and some exceeding good work, and very pleasant to see them do it, till it was late quite dark, and the mistresse of the shop took us into the kitchen and there talked and used us very prettily, and took her for my wife, which I owned and her big belly, and there very merry, till my thing done,

and then took coach and home … But now comes our trouble, I did begin to fear that 'su marido' [her husband] might go to my house to 'enquire pour elle', and there, 'trouvant' my 'muger' [finding my wife] at home, would not only think himself, but give my 'femme' occasion to think strange things. This did trouble me mightily, so though 'elle' would not seem to have me trouble myself about it, yet did agree to the stopping the coach at the streete's end, and 'je allois con elle' [went with her] home, and there presently hear by him that he had newly sent 'su mayde' [her maid] to my house to see for her mistresse. This do much perplex me, and I did go presently home Betty whispering me behind the 'tergo de her mari',[behind her husband] that if I would say that we did come home by water, 'elle' could make up 'la cose well satis' [something that would satisfy], and there in a sweat did walk in the entry ante my door, thinking what I should say a my 'femme', and as God would have it, while I was in this case (the worst in reference a my 'femme' that ever I was in in my life), a little woman comes stumbling to the entry steps in the dark; whom asking who she was, she enquired for my house. So knowing her voice, and telling her 'su donna' [her mistress] is come home she went away. But, Lord! in what a trouble was I, when she was gone, to recollect whether this was not the second time of her coming, but at last concluding that she had not been here before, I did bless myself in my good fortune in getting home before her, and do verily believe she had loitered some time by the way, which was my great good fortune, and so I in a-doors and there find all well. So my heart full of joy, I to the office awhile, and then home, and after supper and doing a little business in my chamber I to bed, after teaching Barker a little of my song. (Diary 11th February 1667)

In March, Pepys has another go at Mrs Bagwell, but it at last appears as though the time spent on her back has not been wasted and he has honoured his word and found a better position for her husband …

… away to Deptford, and there I a little in the yard, and then to Bagwell's, where I find his wife washing, and also I did 'hazer tout que je voudrais con' her, [did everything I wanted with her] and then sent for her husband, and discoursed of his going to Harwich this week to his charge of the new ship building there, which I have got him … (Diary 4th March 1667)

A couple of days later, Pepys has another narrow squeak, but avoids detection:

Thence by coach home and stayed a very little; and then down by water to Redriffe and walked to Bagwells; where la moher was dentro sed would not have me demorer there parceque Mrs. Batters and one of my ancillas, [where the mother was inside but would not have me stay there because Mrs. Batters and one of my servants] I believe Jane (for she was gone abroad today), was in the town and coming thither; so I away presently, esteeming it a great escape. (Diary 6th March 1667)

Later that month, Pepys is walking to Westminster, complaining that he has met no one 'to spend any time with' and is on his way home when he chances upon Mrs Daniel:

> … in Seething Lane met young Mrs. Daniel, and I stopped; and she had been at my house but found nobody within, and tells me that she drew me for her Valentine this year; so I took her into the coach, and was going to the other end of the town, thinking to have taken her abroad; but remembering that I was to go out with my wife this afternoon, I only did hazer her para tocar my prick con her hand which did hazer me hazer; [make her touch my prick with her hand which did make me do the thing i.e. orgasm] and so to a milliner shop at the corner going into Bishopsgate and Leadenhall-street and there did give her eight pairs of gloves, and so dismissed her … (Diary 25th March 1668)

No doubt Mrs Daniels thought eight pairs of gloves a good price for a quick hand job in Pepys' coach. In the meantime, with his new appointment to take up, Mr Bagwell goes off to Harwich and his wife goes with him. There is not further mention of them in the diary until some ten months later, when on the 6th January 1668 Pepys spots Mrs Bagwell, newly returned to town. On his way home, he tries to find her, having a mind to have his way with her, but fails to find her. On the 15th, he has occasion to go to Deptford, and takes the opportunity to walk up and down outside the Bagwell's house, but no one is home.

On the 6th February, Pepys has another grope with his wife's companion, Mary Mercer, putting his hand under her skirts and touching her thighs. Luckily for him, she takes no offence and simply puts away his hand. He does the same thing with the recently acquired maid, Deb Willett. In April, Pepys accounts record the expenditure of one shilling (5 pence) on '… Mrs. Martin, and there did what I would, she troubled for want of imploy for her husband'.

On the 21st, Pepys is at it again, this time it is the actress Mrs Knipp, whose thighs feel his groping hand probing under her skirts. She puts up only a token resistance and he is 'mightily pleased' to discover that she has very soft skin. On the 23rd, he takes the lady out for an evening drink in Lambeth, where they watch a bonfire burning in honour of the king's coronation day anniversary. Here he manages to 'touch her body all over', whether beneath or over her clothes he does not say.

April comes and with it fresh opportunities arrive:

This afternoon came Mrs. Lowther to me to the office, and there yo did tocar su mamelles [touch her breasts] and did bezar [kiss] them and su boca [her mouth], which she took fort [very] willingly, and perhaps yo posse [I believe] in time a hazer mas [do more] to her. (Diary 13th April 1667)

On the 6th May, he has dinner with Mrs Knipp and Mrs Foster at Mrs Pierce's before going to the theatre. After the play, he returns to her house, where he finds Mrs Knipp asleep on a pallet in the dark. Never one to pass up an opportunity: 'yo did poner mi manos under her jupe and tocar su cosa and waked her.' [I did put my hands under her skirt and touch her thing and waked her.] (Diary 6th May 1668)

The 10th is a Sunday and Pepys takes Mercer, Mrs Lowther and her aged mother-in-law to dinner in Chelsea, [then a village west of London] later dropping the old woman home. Later, they go off to Tower Wharf to buy shoes, although whether Mercer goes with them is not clear. If she did, one wonders what she thought of her master kneeling at the feet of this married woman with his hands up her skirts, where his objective is foiled by her underwear:

… we did send for a pair of old shoes for Mrs. Lowther, and there I did pull the others off and put them on, and did endeavour para tocar su thigh but ella had drawers on, but yo did besar la and tocar sus mamelles, elle being poco shy, but doth speak con mighty kindness to me that she would desire me pour su marido if it were to be done. [did endeavour to touch her thigh but she had drawers on, but I did kiss her and touch her breasts, she not being very shy, but doth speak with mighty kindness to me that she would desire me for her husband if it were to be done]. Here staid a little at Sir W. Penn's, who was gone to bed, it being about 11 at night, and so I home to bed. (Diary 10th May 1668)

The following Saturday he has a mind to see Mrs Knipp again:

… I did go forth by coach to the King's playhouse, and there saw the best part of 'The Sea Voyage', where Knepp I see do her part of sorrow very well. I afterwards to her house; but she did not come presently home; and there je [I] did kiss her ancilla, [I did kiss her maid] which is so mighty belle [pretty] … (Diary 16th May 1668)

Pepys is not having a lot of luck. On the evening of the 29th he has arranged to visit Mrs Bagwell in Deptford, but Mercer brings two musicians home to meet him, and they stay singing and playing until 11.00pm, thereby unintentionally subverting his planned assignation.

His habit of making ladies fondle his penis has lately included Mrs Knepp, and Pepys is concerned that she may have taken offence, luckily however, she seems not to have been discommoded by the experience:

Here I was freed from a fear that Knepp was angry or might take advantage; did parlar the esto that yo did the otra day, quand yo was con her in ponendo her mano upon mi cosa [did speak of this that I did the other day when I was with her in placing her hand upon my thing i.e. penis] -- but I saw no such thing; but as pleased as ever, and I believe she can bear with any such thing. Thence to the New Exchange. ... (Diary 30th May 1668)

Two days later, Pepys spends much of the morning drinking with acquaintances in a Rhenish wine-house before some early afternoon business in Whitehall. This concluded, he pays a visit to the Westminster home of Mrs Martin: '...and did hazer what yo would con her, and did aussi tocar la thigh de su landlady' [and did what I would with her, and did also touch the thigh of her landlady]. (Diary 1st June 1668)

Did Pepys put his hand up the skirts of a woman he has not previously met or simply stroke her leg through her dress? A bold move at any time in history. However, whatever the lady thought about this casual grope is not recorded. The following day, after various visits (and after dusk) he makes his way to Deptford, where:

.... I did by agreement andar a la house de Bagwell; and there, after a little playing and baisando, [kissing] we did go up in the dark a su camera and there fasero la grand cosa upon the bed; and that being hecho, did go away and to my boat again, and against the tide home; got there by 12 a-clock and to bed ...' [... we did go up in the dark to her bedroom and there did the big thing upon the bed; and that being done, did go away ...]. (Diary 2nd June 1668)

The comment that this visit was 'by agreement' is interesting in what it does not tell us. Is Pepys sending messages to Mrs Bagwell and receiving replies? One would assume that there was a system of communicating from the Navy Office to the dockyards at Deptford but surely he would have been tempting fate enclosing private notes to a married woman?

All the way through the rest of 1668, Pepys is engaged in his ill-fated affair with Elizabeth's maid, the 17-year-old Deb Willett. Mrs Bagwell disappears from the diary until 4th March 1669, when for reasons unexplained, Pepys records how he 'slunk out to the Bagwells and there saw her and her mother and our late maid Nell, who cried for joy to see me; but I had no time for pleasure there nor could stay; but after drinking, I back to the yard, having a month's mind [i.e. strong inclination] para have had a bout with Nell – which I believe I could have had – and may another time.' (Diary 4th March 1669)

On the 29th March Pepys is again in Deptford, and has a mind to see Mrs Bagwell, which he succeeds in doing, but only at her door, being inexplicably unable to 'conveniently go into her house, and so lost my labour'. That night he lies in bed fantasizing about their new maid, Matt, who had begun in service with them that day. His fantasies are so strong that 'ella did make me para hazer in mi mano' [she did make me do the thing (orgasm) in my hand].

Mrs Bagwell makes her final appearance in the diary on the 15th April 1669, just a month and a half before the diary is brought to a close, Pepys thinking that the eye strain from which he had long-suffered, and brought on by writing by candle-light, is in fact a precursor to his going blind. He goes to the office in the morning, and there finds the lady waiting for him. She passes him a note inviting him to meet her in Moorfields that same afternoon, where she might speak with him. They meet and talk, although about what Pepys dos not reveal, although there must be a suspicion that the Bagwells have decided that another promotion for Mr Bagwell is due. Nothing else transpires '… it being holiday, and the place full of people, we parted, leaving further discourse and doing to another time.' (Diary 15th April 1669)

Whether that meeting materialized and whether or not Pepys continued to visit Mrs Bagwell we will never know. What is known is that the Bagwells became relatively well to do and a year later are to be found living in a much bigger house in Deptford. The Elizabeth Bagwell thought most likely to have been the Mrs Bagwell of the diary died in 1702 and was buried at St Nicholas, Deptford on 14th August of that year, but this identity is far from certain. However, as the long-term mistress of Samuel Pepys, Mrs Bagwell assured herself a kind of immortality. (See Appendix B 'The Bagwells')

Chapter 15

A Pretty Companion

In September 1667, the diary records Pepys; introduction to a young woman whom it was intended should be his wife's new female companion. Although we are given to believe that Deb Willett was an attractive and well educated young woman aged 17, there is little to indicate that she is destined to become the major object of his extra-marital affections for years to come, an amour that would almost destroy his marriage. The first of 187 diary entries concerning Deb goes:

> This evening my wife tells me that W. Batelier hath been here to-day, and brought with him the pretty girl he speaks of, to come to serve my wife as a woman, out of the school at Bow. My wife says she is extraordinary handsome, and inclines to have her, and I am glad of it — at least, that if we must have one, she should be handsome. But I shall leave it wholly to my wife, to do what she will therein. (Diary 24th September 1667)

When the girl turns up for work three days later, Pepys is in raptures:

> While I was busy at the Office, my wife sends for me to come home, and what was it but to see the pretty girl which she is taking to wait upon her: and though she seems not altogether so great a beauty as she had before told me, yet indeed she is mighty pretty; and so pretty, that I find I shall be too much pleased with it, and therefore could be contented as to my judgement, though not to my passion, that she might not come, lest I may be found too much minding her, to the discontent of my wife. She is to come next week. She seems, by her discourse, to be grave beyond her bigness and age, and exceeding well bred as to her deportment, having been a scholar in a school at Bow these seven or eight years. To the office again, my head running on this pretty girl……. and so with pleasure discoursing with my wife of our journey shortly to Brampton, and of this little girle, which indeed runs in my head, and pleases me mightily, though I dare not own it, and so to supper and to bed. (Diary 27th September 1667)

The next day is Saturday, and Pepys still cannot get Deb out of his mind – in fact, thinking about her has kept him awake most of the night: 'Up, having slept not so much to-night as I used to do, for my thoughts being so full of this pretty little girle that is coming to live with us, which pleases me mightily.' (Diary 28th September 1667)

On Monday, he still cannot get her out of his mind, in spite of having his wicked way with Mrs Martin – literally in passing:

> So to Westminster, where to the Swan … and drank and away to the Hall, and thence to Mrs. Martin's, to bespeak some linen, and there je did avoir all [I did have all] with her, and drank, and away, having first promised my goddaughter a new coat-her first coat. So by coach home, and there find our pretty girl Willet come, brought by Mr. Batelier, and she is very pretty, and so grave as I never saw a little thing in my life. Indeed I think her a little too good for my family, and so well carriaged as I hardly ever saw. I wish my wife may use her well. (Diary 30th September 1667)

The next day comes the first of sixteen diary entries concerning Deb during the month of October:

> After dinner took coach and to my wife, who was gone before into the Strand, there to buy a nightgown, where I found her in a shop with her pretty girle, and having bought it away home. … So thence late in the dark round by the wall home by coach, and there to sing and sup with my wife, and look upon our pretty girle, and so to bed. (Diary 1st October 1667)

Most of the entries at this stage are innocuous enough, and of a generally complimentary nature: '… and so home, to supper, and walk in the garden with my wife and girle, with whom we are mightily pleased …'

'… so my wife and she in their morning gowns, very handsome and pretty, and to my great liking.'

But women have an instinct about these things, and Mrs Pepys has already begun to smell a rat. On Tuesday 15th October the three go to the Duke of York's playhouse:

> But here, before the play begun, my wife begun to complain to me of Willet's confidence in sitting cheek by jowl by us, which was a poor thing; but I perceive she is already jealous of my kindness to her, so that I begin to fear this girle is not likely to stay long with us. (Diary 15th October 1667)

Another month goes by with only passing references to the girl, then we learn that Deb has begun to provide more personal services for her master: 'And then to supper, and after supper he went away, and so I got the girl to comb my head, and then to bed, my eyes bad.' (Diary 15th November 1667)

Into December, and Pepys entry for Wednesday 4th demonstrates clearly his sexual predatory nature, when he tries (unsuccessfully) to pick up two different women, one after the other:

Thence into the House [Parliament], and there spied a pretty woman with spots on her face,[i.e. black patches] well clad, who was enquiring for the guard chamber; I followed her, and there she went up, and turned into the turning towards the chapel, and I after her, and upon the stairs there met her coming up again, and there kissed her twice, and her business was to enquire for Sir Edward Bishop, one of the serjeants at armes. I believe she was a woman of pleasure, but was shy enough to me, and so I saw her go out afterwards, and I took a hackney coach, and away. (Diary 4th December 1667)

I to Westminster Hall, and there walked, and thence towards White Hall by coach, and spying Mrs. Burroughs in a shop did stop and 'light and speak to her; and so to White Hall, where I 'light and went and met her coming towards White Hall, but was upon business, and I could not get her to go any whither and so parted, and I home with my wife and girle. (Diary 4th December 1667)

On Saturday, Deb's aunt comes to visit, presumably to see how she is settling in. Pepys clearly fancies the aunt as well:

All the morning at the office, and at noon home to dinner with my clerks, and while we were at dinner comes Willet's aunt to see her and my wife; she is a very fine widow and pretty handsome, but extraordinary well carriaged and speaks very handsomely and with extraordinary understanding, so as I spent the whole afternoon in her company with my wife, she understanding all the things of note touching plays and fashions and Court and everything and speaks rarely, which pleases me mightily, and seems to love her niece very well, and was so glad (which was pretty odde) that since she came hither her breasts begin to swell, she being afeard before that she would have none, which was a pretty kind of content she gave herself. (Diary 7th December 1667)

It has taken a while, but with his wife out of the way and sick in bed, Pepys ventures to give Deb a kiss:

(Lord's day). Up, and my wife, poor wretch, still in pain, [she was suffering a gastric upset] and then to dress myself and down to my chamber to settle some papers, and thither come to me Willet with an errand from her mistress, and this time I first did give her a little kiss, she being a very pretty humoured girle, and so one that I do love mightily. (Diary 22nd December 1667)

When Pepys says 'one that I do love mightily' it is safe to assume that what he really means is 'lust after'! Like many a wife before and since, Elizabeth Pepys knows that something is up, but cannot quite identify what it is that is going on.

Pepys makes an (innocent) visit to two ladies of his acquaintance, one of them an actress, and tells his wife where he has been:

> I took leave and left them there, and so to my bookseller's, and paid for the books I had bought, and away home, where I told my wife where I had been. But she was as mad as a devil, and nothing but ill words between us all the evening while we sat at cards — W. Hewer and the girl by — even to gross ill words, which I was troubled for, but do see that I must use policy to keep her spirit down, and to give her no offence by my being with Knepp and Pierce, of which, though she will not own it, yet she is heartily jealous. At last it ended in few words and my silence (which for fear of growing higher between us I did forbear), and so to supper and to bed without one word one to another. (Diary 30th December 1667)

This marital spate is soon over however, as the very next day Pepys records that the year ends on a calmer note and all seems right with the world once again: '… and so home to supper and to bed, good friends with my wife. Thus ends the year, with great happiness to myself and family as to health and good condition in the world, blessed be God for it!' (Diary 31st December 1667)

The little personal evening services that Deb has been providing have obviously become the norm:

> … and then home to supper, and so by the fireside to have my head combed, as I do now often do, by Deb., whom I love should be fiddling about me, and so to bed. (Diary 11th January 1668)
>
> … and so the girl to comb my head till I slept, and then to bed. (Diary 26th January 1668)
>
> After dinner, my head combed an hour, and then to work again. (Diary 2nd February 1668)

On Thursday, a party visit the theatre and then go to supper before taking a coach home. On the way and despite his wife being in the coach, Pepys has a casual grope of one of the ladies:

> This evening coming home I did put my hand under the coats of Mercer [Mary Mercer – Elizabeth Pepys companion 1664–66] and did touch her thigh, but then she did put by my hand and no hurt done, but talked and sang and was merry. (Diary 6th February 1668)

The entries relating to Deb throughout March concern her accompanying Elizabeth on shopping trips or visits to the theatre. At the end of the month, Pepys is planning his wife's forthcoming trip to his father's house in Brampton:

... I called Deb to take pen, ink, and paper and write down what things came into my head for my wife to do, in order to her going into the country; and the girl writing not so well as she would do, cried, and her mistress construed it to be sullenness and so was angry, and I seemed angry with her too; but going to bed, she undressed me, and there I did give her good advice and beso la, ella weeping still [kissed her, she weeping still]; and yo did take her, the first time in my life, sobra mi genu and did poner mi mano sub her jupes and toca su thigh [spare my (?). ... and did put my hand under her skirts and touched her thigh] which did hazer [give] me great pleasure; and did no more, but besando-la [kissing her] went to my bed. (Diary 31st March 1668)

The cat of lust is out of the bag now, and Pepys can no longer resist the temptation to let his wandering hands roam over the body of the hapless maid. Wednesday 1st April dawns and he is up smartly:

Up and to dress myself; and called, as I use, Deb to brush and dress me and there I did again as I did the last night con mi mano [with my hand], but would have tocado su thing [touched her thing] but ella [she] endeavoured to prevent me con [with] much modesty by putting su [her] hand thereabout, which I was well pleased with and would not do too much, and so con [with] great kindness dismissed la [her]. (Diary 1st April 1668)

The next morning, his wife and Deb, together with Betty Turner and Jane, prepare to leave on their trip to the home of Pepys senior. Pepys gives Deb ten shillings (50p) 'to oblige her to please her mistress (and yo did besar her mucho).' [did kiss her much].

Dropping them at Cheapside, he takes leave of them, but with his wife close by decides to 'not besando [not kiss] Deb, which I had a great mind to'. [His wife was close by]. (Diary 2nd April 1668)

With temptation temporarily removed, Pepys can look forward to a few weeks as a bachelor, not an opportunity he intends to waste; whilst his wife is out of town he kisses, gropes and otherwise assaults Mrs Davenport, Mrs Burroughs, Mrs Turner, Mrs Knipp (and her maid), Mrs Shrewsbury and Mrs Markham.

Chapter 16

Caught Red-Handed

Whether or not Pepys continued to put his hands under the skirts of the hapless Deb upon her return from Brampton, whilst she brushed his hair and helped him undress, is not recorded. It is likely that it had become so commonplace that he no longer bothered to record it. Through June and July, the only diary references to her again relate to the accompanying of her employers to the theatre or on shopping trips. Then on 6 August, Pepys takes his wife and Deb with him on a trip by coach to Surrey, visiting Guildford and Hindhead. Presumably Elizabeth must have fallen asleep in the coach, for Pepys records that he took advantage of an opportunity:

'This day yo [I] did first with my hand tocar la cosa de [touch the privates of] our Deb in the coach – ella [she] being troubled at it – but yet did give way to it.' (Diary 6th August 1668)

It seems that Deb has become resigned to the fact that her master enjoys touching her up, long since a regular feature of his evening grooming: '… and all the while Deb did comb my head and I did tocar her with my mano para mi great pleasure.' [touch her with my hand to my great pleasure]. (Diary 10th August 1668)

Just over a week later, matters escalate, as they have a tendency to do in matters of the flesh:

This night yo did hazer [I did make] Deb tocar mi thing [touch my penis] with her hand after yo was in lecto [I was reading] – with great pleasure. (18th August 1668)

… and then Deb to comb my head; and here I had the pleasure para touch the cosa [private parts] of her and all about, with little opposition; and so to bed. (Diary 13th August 1668)

This could only lead to great trouble, and sure enough, the inevitable happens. Elizabeth, who has long suspected that something was going on, walks in and catches her husband in flagrante. A domestic storm breaks around Pepys head of such magnitude as can only be generated by a betrayed wife:

… and after supper, to have my head combed by Deb, which occasioned the greatest sorrow to me that ever I knew in this world; for my wife, coming up suddenly, did find me imbracing [sic] the girl con my hand sub su coats; and endeed [sic] I was with my main [hand] in her cunny. I was at a wonderful loss upon it, and the girl also; and I endeavoured to put it off, but my wife was struck mute and grew angry, and as her voice came to her, grew quite out of order; and I do say little, but to bed; and my wife said little also, but could not sleep all night; but about 2 in the morning waked me and cried, and fell to tell me as a great secret that she was a Roman Catholique, and had received the Holy Sacrament; which troubled me but I took no notice of it, but she went on from one thing to another, till at last it appeared plainly her trouble was at what she saw; but yet I did not know how much she saw and therefore said nothing to her. But after her much crying and reproaching me with inconstancy and preferring a sorry girl before her, I did give her no provocations but did promise all fair usage to her, and love, and foreswore any hurt that I did with her – till at last she seemed to be at ease again; and so toward morning a little sleep; and so I, with some little repose and rest, rose, and up and by water to White-hall, but with my mind mightily troubled for the poor girl, whom I fear I have undone by this, my wife telling me that she would turn her out of door. (Diary 25th October 1668)

Pepys clearly realises that the matter is far from over as far as Elizabeth is concerned, and he is absolutely right. After meetings with the Duke of York and Lord Sandwich, he heads homeward for the midday meal:

Thence by coach home and to dinner, finding my wife mightily discontented and the girl sad, and no words from my wife to her. So after dinner, they out with me about two or three things; and so home again, I all the evening busy and my wife full of trouble in her looks; and anon to bed – where about midnight, she wakes me and there falls foul on me again, affirming that she saw me hug and kiss the girl; the latter I denied, and truly; the other I confessed and no more. And upon her pressing me, did offer to give her under my hand that I would never see Mrs. Pierce more, nor Knepp, but did promise her perticular [sic] demonstrations of my true love to her, owning some indiscretion in what I did, but that there was no harm in it. She at last on these promises was quiet, and very kind we were, and so to sleep; and in the morning up, but with my mind troubled for the poor girl, with whom I could not get opportunity to speak; but to the office, my mind mighty full of sorrow for her … (Diary 27th October 1668)

Even now the storm has not passed, for following an afternoon spent in the office, Pepys once more returns home, where:

… my wife towards bedtime begin to be in a mighty rage from some new matter that she had got in her head, and did most part of the night in bed rant at me in most high terms, of threats of publishing my shame; and when I offered to rise, would have rose too, and caused a candle to be lit, to burn by her all night in the chimney while she ranted; while I, that knew myself to have given some grounds for it, did make it my business to appease her all I could possibly, and by good words and fair promises did make her very quiet; and so rested all night and rose with perfect good peace, being heartily afflicted for this folly of mine that did occasion it; but was forced to be silent about the girl, which I have no mind to part with, but much less that the poor girl should be undone by my folly. So up, with mighty kindness from my wife and a thorough peace; and being up, did by a note advise the girl what I had done and owned, which note I was in pain for till she told me that she had burned it. (Diary 28th October 1668)

At last it seems that some equilibrium has returned to the Pepys household: '… and at night to supper and to bed, my wife and I at good peace, but yet with some little grudgeings [sic] of trouble in her, and more in me, about the poor girl.' (Diary 25th – 29th October 1668)

The next day Pepys sleeps well, but with a troubled heart as he perceives that Elizabeth's mind is still not at ease over the matter. The diary ends the month with a confession of guilt, shame and yet another future resolve:

So ends this month, with some quiet of my mind, though not perfect, after the greatest falling out with my poor wife, and through my folly with the girl, that ever I had; and I have reason to be ashamed and sorry of it – and more, to be troubled for the poor girl's sake; whom I fear I shall by this means prove the ruin of – though I shall think myself concerned both to love and be a friend to her. (Diary 31st October 1668)

Pepys is a master of self-delusion and if he thinks he has mollified his wife and can continue to be friends with Deb, he is due for a sharp awakening, which is not long in coming!

Chapter 17

The Storm Continues Unabated

The first day of November 1668 is a Sunday, and ends in much the same way as all the days of the previous week. Pepys goes to bed with an unquiet mind about Deb's fate, fearing that Elizabeth will 'put her away' but realising that there will be no return to a peaceful existence until she is gone. On Tuesday, his wife tells him that she has already taken the first steps to put in train Deb's departure:

> So home, and there to supper; and I observed my wife to eye my eyes whether I did ever look upon Deb; which I could not, but do now and then (and to my grief did see the poor wretch look on me and see me look on her, and then let drop a tear or two; which doth make my heart relent at this minute that I am writing this, with great trouble of mind, for she is endeed [sic] my sacrifice, poor girl); and my wife did tell me in bed, by the by, of my looking on other people, and that the only way is to put things out of sight; and this I know she means by Deb, for she tells me that her aunt was here on Monday and she did tell her of her desire of parting with Deb; but in such kind terms on both sides, that my wife is mightily taken with her. I see it will be, and it is but necessary; and therefore, though it cannot but grieve me, yet I must bring my mind to give way to it. (Diary 3rd November 1668)

On Wednesday, Deb goes off with some friends and Pepys suspects that she is looking for alternative employment. On returning home at night, he finds that she has not returned and wonders if she has already gone, but dare not broach the subject with Elizabeth. Most nights are disturbed with her continued complaints and Pepys takes to working late at the office rather than go home to yet another row. Deb returns home but hides herself in her room; Pepys manages to communicate with her by flinging her a note, telling her that he continues to deny ever having kissed her. However, Elizabeth is watching his every move, from his rising to his going out of the front door. All week, the matter continues to fester:

> … then home by coach, with my mind still troubled and finding no content, my wife being still troubled, nor can be at peace while the girl is there.…
> (Diary 6th November 1668)

… the poor girl not appearing at supper, but hides herself in her chamber – so that I could wish in that respect that she was out of the house, for our peace is broke to all of us while she is here. (Diary 8th November 1668)

Then on Tuesday the 10th, marital matters go from bad to worse, as he discovers how many other men have been trying to seduce his physically attractive wife behind his back:

… and so home to dinner, where I find my wife mightily troubled again, more than ever, and she tells me that it is from examining the girl and getting a confession now from her of all, even to the very tocando su thing [touching her 'thing', i.e. private parts] with my hand – which doth mightily trouble me, as not being able to see the consequences of it as to our future peace together. So my wife would not go down to dinner, but I would dine in her chamber with her; and there, after mollifying her as much as I could, we were pretty quiet and eat; and by and by comes Mr. Hollier, and dines there by himself after we had dined. And he being gone, we to talk again, and she to be troubled, reproaching me with my unkindness and perjury, I having denied my ever kissing her – as also with all her old kindnesses to me, and my ill-using of her from the beginning, and the many temptations she hath refused out of faithfulness to me; whereof several she was perticular [sic] in, and especially from Lord Sandwich by the solicitation [sic] of Captain Ferrer; and then afterward, the courtship of my Lord Hinchingbrooke, even to the trouble of his Lady. All of which I did acknowledge and was troubled for, and wept; and at last pretty good friends again, and so I to my office and there late, and so home to supper with her. … (Diary 10th November 1668)

The respite is short-lived however, as Elizabeth's rage has far from run its course. Pepys is learning the truth of the old adage that hell hath no fury like a woman scorned:

… and so to bed, where, after half-an-hour's slumber, she wakes me and cries out that she should never sleep more, and so kept raving until past midnight, that made me cry and weep heartily all the while for her, and troubled for what she reproached me with as before; and at last, with new vows, and particularly [sic] that I would myself bid the girl be gone and show my dislike to her – which I will endeavour to perform, but with much trouble. And so, this appeasing her, we to sleep as well as we could till morning. (Diary 10th November 1668)

The next day finds Pepys in his office, from whence he returns home to dinner (taken at noon in seventeenth-century England), only to find his wife refusing to dine with him. Later that evening after supper, he and Elizabeth retire to bed. …

… where after lying a little while, my wife starts up, and with expressions of affright and madness, as one frantic, would rise; and I would not let her, but burst out in tears myself; and so continued almost half the night, the moon shining so that it was light; and after much sorrow and reproaches and little ravings (though I am apt to think they were counterfeit from her), and my promise again to discharge the girl myself, all was quiet again, and so to sleep. (Diary 11th November 1668)

The next day, Pepys knows he must do the deed as promised if he is not to find his domestic life in ruins. His dinner guest leaves and the deed can be put off no longer; Deb must be sent away. …

And so having dined, we parted, and I to my wife to sit with her a little; and then called her and Willett to my chamber, and there did with tears in my eyes, discharge her and advise her to be gone as soon as she could, and never to see me or let me see her more while she was in the house; which she took with tears too, but I believe understands me to be her friend; and I am apt to believe, by what my wife hath of late told me, is a Cunning girl, if not a slut. (Diary 12th November 1668)

The following day, after a long day's business, Pepys returns home, to be told by his wife that Deb has found a place to go, and will be gone tomorrow morning. Unbelievably, Pepys seems to have learned nothing from his recent experiences:

This troubled me; and the truth is, I have a great mind for to have the maidenhead of this girl, which I should not doubt to have if yo could get time para be con her [sic] – but she will be gone and I know not whither. (Diary 13th November 1668)

For all his vows and undertakings to his wife, Elizabeth clearly does not trust him and it is not difficult to see why! She now has the upper hand and clearly intends to keep it that way:

Before we went to bed, my wife told me she would not have me see her or give her her wages; and so I did give my wife £10 for her year and half-a-quarter's wages, which she went into her chamber and paid her; and so to bed, and there, blessed be God, we did sleep well and with peace, which I have not done in now almost twenty nights together. (Diary 13th November 1668)

If Pepys' thought that the matter was now reconciled in his wife's mind, he soon finds out how much he is sadly mistaken:

Up, and had a mighty mind to have seen or given a note to Deb or to have given her a little money; to which purpose I wrapped up 40s in a paper;

thinking to give her; but my wife rose presently, and would not let me be out of her sight; and went down before me into the kitchen, and came up and told me that she was in the kitchen, and therefore would have me go round the other way; which she repeating, and I vexed at it, answered her a little angrily; upon which she instantly flew out into a rage, calling me dog and rogue, and that I had a rotten heart; all which, knowing that I deserved it, I bore with; and word being brought presently up that she was gone away by coach with her things, my wife was friends; and so all quiet, and I to the office with my heart sad, and find that I cannot forget the girl, and vexed I know not where to look for her. … (Diary 14th November 1668)

Pepys knows that the departure of Deb is unlikely to be the end of the matter. Not only can he not get his mind off the girl and his dishonourable intentions towards her, but the sad fact that his wife is never going to forget the affair:

… and more troubled to see how my wife is by this means likely for ever to have a hand over me, that I shall ever be a slave to her; that is to say, only in matters of pleasure, but in other things she will make her business, I know, to please me and keep me right to her … (Diary 14th November 1668)

Before closing his diary for this memorable day, Pepys makes an interesting observation:

And so at night home to supper, and there did sleep with great content with my wife. I must here remember that I have lain with my moher (wife) as a husband more times since this falling-out then in I believe twelve months before – and with more pleasure to her then I think in all the time of our marriage before. (Diary14th November 1668)

There has been much speculation over why and how Elizabeth's previously low libido had been stimulated by the events concerning Deb Willett. Perhaps it was the images created in her imagination of her husband's lascivious behaviour with the servant girl; perhaps it was brought on by the adrenalin generated by her uncontrollable rages, or similarly by her new-found dominance over her husband. Whatever it was, it has clearly regenerated their physical relationship. Pepys is able to record that on the morning of Sunday, 15th November he got up '… after long lying with pleasure talking with my wife'. Nevertheless, in playing with matches he has had his fingers badly, but not fatally, burnt. Sadly, he has not learned his lesson. There are still more matches in the box, and Pepys is hell bent on striking them!

Chapter 18

Hell Hath No Fury

Even before that Sunday is out, Pepys is again beginning to hanker after the servant girl: '… less troubled about Deb then I was, though yet I am troubled I must confess, and would be glad to find her out – though I fear it would be my ruin.' (Diary 15th November 1668)

Obviously the threat of ruin is soon pushed to the back of his mind, for the very next day, Pepys does some business in the office and then begins a search for Deb's whereabouts: 'I away to Holborne about Whetstones-park, where I never was in my life before, where I understand by my wife's discourse that Deb is gone …' (Diary 16th November 1668)

As the search proceeds, Pepys mind is becoming more and more fixed upon further deceiving his wife about Deb: '… pretty pleasant and at ease in my mind, being in hopes to find Deb, and without trouble or the knowledge of my wife.' (Diary 17th November 1668)

Elizabeth obviously has a better understanding of her husband's dishonourable intentions than he suspects:

Lay long in bed, talking with my wife, she being unwilling to have me go abroad, being and declaring herself jealous of my going out, for fear of my going to Deb; which I do deny – for which God forgive me, for I was no sooner out about noon but I did go by coach directly to Somerset-house and there enquired among the porters there for Dr. Allbun … (Diary 15th November 1668)

The search for Deb through the offices of Dr Allbun proves to be successful:

… at last he comes back and tells me she is well, and that I may see her if I will – but no more. So I could not be commanded by my reason, but I must go this very night; and so by coach, it being now dark, I to her, close by my tailor's; and there she came into the coach to me, and yo did besar her and tocar her thing [and I did kiss her and touch her thing] but ella [she] was against it and laboured with much earnestness, such as I believed to be real; and yet at last yo [I] did make her tener mi cosa in her mano, while mi mano was sobra her pectus, [did make her take my member in her hand, while my

hand was under her clothes] and so did hazer with grand delight. (Diary 18th
November 1668)

Pepys then has the audacity to advise her not to allow any other man to do what he
does, gives her 20s [£1] and instructions that – should she move lodgings – to leave
her new address for him with his booksellers. Returning home, Pepys tells his wife
'… a fair tale, God knows, how I spent the whole day; with which the poor wretch
was satisfied.' He is about to be sadly disillusioned!

The next morning, Pepys rises and goes to his office with his 'heart full of joy to
think in what a safe condition all my matters now stand between my wife and Deb
and me …' At noon, he returns home to see how the refurbishment of his bedroom
is proceeding, only to find his wife sitting sad in the dining-room. …

> … which inquiring into the reason of, she begun to call me all the rotten-
> hearted rogues in the world, letting me understand that I was with Deb
> yesterday; which, thinking impossible for her ever to understand, I did a
> while deny; but at last did, for the ease of her mind and hers, and for ever to
> discharge my heart of this wicked business, I did confess all; and above-stairs
> in our bedchamber there, I did endure the sorrow of her threats and vows
> and curses all the afternoon. And which was worst, she swore by all that was
> good that she would slit the nose of this girl, and be gone herself this very
> night from me; and did there demand (3 or £400) of me to buy my peace,
> that she might be gone without making any noise, or else protested that she
> would make all the world know of it. So, with most perfect confusion of face
> and heart, with sorrow and shame, in the greatest agony in the world, I did
> pass this afternoon, fearing that it will never have an end. … (Diary 19th
> November 1668)

At last, Pepys calls upon his old friend and colleague William Hewer (Pepys'
manservant and later clerk, before embarking on a successful career of his own and
ultimately the executor of Pepys' will) to mediate on his behalf:

> So with most perfect confusion of face and heart, and sorrow and shame, in
> the greatest agony in the world I did pass this afternoon, fearing that it will
> never have an end; but at last I did call for W. Hewer, who I was forced to
> make privy now to all, and the poor fellow did cry like a child, [and] obtained
> what I could not, that she would be pacified upon condition that I would give
> it under my hand never to see or speak with Deb, while I live, as I did before
> with Pierce and Knepp, and which I did also, God knows, promise for Deb.
> too, but I have the confidence to deny it to the perjury of myself. So, before it
> was late, there was, beyond my hopes as well as desert, a durable peace; and
> so to supper, and pretty kind words, and to bed, and there je did hazer con

elle to her content, and so with some rest spent the night in bed, being most absolutely resolved, if ever I can master this bout, never to give her occasion while I live of more trouble of this or any other kind, there being no curse in the world so great as this of the differences between myself and her, and therefore I do, by the grace of God, promise never to offend her more, and did this night begin to pray to God upon my knees alone in my chamber, which God knows I cannot yet do heartily; but I hope God will give me the grace more and more every day to fear Him, and to be true to my poor wife. This night the upholsters did finish the hanging of my best chamber, but my sorrow and trouble is so great about this business, that it puts me out of all joy in looking upon it or minding how it was. (Diary 19th November 1668)

Fearing that should his wife manage to communicate with Deb and that in that event, Deb would deny all, the situation would become even worse. He sends word to her that he has confessed to everything and that the cat is well and truly out of the bag. As part of the deal with Elizabeth, Will Hewer is to accompany him everywhere as a chaperone when she is not with him:

This morning up, with mighty kind words between my poor wife and I; and so to White Hall by water, W. Hewer with me, who is to go with me everywhere, until my wife be in condition to go out along with me herself; for she do plainly declare that she dares not trust me out alone, and therefore made it a piece of our league that I should always take somebody with me, or her herself, which I am mighty willing to, being, by the grace of God, resolved never to do her wrong more. (Diary 20th November 1668)

Pepys puts his cards on the table with Will Hewer, who is obviously taking no chances and goes and checks his story with Deb:

… and so to White Hall, in my way I telling him plainly and truly my resolutions, if I can get over this evil, never to give new occasion for it. He is, I think, so honest and true a servant to us both, and one that loves us, that I was not much troubled at his being privy to all this, but rejoiced in my heart that I had him to assist in the making us friends, which he did truly and heartily, and with good success, for I did get him to go to Deb. to tell her that I had told my wife all of my being with her the other night, that so if my wife should send she might not make the business worse by denying it. While I was at White Hall with the Duke of York, doing our ordinary business with him, here being also the first time the new Treasurers. W. Hewer did go to her and come back again, and so I took him into St. James's Park, and there he did tell me he had been with her, and found what I said about my manner of being with her true, and had given her advice as I desired. I did there enter into more talk about my wife and myself, and he did give me great assurance of several particular cases to which my wife had from time to time made him privy of her loyalty and truth to me after many and great temptations, and I believe them truly. I did also discourse the unfitness of my leaving of my employment now in many respects to go into the country, as my wife desires, but that I would labour to fit myself for it, which he thoroughly understands, and do agree with me in it. (Diary 20th November 1668)

Returning home, Pepys hopes for a quiet and peaceful reception; sadly his hopes could not be further from the reality:

But when I come home, hoping for a further degree of peace and quiet, I find my wife upon her bed in a horrible rage afresh, calling me all the bitter names; and rising, did fall to revile me in the bitterest manner in the world, and could not refrain to strike me and pull my hair; which I resolve to bear with, and had good reason to bear it. So I by silence and weeping did prevail with her a little to be quiet, and she would not eat her dinner without me; but yet by and by into a raging fit she fell again worse than before, that she would slit the girl's nose. … (Diary 20th November 1668)

Once more, Will Hewer is required to make the peace:

… at last W. Hewer come in and come up, who did allay her fury, I flinging myself, in a sad desperate condition, upon the bed in the blue room, and there lay while they spoke together; and at last it come to this, that if I would call Deb. whore under my hand and write to her that I hated her, and would never see her more, she would believe me and trust in me, which I did agree to, only as to the name of whore I would have excused, and therefore wrote to her sparing that word, which my wife thereupon tore it, and would not be satisfied till, W. Hewer winking upon me, I did write so with the name of a whore as that I did fear she might too probably have been prevailed upon to have been a whore by her carriage to me, and therefore as such I did resolve never to see her more. This pleased my wife, and she gives it W. Hewer to carry to her with a sharp message from her. So from that minute my wife begun to be kind to me, and we to kiss and be friends, and so continued all the evening, and fell to talk of other matters, with great comfort, and after supper to bed.

More visitors come and go, and Pepys ends the day with more of the usual promises and resolutions:

I to my wife again, and so spent the evening with very great joy, and the night also with good sleep and rest, my wife only troubled in her rest, but less than usual, for which the God of Heaven be praised. I did this night promise to my wife never to go to bed without calling upon God upon my knees by prayer, and I begun this night, and hope I shall never forget to do the like all my life; for I do find that it is much the best for my soul and body to live pleasing to God and my poor wife, and will ease me of much care as well as much expense. (Diary 20th November 1668)

The next day begins with a degree of equilibrium, and Hewer seems to have completed his task in taking Pepys' letter to Deb. Even when he goes home, things seem to have returned to normal:

Up, with great joy to my wife and me, and to the office, where W. Hewer did most honestly bring me back the part of my letter to Deb. wherein I called her whore, assuring me that he did not shew it her, and that he did only give her to understand that wherein I did declare my desire never to see her, and did give her the best Christian counsel he could, which was mighty well done of him. But by the grace of God, though I love the poor girl and wish her well, as having gone too far toward the undoing her, yet I will never enquire after or think of her more, my peace being certainly to do right to my wife...... home to my wife, where I find my house clean now, from top to bottom, so as I have not seen it many a day, and to the full satisfaction of my mind, that I am now at peace, as to my poor wife, as to the dirtiness of my house, and as to seeing an end, in a great measure, to my present great disbursements upon my house, and coach and horses. (Diary 21st November 1668)

The next day is Sunday, and Elizabeth is obviously making an effort, as she spends the whole day 'making herself clean, after four or five weeks being in continued dirt'. On Wednesday he and Elizabeth go to the theatre and Pepys is uncomfortable that she will spot him 'looking about'. However, matters are still calm when the following Sunday comes around, although Deb is still on his mind:

Lay long in bed with pleasure with my wife, with whom I have now a great deal of content, and my mind is in other things also mightily more at ease, and I do mind my business better than ever and am more at peace, and trust in God I shall ever be so, though I cannot yet get my mind off from thinking now and then of Deb., but I do ever since my promise a while since to my wife pray to God by myself in my chamber every night, and will endeavour to get my wife to do the like with me ere long ... (Diary 29th November 1668)

Things are still bubbling underneath the apparent calm, and come to the surface when Elizabeth catches Pepys talking in his sleep:

Up, after a little talk with my wife, which troubled me, she being ever since our late difference mighty watchful of sleep and dreams, and will not be persuaded but I do dream of Deb., and do tell me that I speak in my dreams and that this night I did cry, Huzzy, and it must be she, and now and then I start otherwise than I used to do, she says, which I know not, for I do not know that I dream of her more than usual, though I cannot deny that my thoughts waking do run now and then against my will and judgment upon her, for that only is wanting to undo me, being now in every other thing as to my mind most happy, and may still be so but for my own fault, if I be catched loving anybody but my wife again. (Diary 5th December 1668)

Then on Monday 7th December, Pepys is in his new coach when …

… This afternoon, passing through Queen's Street, I saw pass by our coach on foot Deb., which, God forgive me, did put me into some new thoughts of her, and for her, but durst not shew them, and I think my wife did not see her, but I did get my thoughts free of her soon as I could. (Diary 7th December 1668)

Sadly, the matter will just not go away, even when Pepys has remained blameless. …

And so home, where I have a new fight to fight with my wife, who is under new trouble by some news she hath heard of Deb's being mighty fine, and gives out that she has a friend that gives her money, and this my wife believes to be me, and, poor wretch! I cannot blame her, and therefore she run into mighty extremes; but I did pacify all, and were mighty good friends, and to bed, and I hope it will be our last struggle from this business, for I am resolved never to give any new occasion, and great peace I find in my mind by it. So to supper, she and I to bed. (Diary 18th December 1668)

And new jealousies continue to surface …

It was, that she did believe me false to her with Jane [Pepys' maid 1658 to 1661 – married his clerk Tom Edwards in 1669 and Pepys was godfather to their son] and did rip up three or four silly circumstances of her not rising till I come out of my chamber, and her letting me thereby see her dressing herself; and that I must needs go into her chamber and was naught with her; which was so silly, and so far from truth, that I could not be troubled at it, though I could not wonder at her being troubled, if she had these thoughts, and therefore she would lie from me, and caused sheets to be put on in the blue room, and would have Jane to lie with her lest I should come to her. At last, I did give her such satisfaction, that we were mighty good friends, and went to bed betimes … (Diary Sunday, 7th February 1669)

So to Cox's, and thence walked with Sir J. Smith back to Redriffe; and so, by water home, and there my wife mighty angry for my absence, and fell mightily out, but not being certain of anything, but thinks only that Pierce or Knepp was there, and did ask me, and, I perceive, the boy, many questions. But I did answer her; and so, after much ado, did go to bed, and lie quiet all night; but [she] had another bout with me in the morning, but I did make shift to quiet her, but yet she was not fully satisfied, poor wretch! in her mind, and thinks much of my taking so much pleasure from her; which, indeed, is a fault, though I did not design or foresee it when I went. (Diary 4th March 1669)

A few days later he returns home from the office, expecting to find his wife in a good humour. On the contrary, she is sitting alone in her closet in a furious temper, having heard that 'Deb's living very fine, and with black spots, and speaking ill words of her mistress …' (Diary 12th March 1669)

Having pacified her, all continues calm, Pepys recording on the 29 March that all the household staff having been employed since Debs' departure, no one now recalls the trouble that had arisen between himself and his wife. However, the London of Pepys' day is not a large city, and fate intervenes once more …

But here being in the court-yard, God would have it, I spied Deb., which made my heart and head to work, and I presently could not refrain, but sent W. Hewer away to look for Mr. Wren (W. Hewer, I perceive, did see her, but whether he did see me see her I know not, or suspect my sending him away I know not, but my heart could not hinder me), and I run after her and two women and a man, more ordinary people, and she in her old clothes, and after hunting a little, find them in the lobby of the chapel below stairs, and there I observed she endeavoured to avoid me, but I did speak to her and she to me, and did get her pour dire me ou she demeurs [get her to tell me where she stays] now, and did charge her para say nothing of me that I had vu elle [seen her], which she did promise, and so with my heart full of surprize and disorder I away … But, God forgive me, I hardly know how to put on confidence enough to speak as innocent, having had this passage to-day with Deb., though only, God knows, by accident. But my great pain is lest God Almighty shall suffer me to find out this girl, whom indeed I love, and with a bad amour, but I will pray to God to give me grace to forbear it. So home to supper, where very sparing in my discourse, not giving occasion of any enquiry where I have been to-day, or what I have done, and so without any trouble to-night more than my fear, we to bed. (Diary 13th April 1669)

Deb is a very young woman of nineteen years, clearly fond of Pepys, but obviously frightened by his bullying, already having lost her employment, her home and possibly her reputation as a result of his persistent sexual harassment. Once again however, fate denies her the chance to shake him off, and this time, Pepys is prepared to use his superior physical strength to get his way:

> Thence I away, and through Jewen Street, my mind, God knows, running that way, but stopped not, but going down Holburn-hill, by the Conduit, I did see Deb. on foot going up the hill. I saw her, and she me, but she made no stop, but seemed unwilling to speak to me; so I away on, but then stopped and 'light, and after her and overtook her at the end of Hosier lane in Smithfield, and without standing in the street desired her to follow me, and I led her into a little blind alehouse within the walls, and there she and I alone fell to talk and baiser la and toker su mammelles [kiss her and touch her breasts], but she mighty coy, and I hope modest, but however, though with great force, did hazer ella par su hand para tocar mi thing, nut ella was in great pain para be brought para it [did make her touch my thing with her hand but she was in great pain to be made to do it]. I did give her in a paper 20s, and we did agree para meet again in the Hall at Westminster on Monday next; and so, giving me great hopes by her carriage that she continues modest and honest, we did there part. … (Diary 15th April 1669)

… leaving Pepys riddled with guilt and fearful lest Elizabeth discover that he has yet again broken his oath and seen Deb yet again. …

> Thence home, and to my business at the office, to finish it, but was in great pain about yesterday still, lest my wife should have sent her porter to enquire anything, though for my heart I cannot see it possible how anything could be discovered of it, but yet such is fear as to render me full of doubt and disgust. (Diary 16th April 1669)
> … and my wife being come home we to talk and to sup, there having been nothing yet like discovery in my wife of what hath lately passed with me about Deb., and so with great content to bed. (Diary 19th April 1669)

Pepys' hankering after Deb still has not gone away, neither has Elizabeth's jealousy …

> … walked home round by the Excise Office, having by private vows last night in prayer to God Almighty cleared my mind for the present of the thoughts of going to Deb at Greenwich, which I did long after. … Thence with my wife abroad, with our coach, most pleasant weather; and to Hackney, and into the marshes, where I never was before, and thence round about to Old Ford and Bow; and coming through the latter home, there being some young gentlewomen at a door, and I seeming not to know who they were, my wife's jealousy told me presently that I knew well enough it was that damned place where Deb. dwelt, which made me swear very angrily that it was false, as it

was, and I carried [her] back again to see the place, and it proved not so, so I continued out of humour a good while at it, she being willing to be friends, so I was by and by, saying no more of it. (Diary 7th May 1669)

Deb is the last woman to make an appearance in the diary, in the very last entry that Pepys was to make:

And thus ends all that I doubt I shall ever be able to do with my own eyes in the keeping of my journall, I being not able to do it any longer, having done now so long as to undo my eyes almost every time that I take a pen in my hand; and therefore, whatever comes of it, I must forbear; and therefore resolve from this time forward to have it kept by my people in long-hand, and must therefore be contented to set down no more than it is fit for them and all the world to know; or if there be anything (which cannot be much, now my amours to Deb are past, and my eyes hindering me in almost all other pleasures), I must endeavour to keep a margin in my book open, to add here and there a note in short-hand with my own hand. (Diary 31st May 1669)

Were Pepys 'amours' with Deb really over at this point and did he ever see her again? We do not know for certain. It must seem likely however that their association continued in one form or another after the diary period. It is now generally thought that Deb continued to live in the same area as Pepys and we know that she married one Jeremiah Wells, a theology graduate, in January 1670. They obviously remained in touch as Wells later corresponded with Pepys, who subsequently assisted him in securing employment as a ship's chaplain. Sadly, the union of Mr and Mrs Wells was short-lived; Debs died in 1678 at the age of 27 and Jeremiah died only eighteen months later.

Chapter 19

Some That Got Away

By no means did all the women that came to the attention of Pepys' roving eye succumb to his charms. Many escaped the worst excesses of his lascivious attentions, either because the right circumstances for a dalliance never presented themselves, or the lady simply did not fancy him.

Rebecca Jowles was the daughter of John Allen, the Clerk of the Ropeyard in the naval docks at Chatham and the wife of Henry Jowles, a naval lieutenant. She appears on a dozen or more occasions throughout the diary period from April 1661, when Pepys sees the young Miss Allen for the first time and is smitten: '… very tall and … very handsome, so much as I could not forbear to love her exceedingly, having, among other things, the best hand that ever I saw.' (Diary 9th April 1661)

More than two years later, and in spite of the fact that she has married and given birth, Pepys is still lusting after her:

> Here I saw Mrs. Becky Allen, who hath been married, and is this day churched, after her bearing a child. She is grown tall, but looks very white and thin, and I can find no occasion while I am here to come to have her company, which I desire and expected in my coming, but only coming out of the church I kissed her and her sister and mother-in-law. (Diary 12th July 1663)

Mrs Jowles puts in occasional appearances in the diary without Pepys' desires being satisfied. Then in March 1669, circumstances appear favourable and with typical Pepysian cunning, he makes an attempt upon her virtue:

> '… took occasion, in my way, at St. Margett's, to pretend to call to see Captain Allen to see whether Mrs. Jowles, his daughter, was there; and there his wife come to the door, he being at London, and through a window, I spied Jowles, but took no notice of he but made excuse till night, and then promised to come and see Mrs. Allen again, and so away, it being a mighty cold and windy, but clear day. … and after dinner a barber come to me, and there trimmed me, that I might be clean against night, to go to Mrs. Allen. And so, staying till about four o'clock, we set out, I alone in the coach going and coming; and in our way back, I 'light out of the way to see a Saxon monument. … So homeward, and stopped again at Captain Allen's, and there 'light, and sent

the coach and Gibson home, and I and Coney staid; and there comes to us Mrs. Jowles, who is a very fine, proper lady, as most I know, and well dressed. Here was also a gentleman, one Major Manly, and his wife, neighbours; and here we staid, and drank, and talked, and set Coney and him to play while Mrs. Jowles and I to talk, and there had all our old stories up, and there I had the liberty to salute her often, and pull off her glove, where her hand mighty moist, and she mighty free in kindness to me, and je [I] do not at all doubt that I might have had that that I would have desired de elle [her] had I had time to have carried her to Cobham, as she, upon my proposing it, was very willing to go, for elle [she] is a whore, that is certain, but a very brave and comely one. Here was a pretty cozen of hers come in to supper also, of a great fortune, daughter-in-law to this Manly, mighty pretty, but had now such a cold, she could not speak. Here mightily pleased with Mrs. Jowles, and did get her to the street door, and there to [touch?] her su [her] breasts, and baiser [kissed] her without any force, and credo [believed] that I might have had all else, but it was not time nor place. Here staid till almost twelve at night, and then with a lanthorn from thence walked over the fields, as dark as pitch, and mighty cold, and snow, to Chatham, and Mr. Coney with great kindness to me: and there all in bed before I come home, and so I presently to bed. (Diary 24th March 1669)

As far as we know, the right time and place was never to present itself, as Rebecca Jowles does not appear again in the remaining two months of the diary.

Jane Welsh was the assistant to Richard Jervas, Pepys' regular barber. In July 1664, Pepys takes his periwig in to be cleaned of nits and contrives to get Jane alone by way of a typical Pepys' subterfuge:

Here meeting his mayd Jane, that has lived with them so long, I talked with her, and sending her of an errand to Dr. Clerk's, did meet her, and took her into a little alehouse in Brewers Yard, and there did sport with her, without any knowledge of her though, and a very pretty innocent girl she is. (Diary 18th July 1664)

So I walked to Westminster, and there at my barber's had good luck to find Jane alone; and there I talked with her and got the poor wretch to promise to meet me in the abbey on tomorrow come sennit, telling me that her maister and mistress have a mind to get her a husband, and so will not let her go abroad without them — but only in sermon time a-Sundays she doth go out. (Diary 3rd September 1664)

Throughout the rest of the year, Pepys attempts to arrange assignations with Jane, but more often than not, she stands him up, and even when he does get her alone, a few kisses is all he achieves:

… and thence to Gervas's, and there find I cannot prevail with Jane to go forth with me, but though I took a good occasion of going to the Trumpet she declined coming, which vexed me. 'Je avait grande envie envers elle, avec vrai amour et passion'. [I longed for her with real love and passion.] (Diary 9th December 1664)

Never a man to take no for an answer, Pepys tries repeatedly in the new year to make an assignation with her, but is either stood up or rebutted on nearly every occasion. Despite advice from her master and Pepys, she runs off with her boyfriend, a poor fiddler, and disappears from the pages of the diary until more than a year later, when Pepys by chance comes across her in the street. Taking her for a drink, he hears the whole sorry tale, but has obviously lost all interest in her:

… met her at Lambeth, and there drank with her; she telling me how he that was so long her servant, did prove to be a married man, though her master told me (which she denies) that he had lain with her several times in his house. There left her 'sans essayer alcune cose con elle', [without trying anything else on with her]. (Diary 18th April 1666)

The Swan Inn stood in New Palace Yard adjacent to the Houses of Parliament, one of Pepys favourite watering holes. At least part of the attractiveness of the establishment may be found in the two serving girls, sisters Sarah and Frances Udall. Initially, Sarah attracts Pepys attention, being 'sported' with whenever he visits, such games consisting of some teasing and a little groping. However, some eleven months after her first appearance in the diary, Pepys tries something a little more serious:

So it being not dinner time, I to the Swan, and there found Sarah all alone in the house and I had the opportunity a hazer what I tena a mind á hazer con ella [to do what I had a mind to do with her], only con [with] my hands -- but she was vexed at my offer a tocar la under sus jupes [to touch her under her skirts]; but I did once, nonobstant [despite] all that. (Diary 27th November 1665)

Sarah has clearly drawn a line and she doesn't appear again until the following March when Pepys briefly mentions that 'after dinner had opportunity of being pleased with Sarah'. All through 1666 Pepys mentions her whenever he visits the Swan, but other than a kiss or two, clearly isn't making any progress. Then in November, he discovers the reason for her lack of interest: '… thence by water to Westminster, and there at the Swan find Sarah is married to a shoemaker yesterday, so I could not see her, but I believe I shall hereafter at good leisure.'

The fact that Sarah is now a married woman only seems to give Pepys a fresh incentive to pursue his lustful objective:

I did go drink at the Swan, and there did meet with Sarah, who is now newly married; and there I did lay the beginnings of a future amor con ella [love with her], which in time may come para laisser me hazer alguna cosa con elle [let me play some thing with her]. (Diary 30th November 1666)

In the meantime, he turns his attention to Sarah's sister, Frances: 'I to the Swan, and there did the first time 'baiser' [kiss] the little sister of Sarah. (Diary 3rd December 1666)

Sarah is very clearly not interested in entertaining this dirty old man, other than serving him as a customer of the inn, and after this entry, she gradually fades from the diary: 'Thence to the Swan, and there I sent for Sarah and mighty merry we were, but contra [against] my will were very far from hazer algo [doing anything]. (Diary 18th December 1666)

Chapter 20

Last Love

Pepys made the final entry in his diary on 31st May 1669, thinking that he was going blind. In fact, it proved to be chronic eye-strain and he retained his sight until the end of his life. Although he kept later diaries, they relate only to specific subjects of importance in his public life, for example, the 'Tangier Journal of 1683' ... Sadly, we have no personal references to his private life and loves after that final entry in which he asks God to prepare him for the loss of his sight: 'And so I betake myself to that course which [is] almost as much as to see myself go into my grave – for which, and all the discomforts that will accompany my being blind, the good God prepare me.' (Diary 31st May 1669)

Given what we know from his own admissions about his private (and less than private) lusts, it is difficult to believe that after the death of his wife Elizabeth on the 10th November 1669, Pepys pursued a celibate existence. What records there are identify only one woman who might qualify as a lover in his life after that date, but without the candour of the diary we are left to make what assumptions we may about the nature of their relationship. Nonetheless, Pepys tantalisingly leaves us with one final illuminating clue. In May 1703, only a few days before his death, he enters a codicil to his will:

> Item: Whereas I hold myself obliged on this occasion to leave behind me the most full and lasting acknowledgement of my esteem respect and gratitude to the Excellent Lady Mrs. Mary Skyner for the many important Effects of her Steddy friendship and Assistances during the whole course of my life, within the last thirty three years; I doe give and devise unto the said Mrs.Mary Skyner One Annuity or yearly payment of Two hundred pounds of lawful money of England for and during the terms of her natural Life.

When he died, Pepys was owed the extraordinary sum of £28,007 2s 1p by the Crown, which according to the National Archive, is more than £2,000,000 in today's purchasing power. Of these monies, his will directed that £5,000 should go to Mary Skinner; however, none of these monies due was ever paid. The reference in this codicil dates the beginning of their relationship to the year following Elizabeth's death. Who was this woman whom Pepys held in such high esteem and what exactly was their relationship?

A clue comes unexpectedly in the court records of the Old Bailey. On Michaelmas Day, the 29th September 1693. Pepys was on the road to Chelsea in a coach with his nephew (and ultimately his heir) John Jackson, Mrs Mary Skinner and some other ladies, when they were held up and robbed. The robbers were subsequently caught, tried and executed. The court recorded that 'my lady Pepys saved a bag of money that she had about her.' Whether she was deliberately misrepresented as Mrs Pepys or the court clerk simply made such an assumption, it is impossible to say, but in any event, the entry is revealing.

Another diarist, the distinguished scientist, Robert Hooke, also gives the game away in an even earlier entry in his diary dated 15th December 1676 in which he records that he '… gave Mrs. Pepys a recipe for making varnish.' Surely a Freudian slip revealing how Mary was regarded by friends and associates – one who fulfilled a much greater role than friend or housekeeper. John Evelyn and his wife certainly regarded Samuel Pepys and Mary as man and wife, which, given the former's well acknowledged sense of propriety, speaks volumes for the otherwise respectability of the Pepys household. Many of the letters to Pepys from Evelyn close with a salutation to Mrs Skinner, hardly something he was likely to do had she been merely a housekeeper or servant: '… so becoming a New Yeares Gift as my wishing Mr. Pepys this an happy-one, and many more, with the same to Mrs. Skinner from our fire-side.' (Letter John Evelyn to Samuel Pepys 1st January 1700)

Again later the same year. … 'Your prayers I neede not beg, you are so charitable. But mine, my wife's, and all our most humble services to you, Mrs. Skinner, Mr. Ewers, I beseech you to present……' (Letter John Evelyn to Samuel Pepys 22nd July 1700)

Confirmation that Pepys thought of her as much more than a servant is evidenced by his many references to her in his own correspondence, such as when he sends her personal greetings to Mrs Evelyn: 'Your most affectionately faithful and obedient servant, SP. Mrs. Skinner prays to bee thought noe lesse soe to my Lady …' (Letter Samuel Pepys to John Evelyn 24th December 1701)

There is other clear evidence of her role in managing Pepys' household. When he discharged the difficult housekeeper Mrs Fane from his service, Mary persuaded him to give her a second chance. Whenever he was ill, she acted as his amanuensis, replying to his correspondence and dealing with his day-to-day affairs. When nephew John Jackson went on the Grand Tour of the continent, Pepys commissioned him to buy small gifts for her as he travelled, and to be certain to send her greetings whenever he wrote.

In addition to being his business manager, amanuensis, and probably de facto wife, she was also his nurse. On the 7th August 1770 Pepys wrote to John Evelyn: 'I cannot give myself the scope I otherwise should in talking now to you at this distance, on account of the care extraordinary I am now under from Mrs. Skinner's being suddenly fallen very ill.'

So how and where did Mary and Samuel meet? Mary was the daughter of one Daniel Skinner, a merchant who lived with his wife in Mark Lane and worshipped at St Olave's, a city church attended regularly by Samuel and Elizabeth and where they are both buried. The portrait of her by an unknown artist, in the possession of the Pepys Library in Magdalene College, Cambridge, shows a serious, good looking woman with dark eyes and an aquiline nose, hair set into ringlets and a single pearl necklace setting off her fashionably low-cut silk gown.

Some clues to their relationship are provided in a letter of July 1676 to Pepys, written in Latin, from a young Daniel Skinner, a Fellow of Trinity College, Cambridge. In the letter, Daniel makes reference to Pepys' love for his sister originating from some years past and the previous kindnesses he had then received from Pepys. It also makes reference to angry accusations made by Mr and Mrs Skinner senior against Pepys – presumably in respect of his relationship with their daughter. Mary had actually been brought up by Mrs Skinner's childless sister in Hertfordshire who was married to a Lincolnshire baronet, and therefore relatively wealthy. It seems safe to assume that Mary must have regularly visited her natural parents, with whom she remained on very good terms, and they in turn undoubtedly knew Pepys and his wife as all four were regular worshippers at the same church, of which Pepys was a major beneficiary. How natural that the Skinners would introduce them to their grown up daughter.

Although they were both free to do so, Pepys never married Mary although his relationship with her parents was eventually mended. Perhaps his marriage to Elizabeth had been sufficiently turbulent to put him off repeating the experience or perhaps he felt that she was compromised by entering a relationship with him outside marriage – years earlier he had referred to Lord Brouncker's much loved live-in mistress as a whore. Nevertheless, she remained his close companion and confident for thirty-three years and was at his side when he died. Almost the last conscious action of the dying Pepys was to call her and John Jackson to his bedside and bidding them remain good friends, take her by the hand and kiss her. His last words according to John were 'God be gracious to me', he then blest everyone in the room and prayed God to reward them all. Turning his face towards Mary Skinner he said 'and thee in particular my dear child'. He passed away that night at forty-seven minutes past three o'clock.

After Pepys' death, Mary returned to live in lodgings in Westminster, where she kept a portrait of him on her wall and wore a diamond encrusted heart shaped mourning ring she had had made.

Sadly, Mary Skinner has no voice in history, so whether her role in Pepys' life extended further than that of 'friendship and assistance' remains speculative. Her memories of their life together remain unrecorded by her or anyone else and they died with her when she passed away twelve years later, to be buried on the 18th October 1715, as she had wished, close to her foster-mother in Hatfield. Nowhere does there appear to be any reference to her being the de facto second Mrs Samuel Pepys and as such the woman with whom he shared his life for the last three decades of his life.

Chapter 21

Shame & Remorse?

In judging Samuel Pepys there is a temptation to do so against twenty-first century western values of morality and gender equality, but how would the society of Pepys' own time have viewed his attitude and behaviour towards women? The period following the restoration of the monarchy in 1660 is popularly perceived to be one of liberalization, led by a 'merry monarch' who had freed England from the oppressive and puritanical rule of Oliver Cromwell. Under the governance of the Commonwealth, all forms of public entertainment, including theatres, had been closed and what were regarded as idolatrous representations of divine or human figures had been destroyed, including many irreplaceable medieval church paintings, windows and statuary.

Both public and private morals had been scrutinised under the Puritans and in 1650, the 'Act for the Suppression of the Detestable Sins of Inceste, Adulterie & Fornication' had prescribed that couples found guilty of such offences should be publicly whipped and branded (although in practice the male party often escaped with only a financial penalty). Clothes were black and unadorned and church attendance was mandatory. When Charles Stuart returned from exile in Holland in May 1660, the change in society was immediate and palpable. 'The change is so great' wrote Lady Derby, 'that I can hardly believe it'. However, the joyful enthusiasm with which he was welcomed did not last long. By August 1661, Pepys was recording a conversation concerning 'the lewdnesse and beggary of the court……. which I fear will bring all to ruine again' (Diary 17th August 1661). Summing up at the end of that same month, he observed that '… at Court things are in very ill condition, there being so much aemulacion, poverty, and the vices of swearing, drinking and whoring …' (Diary 31st August 1661).

The king sat at the centre of this licentious assembly, setting an example that many of his courtiers were more than happy to follow.

The diarist John Evelyn wrote: 'I can never forget the inexpressible luxury and profaneness, gaming, and all dissoluteness, and as it were total forgetfulness of God…. the King sitting and toying with his concubines….' Even several years later, Pepys is still bewailing 'the wantonness of the court' and how the king with his concubines 'doth spend most of his time in feeling and kissing them naked all over their bodies in bed – and contents himself, without doing the other thing but as he finds himself inclined; but this lechery will never leave him.' (Diary 16th October 1665)

The republican poet John Ayloffe wrote that the king sat 'besieged by whores, buffoons and bastard chits'. This statement contains more than a grain of truth – Charles is thought to have fathered at least twenty illegitimate children of which he acknowledged fourteen. The mothers ranged in status from actress to duchess, one of whom in the person of the Duchess of Portsmouth gave birth to a son who became Charles Lennox, 1st Duke of Richmond and an ancestor of Diana, Princess of Wales.

At a time when there was insufficient funds in the national exchequer to pay the navy seamen engaged in fighting the war against the Dutch, Charles's mistresses were costing a fortune – Barbara Palmer, 1st Duchess of Cleveland was said to have once lost the immense sum of £20,000 at cards in a single evening (equivalent to about 1.5 million pounds in 2016).[4] This licentious behaviour and scandalous waste caused much public resentment, and the poets, both professional and anonymous, were soon quick to put pen to paper, Barbara's allegedly insatiable sexual appetite being an early target:

> The number can never be reckoned;
> She's fucked the great and the small,
> From good King Charles the Second
> To honest Jacob Hall
> [Jacob Hall was a circus tightrope walker.]

Barbara remained Charles's official mistress until 1670 and bore him six children, the king ensuring their ennoblement by creating her husband Earl of Castlemaine. None of this inhibited the anonymous rhymers; one such ode scribbled on the back of a door so enraged the king that he (unsuccessfully) offered £1,000 reward for the identity of the culprit (although the Earl of Rochester has to be a likely candidate):

> Castlemaine I say is much to be admired,
> Although she ne're was satisfied or tired;
> Full forty men a day provided for this whore:
> Yet like a bitch she wags her tail for more.

Was this new licentiousness and liberty imitated or approved of by the population at large? John Wilmot, the Earl of Rochester, later banished for writing obscene

---

4. National Archive recommends multiplying by a factor of 75 to obtain a modern value for 17C values, but this takes no account of changing purchasing power or relative prices.

and scurrilous odes about the king, gives a clue to the disillusionment and sorrow felt by many at the moral turpitude of the king and his court:

> Chaste, pious, prudent Charles the Second,
> The miracle of thy restoration
> May like to that of quails be reckoned,
> Rained upon the Israelitish nation;
> The wished-for blessing from heaven sent
> Became their curse and punishment.

Were the sexual promiscuity of the king to be reflected amongst the general population, in an age without reliable contraception, the rate of illegitimate births might have been expected to rise, although not perhaps to the level achieved by Charles! In fact, this is far from the case; illegitimate births per thousand deliveries actually fell during the Restoration period, from an average of 2.06 in the 1630s to 1.30 in the 1670s. (P.Laslett, *Family Life & Illicit Love*, Cambridge University Press 1977)

It begins to appear that, as is often suspected to be the case in our own day and age, there was one rule for the rich and another for the poor. This was certainly so in seventeenth-century England; in May 1681 the Duke of York intervened to save the Lady Sophia Lindsay from being publicly whipped through the streets of Edinburgh, to which she had been sentenced as a punishment for assisting in the escape of her father-in-law, the Earl of Argyle, who was facing a charge of treason. Instead, she was saved the public humiliation (but not the pain) by being privately birched by the Sergeant-at-Arms in a room in Edinburgh Castle.

Although Charles may not have been too concerned about fathering illegitimate children, the consequences for a single woman in the Restoration period, (or indeed a married woman conceiving in an adulterous relationship), would have been disastrous. When Pepys thought he had made one of his mistresses pregnant, it threw him into a major panic until it proved to be a false alarm. In seventeenth century England, marriage and sexual morals played a far more important social role than they do now, with a family centred around a married couple representing the basic social unit. Society was still strongly influenced by strict Puritan values; publicly inflicted corporal punishment awarded by ecclesiastical courts for adulterous relationships had only been abolished in 1641, but moral lapses still continued to be prosecuted by the civil courts; at Hastings in 1669, one George Laby was ordered to pay half a crown (12½ pence) per week maintenance for his illegitimate child whilst the mother, a servant girl named Anne Perk, was sentenced to be stripped naked upwards from the waist and publicly flogged at the whipping post as a punishment for her lewd behaviour.

Sexual integrity and the status of a married person gave a woman respectability and social prestige, evidenced by the fact that the law only recognised women in one of three ways; maid, wife or widow. This, coupled with the fact that it was difficult for women to find ways of making an independent living, meant that securing and retaining a husband was a matter of great importance. Almost all of Pepys' women, whether married or not, took a great deal of persuading before they succumbed, or indeed, when blandishments or bribery failed, they had to be forced into submission.

Given that the licentiousness of the king and court were not reflected in the sexual behaviour of the general public, how would others have reacted to Pepys' treatment of women? Would they have thought it offensive, immoral or simply normal behaviour? Pepys himself pretty well answers the question in a diary entry made in June 1663:

> … and then came again to the [Westminster] hall and fell in talk with Mrs. Lane and after great talk that she never went abroad with any man as she heretofore used to do, I with one word got her to go with me and to meet me at the further Rhenish wine-house – where I did give her a Lobster and do so towse [to handle roughly, dishevel] her and feel her all over, making her believe how fair and good a skin she had; and endeed [sic] she hath a very white thigh and leg, but monstrous fat. When weary, I did give over, and somebody having seen some of our dalliance, called aloud in the street, 'Sir, why do you kiss the gentlewoman so?' and flung a stone at the window – which vexed me – but I believe they could not see me towsing her; and so we broke up and out the backway, without being observed I think; and so she towards the hall and I to White-hall. … (Diary 29th June 1663)

Several things about the incident may be deduced from this passage; Pepys did not want to be seen with Mrs Lane and made her travel separately to their pre-arranged assignation, a short distance away; a passer-by observes his treatment of the woman – groping her, raising her skirts and petticoats high enough to observe and fondle her thighs – and strongly and vocally disapproved of his behaviour. When leaving, they sneak out of the back entrance and go their separate ways so as not to be observed (presumably by someone who might recognise them – London was a comparatively small place in the seventeenth century with a population of about 250,000 in 1600). Finally, lobster was clearly as much of an expensive treat to offer a lady then as it is now!

Did Pepys feel any shame or remorse for his adulterous and illicit relationships? He certainly had a completely different set of values when it came to judging the behaviour of others. When in 1666 he heard tell of an attempted rape by his colleague at the Admiralty and staunch puritan John Creed, he was (slightly) outraged: '… an odde story lately told of him for a great truth, of his endeavouring to lie with a woman at Oxford, and her crying out saved her; and this being publicly known, doth a little make me hate him.' (Diary 18th February 1666)

As usual with Pepys, his early concerns seem to be principally with money: 'Besides too, I do perceive more and more that my time of pleasure and idleness of any sort must be flung off, to attend the getting of some money …' (Diary 30th June 1663)

However, throughout the diary period, a pattern emerges of Pepys continuing to act and treat women in a reprehensible manner, afterwards expressing shame or remorse and vowing to amend his ways. As with all Pepys resolutions and professions of shame, those concerning Mrs Lane for example, were short lived:

> By and by Mrs. Lane comes; and my bands not being done, she and I parted and met at the Crowne in the palace-yard, where we eat (a chicken I sent for) and drank and were mighty merry, and I had my full liberty of towsing her and doing what I would but the last thing of all; for I felt as much as I would and made her feel my thing [penis] also, and put the end of it to her breast and by and by to her very belly – of which I am heartily ashamed. But I do resolve never to do more so. (Diary 18th July 1663)
>
> I went by water to Westminster-hall; and there finding Mrs. Lane, took her over to Lambeth where we were lately, and there did what I would with her but [i.e. except] only the main thing, which she would not consent to, for which God be praised; and yet I came so near, that I was provoked to spend [i.e. ejaculate]. But I trust in the Lord I shall never do so again while I live. (Diary 23rd September 1663)
>
> … I by water to Westminster-hall and there did see Mrs. Lane, and de la, elle and I to the cabaret [tavern] at the Cloche in the street du roy; [King's Road] and there, after some caresses, je l'ay foutee sous de la chaise deux times,[I fucked her twice under the chair], and the last to my great pleasure;.… and although I did make grand promises a la contraire, nonobstant je ne la verrai pas long time [on the contrary, notwithstanding I will not see her for a long time]. (Diary 16th January 1664)

Despite vowing not to see her again, at least for a long time, only a few months later he is taking her to Lambeth once again where '… there eat and drank and had my pleasure of her twice'. (Diary 23rd July 1664)

In spite of his many resolutions to modify his behaviour, three years later he is still misbehaving indiscriminately with both married women and adolescent serving girls:

> … and so away to Mrs. Martin's lodging, who was gone before expecting me; and there yo haze what yo vellem cum her [did what I would with her] and

drank; and so by coach home (but I have forgot that I did in the morning go to the Swan; and there tumbling of la little fille [the little girl – Frances Udall], son uncle [her uncle and the landlord William Herbert] did trouver her cum su neckcloth off [her uncle did find her with her neckcloth off], of which I was ashamed ... (Diary 20th May 1667)

In spite of his invariable sense of shame after an illicit episode, Pepys seems to be well aware that his nature drives him again and again to commit immoral acts, which he later regrets:

... I going down to Deptford; and Lord, to see with what itching desire I did endeavour to see Bagwell's wife, but failed, for which I am glad; only, I observe the folly of my mind, that cannot refrain from pleasure at a season ... (Diary 16th May 1666)

... but my love of pleasure is such, that my very soul is angry with itself for my vanity in so doing ... (Diary 6th June 1666)

To what extent does Pepys behaviour reflect that of men generally in his time? There is nothing to suggest that Mrs Lane's apparent willingness to accommodate Pepys' sexually motivated attention is behaviour common to most seventeenth-century women. Indeed, whether it be from a sense of morality or a fear of pregnancy, most of the women who became the subject of his lustful desires strongly resisted his advances and some (but by no means all) only succumbed when he resorted to bribery or physical force. In an age before formal policing, human activity could only be regulated by commonly accepted modes of behaviour, in turn dictated by a fear of the consequences, mortal or immortal. As has been illustrated elsewhere, Pepys was not averse to employing physical force to achieve his desires, resorting to rape when the lady became completely intractable: '... it being dark, did privately entrer en la maison de la femme de Bagwell, [privately enter the house of Bagwell's wife] and there I had sa compagnie [her company], though with a great deal of difficulty; neanmoins, enfin je avais ma volonte d'elle [however, finally I had my way with her]. (Diary 20th February 1665)

Any temptation to believe that Mrs Bagwell gave in peacefully is dispelled by the diary entry for the following day (where for no apparent reason, Mrs Bagwell has become anonymous): 'Up and to the office (having a mighty pain in my forefinger of my left hand, from a strain that it received last night in struggling avec la femme que je [with the woman that I] mentioned yesterday.' (Diary 21st February 1665)

Not only was Pepys prepared to use force against women, he was clearly turned on by the experience, or even by observing its use by others:

This night late, in my coach coming up Ludgate Hill, I saw two gallants and their footmen taking a pretty wench which I have much eyed lately, set up shop upon the hill, a seller of ribband [sic] and gloves. They seemed to drag her by some force, but the wench went and I believe had her turn served; but God forgive me, what thoughts and wishes I had of being in their place.'
(Diary 3rd February 1664)

Why didn't the women who had been raped or forced to commit obscene acts by Pepys bring actions against him? Almost certainly, because then as now, 'it was extremely difficult for women to bring charges of rape against men, and the women who did so often faced dire social consequence and future violence even in cases or where the rape was known to have occurred.' (Garthine Walker, *Crime, Gender and Social Order in Early Modern England*, Cambridge University Press, 2003)

The seventeenth-century Lord Chief Justice Sir Matthew Hale summed it up perfectly, in words that still resonate today:

It is true that rape is a most detestable crime, and therefore ought severely and impartially to be punished with death; but it must be remembered, that it is an accusation easily to be made, hard to be proved, but harder to be defended by the party accused, though innocent.

Women were in an even worse bind if they became pregnant as a result of such an assault. There was a view that women could only become pregnant if they experienced orgasm – Pepys was fearful whenever he made a woman 'come' that she might have conceived as a result, a belief set out in a posthumous book published in 1627: 'Rape is the carnal abusing of a woman against her will. But if the woman conceive upon any carnal abusing of her, that is no rape, for she cannot conceive unless she consent.' (Sir Henry Finch, *Law or Discourse Thereof*, 1627)

In summary, it appears that the well-documented licentious behaviour of Charles II and his court was not reflected in the behaviour of the population as a whole, who broadly continued to uphold values and moral codes that largely apply in western society to this day. Pepys seems to be secure in believing that there would not be any adverse consequences from his forcing his attentions on unwilling women, formal complaints being unlikely; his attempts to conceal these activities centered upon the desire to keep the truth from his wife. Neither do these assignations appear to have interfered with his business activities, although he sometimes mentions in passing a suspicion that he has lost time in his pursuit of pleasure:

… and did to the joy of my soul dispatch much business – which doth make my heart light and will enable me to recover all the ground I have lost (if I have by my late minding my pleasures lost any) and support myself. (Diary 12th January 1667)

Pepys usually worked until dinner – taken around midday and then in common with many of his social class reserved the afternoon for leisure activities – the theatres were open in the afternoons to take advantage of natural light. He would then return to the office and work again often until late in the evening. Being largely his own boss, no one needed to know where he was at any given moment and many of his colleagues did little or no work at all. Furthermore, his sexual assignations were often fitted in with work-related occasions, for example, trips to the naval yards at Deptford usually included a visit to Mrs Bagwell.

In addition to his serial adultery, the range of Pepys' sexual malpractice covers the entire spectrum; from unsolicited kissing, through groping under skirts and petticoats and down bodices to compelling his victims to commit obscene acts upon his person, in both private and public venues. Finally, at the top of the scale, he frequently employed physical violence in order to compel women to submit to his lustful desires: 'Alone with her, I tried to do what I wanted, and against her struggles I did it, though not to my satisfaction.' (Diary 20th December 1664).

There can be little doubt that, by the standards of modern times, Pepys would be regarded as a serious sex offender.

Chapter 22

Postscript

Pepys did not go blind after May 1669 as he had anticipated, but lived on with his sight intact for another thirty-four years. He enjoyed further advancements, survived political plots and perils, served in various constituents as a Member of Parliament, as well as serving as President of the Royal Society. Having witnessed the execution of Charles I, he lived on through the reigns of Charles II, James II, William and Mary saw James' daughter Anne ascend the throne.

Samuel Pepys died on the 26th May 1703 at his home in Clapham (now a borough but then a village just south of London). Mary Skinner, his long-standing friend, his colleague Will Hewer and his nephew John Jackson were with him at the end. He was given the last sacraments by another old friend, George Hickes, a former Dean of Worcester. After a painful struggle that lasted the greater part of two days, he died of what is now thought to have been kidney failure at forty-seven minutes past three o'clock in the morning. He was 70 years old.

George Hickes conducted the funeral in the church of St Olave in the City of London, which had been Pepys's own church when he and Elizabeth lived in Seething Lane and where they had worshipped regularly in the special Navy Office gallery. When Elizabeth died in 1669 he buried her in that same church and the bust he had made of her still looks across with the hint of a frown to the pew where she and her errant husband used to sit.

A year or two before Pepys died, his life-long friend John Evelyn had written to him, looking forward to the two of them meeting again 'in those regions of peace and love and lasting friendships … that Royal Society above'. On the day of Pepys' death, Evelyn wrote in his own diary:

> This day died Mr. Samuel Pepys, a very worthy, industrious and curious person, none in England exceeding him in knowledge of the navy, in which he had passed through all the most considerable offices, Clerk of the Acts and Secretary of the Admiralty, all which he performed with great integrity. When King James II went out of England, he laid down his office, and would serve no more; but withdrawing himself from all public affairs, he lived at Clapham with his partner, Mr. Hewer, formerly his clerk, in a very noble house and sweet place, where he enjoyed the fruit of his labours in great prosperity. He was universally beloved, hospitable, generous, learned in many

things, skilled in music, a very great cherisher of learned men of whom he
had the conversation.

John Evelyn himself passed away three years later. As far as we are aware he never
knew that his friend of forty years and fellow diarist Samuel Pepys, the celebrated
member of the establishment and respectable pillar of society, was a man who had
taken every opportunity that came his way to 'love a pretty wench in a corner' or
at very least, to kiss her and put his hand up her skirts.

The School of Venus

W ritten pornography was far from uncommon in the England of the seventeenth century. Novels, travelogues, philosophy, and even botanical treatises could all be found with extended erotic passages. After many years of puritanical repression, the England of Charles II rediscovered old liberties (and libertines) and publishers found that there was a ready market for all forms of pornography. *The School of Venus, or the Ladies Delight, Reduced into Rules of Practice* was published in England in 1680, and is an hilarious, lewd, racy, and copiously illustrated sex manual, originally published in France as *L'escholle des Filles* [School for Girls].

In January 1668, Pepys records that he paid one of his regular visits to his bookseller:

> [I] stopped at Martin's, my bookseller, where I saw the French book which I did think to have had for my wife to translate, called L'escholle des Filles, but when I come to look in it, it is the most bawdy, lewd book that ever I saw … I was ashamed of reading in it. (Diary 13th January 1668)

Not everyone approved of the lax moral climate originating in the court of the 'merry monarch' – in 1650, only 1 per cent of live births took place outside marriage and the last execution for adultery in England had taken place only in 1654. In many cases, books with sexual content were published with different title pages or covers to fool the authorities, which is why Pepys may have genuinely considered purchasing the book in the original French, initially unaware of its true nature.

The book follows a plot line that seems rather simple and naïve by modern standards (although viewers of on-line pornography may disagree). The main narrative introduces two principal characters; Katherine, 'a virgin of admirable beauty' and 'a kins-woman of hers named Frances'. Frances 'come[s] to chat' with Katherine one morning, finding her alone and working 'as if it were a Nunnery'. Frances reproaches her cousin for being 'such a fool [as] to believe you can't enjoy a man's company without being married.' Katherine naively explains that she enjoys the companionship of many men 'my two unkles [sic], my cousins, Mr. Richards and many others' but Frances explains that she means something altogether different. However, by page 34 the narrative has turned into what might now be described as a sex manual: '… sometimes my Husband gets upon me, and sometimes I get upon him, sometimes we do it sideways, sometimes kneeling, sometimes crossways, sometimes backwards … sometimes Wheelbarrow, with one leg upon his shoulders, sometimes we do it on our feet, sometimes upon a stool.'

The book is surprisingly frank about female sexual autonomy, asking 'why should not ones Finger yield a Wench the like pleasure' as a penis and speculating about how the world would be 'if Women govern'd the world and the Church as men do'. Female multiple orgasms are referenced throughout, and there appear to be a few scattered allusions to the clitoris, referred to as 'the top of the cunt' which 'stands out'.

In spite of his alleged shame in reading it, Pepys eventually convinced himself that it would not hurt to read it through just once, in order to confirm that it was as lewd as he thought it to be. Overcoming his embarrassment he returned to the bookseller three weeks later to purchase the book (albeit in a cheap edition):

> Thence away to the Strand to my book-seller's, and there stayed an hour and bought that idle, roguish book, L'escholle des Filles, which I have bought in plain binding (avoiding the bullying of it being better bound) because I resolve, as soon as I have read it, to burn it, that it may not stand in the list of books, nor among them, to disgrace them if it should be found. (Diary 8th February 1668)

Interestingly, the bookseller clearly had a more expensive edition, as well as the copy bought by Pepys – in the plain brown wrapper so familiar to purchasers of pornography in the early twentieth century. An opportunity to peruse the book privately appeared on the following day, Sunday 9 February, when instead of going to church as usual, Pepys takes the book to his office:

> Lords Day. Up, and at my chamber all the morning and the office, doing business and also reading a little of L'escholle des Filles, which is a mighty lewd book, but yet not amiss for a sober man to read over to inform himself of the villainy of the world. (Diary 9th February 1668)

At noon, Pepys returns home to dinner, where he is accompanied by four male friends, who 'sang till almost night, and drank my good store of wine'. He complains about the singing and clearly has other things on his mind. Having eventually got rid of them, and probably somewhat intoxicated, Pepys cannot wait to get back to perusing his new book, which, according to him, he is doing simply 'to inform himself of the villainy of the world': '… I to my chamber, where I did read through L'escholle des Filles; a lewd book, but doth me no wrong to read for information sake …'

However, as always, Pepys is honest and frank with his diary entry and we learn that whilst reading it for 'information sake', the book fulfills another purpose altogether – that for which it was clearly intended: '… but it did hazer my prick para stand all the while, and una vez to decharger …'

Even the strange use of pseudo-Spanish cannot conceal the fact that reading the book gave him an erection and eventually made him ejaculate. Regaining his composure, his puritan upbringing surfaces once more and: '… after I had done it, I burned it, that it might not be among my books to my shame; and so at night to supper and then to bed.' (Diary 9th February 1668)

However, in spite of Pepys' self righteous justification for reading the book, the game is rather given away by his opinion that *L'escholle des Filles* was 'rather worse than Putana Errante', now known to be a prose dialogue dating from 1584 upon which *L'escholle des Filles* is based, and with which he was apparently already wholly familiar.

Pepys' bookseller would no doubt have had a significant stock of pornography on his 'top shelf' or put aside for selected customers. Had he enquired further, Pepys might well have titillated himself by reading *The Practical part of love. Extracted out of the extravagant and lascivious life of a fair but subtle female* first published in 1660. To the English, most devices, diseases and techniques associated with sex have all traditionally originated in France, to wit; french letters; french pox, french kiss. Likewise, as with *The School of Venus* much of the printed pornographic material in the seventeenth century was also said to have originated there, for example; 'The most delightfull and pleasant history of Francion wherein all the vices that usually attend youth are plainly laid open by Monsieur De Moulines Sier De Parc.; done into English by a person of honour' published in 1661.

This is not to say that much of the material was not home grown; *The Crafty Whore* published in 1658 describes; 'the mistery and iniquity of bawdy houses laid open, in a dialogue between two subtle bawds, wherein, as in a mirrour, our city-curtesans may see their soul-destroying art, and crafty devices, whereby they insnare and beguile youth, pourtraied to the life, by the pensell of one of their late, (but now penitent) captives, for the benefit of all, but especially the younger sort. Whereunto is added dehortations from lust drawn from the sad and lamentable consequences it produceth.'

On a rather higher intellectual plane, John Wilmott, Second Earl of Rochester was notorious for his erotic and vitriolic verses. A contemporary of Pepys and a close friend and companion of Charles II, Wilmot was a genuinely brilliant writer of poetry, a wit, a dramatist, a womaniser and a life-long alcoholic, who died in 1680 at the age of 33. Much of his poetry is so obscene, that it was still being censored from anthologies of poetical works in the 1950s. Upon seeing him walking with the king in St James's Park, in yet another outburst of self righteous indignation, Pepys wonders why the monarch is in the company of 'so idle a rogue'.

Wilmot's witty attention was regularly drawn to the members of Charles's court where he spent much of his time, and no one was immune from his acidic eroticism, not even the daughter of the king's personal physician, whose mother was a maid of honour to the Queen:

> Her father gave her dildoes six,
> Her mother made 'em up a score,
> But she loves nought but living pricks
> And swears by God she'll frig no more.

Advice on all matters sexual was not confined to men. Women also had new sources of information on subjects not previously openly discussed. Take for example a book published in 1694 entitled *The Ladies Dictionary: Being a General Entertainment for the Fair Sex*. Those wicked foreigners seem to be in the frame yet again, as the frontispiece goes on to say that it is 'a work never attempted before in English'. The subjects upon which advice is offered have a contemporary familiarity; exercise is recommended 'that the blood may be stirred in the veins' and diet; 'avoid anything that is very salt, sharp, bitter, or too hot' and recommends 'new eggs, veal, mutton, capon etc.' Fruit and vegetables are entirely absent however. The perennial female obsessions with physical appearance and make–up are well catered for, with advice on what to do when 'parts of the body fall away in one part and not in another'. As in modern women's magazines however, the subject quickly moves on to the etiquette of dating; 'is it proper for a woman to yield at the first address' and yet further on to prostitution and the likely outcomes of an adulterous affair; 'the dishonour it puts upon the fair Sex, and revenge it stirs them up to'. For entertainment, it includes some risqué ditties, including this one on a woman's intimate parts:

> Her maiden womb, the dwelling house of pleasure.
> O blest is he may search that secret treasure.

The front cover of the book includes the legend that it comes 'with an addition of a new School of Love, and a present of excellent Similitudes, Comparisons, Fancies and Devices' a list that, with some updating of the language, might not look out of place on the cover of a twenty-first century woman's magazine of a particular genre. Those who think that the internet is the begetter of all things pornographic might look more closely at what their grandfathers (and grandmothers) eight, ten or more times removed might have pored over by candlelight!

Appendix B

The Bagwells

Mr and Mrs Bagwell first enter the diary in July 1663 and make regular appearances therein until April 1669, during which six years Mrs Elizabeth Bagwell continued on and off as one of Pepys' long-term mistresses. William Bagwell was a ship's carpenter and although the diary does not record his given name, we know it to be William as it does identify two of the ships upon which he served. He obviously came from a family of shipwrights – his father, Owen Bagwell, had been foreman of the dockyard at Deptford and is mentioned in *The Secret History of His Majesty's Ship-Yard* published in 1718. His nephew William Sutherland, also described as a kinsman in Mrs Bagwell's will, was a Master Caulker who made several significant contributions to the shipbuilding technology of the day and wrote *The Ship Builders Assistant* which continued in publication until 1840.

As a result of his wife's importuning, and undoubtedly supported by his own abilities, William Bagwell became very successful and relatively wealthy. He and his wife are known to have employed at least one servant and by 1670 were living at Deptford in a larger than average five-hearth house. At his death in 1697 he bequeathed to various beneficiaries quantities of silver in the form of tankards, plates and candlesticks, together with a pocket-watch and a sword and scabbard. The Elizabeth Bagwell thought most likely to have been the Mrs Bagwell of the diary died in 1702 and was buried at St Nicholas, Deptford on 14th August of that year.

The diary fails to reveal Mrs Bagwell's given name, although we can be reasonably certain that it was (ironically) Elizabeth. William's will of 1697 makes reference to 'Elizabeth my well beloved wife' and names a kinsman, one Owen Bagwell as a Trustee. The same Owen Bagwell appears in the 1702 will of an Elizabeth Bagwell of Deptford, who identifies him as 'my husband's kinsman'.

Note: An alternative candidate has been suggested by Guy de la Bedoyère in his work *The Letters of Samuel Pepys*, in which he identifies her as Judith (née Campion), citing a record of the marriage of this woman and a William Bagwell in 1658.

Appendix C

Full Forty Times Over (full libretto)

'Full Forty Times Over' the 'very lewd song' taught to Pepys by Mrs Aynsworth, one-time procuress from Cambridge and latterly the landlady of The Reindeer inn at Bishop's Stafford. Modern readers may struggle to find the lewdness described by Pepys:

Full forty times over I have strived to win,
Full forty times over repulsed have been,
But 'tis forty to one but I'll tempt her agen,
For he's a dull Lover,
That so will give over,
Since thus runs the sport,
Since thus runs the sport.
Assault her but often, and you carry the Fort,
Since thus runs the sport,
Assault her but often, and you carry the Fort.
There's a breach readymade, which still open hath been,
With thousands of thoughts to betray it within,
If you once but approach you are sure to get in,
Then stand not off coldly,
But venter on boldly,
With weapon in hand,
With weapon in hand,
If you once but approach, she's not able to stand,
With weapon in hand,
If you once but approach, she's not able to stand.
Some Lady-birds when down before them you sit,
Will think to repulse you with Fire-balls of wit,
But alas they're but crackers, and seldom do hit,
Then vanquish them after,
With alarms of laughter,
Their Forces being broke,
Their Forces being broke,
And the fire quite out, you may vanquish in smoak,

Their Forces being broke,
And the fire quite out, you may vanquish in smoak.
With pride & with state, some out-works they make,
And with Volleys of frowns drive the enemy back,
If you mind her discreetly she's easie to take,
Then to it, ne'r fear her,
But boldly come near her,
By working about,
By working about,
If you once but approach, she can ne'r hold it out,
By working about,
If you once but approach, she can ne'r hold it out.
Some Ladies with blushes and modesty fight,
And with their own fears the rude foe do affright,
But they'r eas'ly surpriz'd if you come in the night,
Then this you must drive at,
To parley in private,
And then they're o'rthrown,
And then they're o'rthrown.
If you promise them farely, they'll soon be your own,
And then they're o'rthrown,
If you promise them fairly, they'll soon be your own.

Ladies of Pepys' acquaintanceship

Pepys does not always make clear exactly who the ladies are that find themselves the objects of his lustful desires, or with whom he was otherwise acquainted. Due to their status or position in society, some are known to history whilst others are at best simply names that flit anonymously across the pages of the diary, before disappearing again into obscurity. Most of the ladies with whom Pepys became intimately familiar are either servants or women in trade, i.e. of a lower social order than himself. Although he knew and socialized with women from the higher social classes, he rarely if ever made any attempt to seduce them. Also, the majority of the women with whom he had affairs are married or widowed. It is not clear whether this arose by chance, or whether it was a deliberate policy in order to minimise the risk of repercussions.

The diary contains references to 2,835 different people, from princes to paupers, of which 470 are women, so this is a far from complete list of those who crossed his path. The women named here are those with whom Pepys may or may not have had a relationship of one sort or another, but they are women that he thought attractive and mentions this fact in the diary.

Mrs Allen
Wife of Captain John Allen, who was Clerk of the Ropeyard, Chatham 1660/63: 'By and by comes Captain Allen and his son Jowles and his wife, who continues pretty still.' (Diary 1st January 1663)

Betty Archer (unknown)
An otherwise unknown woman that Pepys apparently admired whilst a student at Cambridge university. Pepys continued to see her sister Mary Archer socially during the diary period.

Mrs Aynsworth
Known to Pepys whilst a student at Cambridge, she taught him lewd songs and was once publicly whipped for obscene behaviour. Later in life she became landlady of the Reindeer Inn at Bishops Stafford where Pepys stayed on a number of occasions later in his life.

Mary Backwell

Wife of Alderman Backwell, a goldsmith-banker, and MP at various times between 1673 and 1683. He has been described as the principal founder of the banking system in England. In 1662 Pepys admires her as 'a very pretty woman' but by 1669 has revised his opinion: '… but I do, contrary to my expectation, find her something a proud and vain-glorious woman, in telling the number of her servants and family and expences …' (Diary 12th April 1669)

Mrs (Elizabeth?) Bagwell

Wife of William Bagwell, for whom she importuned Pepys a carpenter's job at sea for her husband. Pepys had a torrid affair with her over several years after 1663. Her first and maiden names are not certain – for several reasons 'Elizabeth' is a strong possibility, although one Judith Campion has also been suggested. (See appendix 'The Bagwells'.)

Mrs Mary Batelier

A seamstress and daughter of Susanna and Joseph Batelier, a wine merchant and customs clerk. The Bateliers were neighbours of the Pepyses living in Crutched Friars and she and her brother William were regular drinking pals of the Pepys. Pepys describes her as 'a very pretty woman' and 'the fair Batelier' but although admiring her, never seems to have made a pass at her, probably because she was too well known to his wife.

Betty (surname unknown)

Maid to the actress Mary Knipp (or Knepp). Pepys always regarded female servants – whether his own or those of other people, as fair game; '… I did give the pretty maid Betty that comes to me half-a-crown for coming, and had a baiser or two-elle [had a kiss or two – she] being mighty jolie.' (Diary 28th September 1668) Half a crown (12 ½pence) was quite a sum in 1668 – probably a good deal more than a week's wages for a maid – and certainly worth a snogging by Pepys.

Mrs Frances Butler

'The great beauty, who is sometimes styled la belle Boteler' (from a footnote on a diary entry in the 1893 edition edited by Henry B. Wheatley). She was unmarried – the appellation is simply a contraction of 'Mistress', the common form of address at the time. Pepys stalked her for some time, but lost touch when she moved house; '… thence to Clerkenwell church, and there, as I wished, sat next pew to the fair Butler, who indeed is a most perfect beauty still; and one I do very much admire myself for my choice of her for a beauty, she having the best lower part of her face that ever I saw all days of my life.' (Diary 2nd October 1664)

Mrs Elizabeth Burroughs

An exceptionally attractive widow of a naval lieutenant, Anthony Burrows, who had been killed in action in 1665. Her mother, Mrs Crofts, kept a shop in Westminster where Elizabeth seems to have worked. An entry in Pepys's private accounts for 1667–8 ('Burroughs … gloves') may refer to a gift that he purchased for Elizabeth; '… then to the office, where I got Mrs. Burroughs sola cum ego – and did tocar su mamelles so as to hazer me hazer.' [Got Mrs. Burroughs on her own – and did touch her breasts so as to make me come.] (Diary 15th January 1667)

Lady Castlemaine (Barbara Palmer)

Born in 1640 Barbara Villiers, only child of William, second Viscount Grandison, married April 14th, 1659, to Roger Palmer, created Earl of Castlemaine, 1661. She became the king's mistress soon after the Restoration, and was in 1670 made Baroness Nonsuch, Countess of Southampton, and Duchess of Cleveland. She had six children by the king, one of them being created Duke of Grafton, and the eldest son succeeding her as Duke of Cleveland. She subsequently married Beau Fielding, whom she prosecuted for bigamy. She died October 9th, 1709, aged 69. Considered a great beauty, Pepys was enthralled by her and had sexual fantasies about her for years – seeing her in her night clothes in chapel, he became so aroused that he 'spent in his breeches'. The diary contains no less than 152 references to her. Whilst once walking in the privy-garden he came upon her underwear drying in the sun and records that he 'saw the finest smocks and linen petticoats of my Lady Castlemaine's, laced with rich lace at the bottom, that ever I saw; and did me good to look upon them.' (Diary 21st May 1662)

Mrs Clerke (a)

Pepys' landlady during his stay in Greenwich whilst the plague was rampant in London; '… to have a place to retreat to for my wife, if the sicknesse should come to Woolwich, am contented to pay dear; so for three rooms and a dining-room, and for linen and bread and beer and butter, at nights and mornings, I am to give her 5l. 10s. per month …' (Diary 11th October 1665)

Mrs Clerke (b)

The wife of a Fenchurch Street milliner that Pepys regularly lusted after, although never seems to have approached; 'and so to church, where, God forgive me! I did most of the time gaze on the fine milliner's wife, in Fenchurch Street, who was at our church to-day.' (Diary 28th February 1668)

Mrs Clifford (unknown)

A 'comrade' of Mrs Pearse, both of whom Elizabeth Pepys appeared to have been jealous and became angry when she knew Pepys had seen them socially; '…at home I found Mrs. Pierce, la belle, and Madam Clifford, with whom I was forced to stay, and made them the most welcome I could; and I was (God knows) very well pleased with their beautiful company, and after dinner took them to the Theatre …' (Diary 9th October 1661)

Mrs Cragg (unknown)
Possibly either Alice, wife of Francis Crake, or Susanna, wife of Thomas Crake, the landlady of Betty Martin (b. Lane) '… hence I to Westminster and to Mrs. Martin's, and did hazer what je would con her, [did what I would with her] and did once toker [touch] la thigh de su [her] landlady. …' (Diary 1st June 1668)

Diana Crisp
Daughter of Mrs Crisp, a neighbour of the Pepyses in Axe Yard. One of Pepys' earliest dalliances;'From thence to Axe Yard to my house, where standing at the door Mrs. Diana comes by, whom I took into my house upstairs, and there did dally with her a great while, and found that in Latin "Nulla puella negat".' [The girl refused nothing]. (Diary 4th September 1660)

Mrs Daniel
The wife of a navy lieutenant John Daniel (who served aboard the warship *Royal Charles*) and the daughter of Mrs Clerke (a) Pepys' landlady during his stay at her home in Greenwich whilst the plague raged in London: '… to Mrs. Clerke's and there I had a good bed, and well received, the whole people rising to see me, and among the rest young Mrs. Daniel, whom I kissed again and again alone. (Diary 11th July 1666)

Frances Davenport
An actress in Knipp's theatre company. This seems to be her only assignation with Pepys: 'I took her to the Lodge, and there treated her and had a deal of good talk, and now and then did baiser la, [kiss her] and that was all, and that as much or more than I had much mind to because of her paint.' (Diary 8th April 1668)

Robin Delkes
The daughter of 'old Delkes' a waterman: 'After he was gone comes by a practice of mine yesterday, old Delkes the waterman with his daughter Robins, and several times to and again, he leaving her with me about getting of his son Robins off, who was pressed yesterday again. And jo haze ella mettre su mano upon my pragma hasta hazerme hazer la costa in su mano. [And I made her put her hand on my thing to touch me until I came in her hand.] Pero ella no voulut permettre que je ponebam meam manum a ella [she would not let me put my hand on her], but I do not doubt but allo k[r]onw de obtenir le …' [I do not doubt but another time I will get it.] (Diary 23rd August 1665)

Mrs Eastwood (unknown)
A widow living in Westminster (see Mrs Fenton).

Mrs Fenton (unknown)
A maid living in Westminster and a relative of Doll Lane, 'and by and by comes a pretty widow, one Mrs. Eastwood, and one Mrs. Fenton, a maid; and here merry kissing and looking on their breasts, and all the innocent pleasure in the world.' (Diary 1st August 1666)

Eleanor 'Nell' Gwyn (also Gwynn, Gwynne)
Actress and a long-time mistress of King Charles II. 'Nelly; a most pretty woman, who acted the great part of Coelia to-day very fine, and did it pretty well: I kissed her, and a mighty pretty soul she is.' (Diary 23rd January 1666)

Betty Hall
Black actress in the same company of players as Nell Gwynne. '... Mrs. Halls which is my little Roman-nose black girl, that is mighty pretty: she is usually called Betty.' (Diary 23rd January 1666)

Mrs Hely (unknown)
Pepys first lady friend, otherwise unidentified, '... and so up and down by Minnes's wood, with great pleasure viewing my old walks, and where Mrs. Hely and I did use to walk and talk, with whom I had the first sentiments of love and pleasure in woman's company, discourse, and taking her by the hand, she being a pretty woman.' (Diary 26th July 1663)

Betty Howlett
(See Betty Mitchell)

Peg Hughes
An actress in the same company as Nell Gwynne, '... But, Lord! their confidence! and how many men do hover about them as soon as they come off the stage, and how confident they are in their talk! Here I did kiss the pretty woman newly come, called Pegg that was Sir Charles Sidly's mistress, a mighty pretty woman, and seems, but is not, modest.' (Diary 7th May 1668)

Mrs Rebecca Jowles (nee Alleyn)
Rebecca Alleyn, aged about 18, daughter of John Allen; Clerk of the Ropeyard, Chatham, Kent. Married in August 1662 to Henry Jowles, of Chatham, aged about 24. (Chester's 'London Marriage Licences', ed. Foster, col. 779) as quoted by Wheatley, 1904. 'Here mightily pleased with Mrs. Jowles, and did get her to

the street door, and there to her su [her] breasts, and baiser [kiss] her without any force, and credo [believe] that I might have had all else, but it was not time nor place.' (Diary 24th March 1668)

Mary Knipp (also Knep, Knepp, Nepp, Knip)

She was one of the first generation of female performers to appear on the public stage during the Restoration period; a singer and a dancer in the King's Company between 1664 and 1678. The dramatist and theatre manager Tom Killigrew told Pepys that she was '… like to make the best actor that ever come upon the stage'. Pepys pursued her for years and although he was successful in intimately fondling and kissing her on various occasions, she never appears to have become his mistress: 'The company all being gone to their homes, I up with Mrs. Pierce to Knipp, who was in bed; and we waked her and there I handled her breasts and did baiser la [kiss her] and sing a song, lying by her on the bed.' (Diary 24th January 1667)

Betty Lane

(See Betty Martin)

Doll Lane

(See Doll Powell)

Mrs Lowther

Margaret Penn, daughter of Admiral Sir William Penn and Margaret Jasper Penn, was born 1636. She married Anthony Sir Thomas Lowther in 1666–67 (see Lady Margaret Penn). Apart from noting that his wife sometimes wore them, this is the only reference in the diary to a woman wearing 'drawers', a new garment in the seventeenth century: '… we did send for a pair of old shoes for Mrs. Lowther, and there I did pull the others off and put them on, and did endeavour para tocar su thigh [to touch her thigh] but ella [she] had drawers on, but yo did besar la and tocar sus mamelles [I did kiss her and touch her breasts], elle [she] being poco [very] shy …' (Diary 10th May 1668)

Mrs Nan Markham

Maid to Lady Penn, allegedly Sir William Penn's mistress before her marriage. As usual with Pepys, servants are fair game '… and being lighted homeward by Mrs. Markham, I blew out the candle and kissed her.' (Diary 27th April 1668)

Betty Martin (nee Lane)

She ran a draper's stall in Westminster Hall, where Pepys sometimes bought linen and where she caught Pepys' amorous attention. She became his mistress in a relationship which continued after she married Samuel Martin in 1664. Her sister, Doll, was also one of Pepys' many other women. (See also Doll Powell)

Betty Mitchell (nee Howlett)
Betty Howlett, daughter of Westminster Hall booksellers, married Michael Mitchel, son of Miles and Ann Mitchell, also booksellers in Westminster Hall. Pepys called her 'his wife' and tried for many years to make her his mistress. Although he succeeded in persuading her to fondle him in an intimate manner on several occasions, she never became his mistress.

Penelope Mordaunt (Countess of Peterborough)
Pepys visited Lady Peterborough regularly in the later diary years, although their relationship was entirely platonic, even though she was apparently something of a tease: 'Thence to my Lady Peterborough, she desiring to speak with me; she loves to be taken dressing herself, as I always find her. …' (Diary 27th January 1668)

Morena (a. Elizabeth Dickens)
Daughter of John Dickens (Dekins or Dicksons, as he spelt the name), was a hemp merchant with an unmarried daughter named Elizabeth. Pepys called her his 'Morena' – the word is Portuguese for a brunette; probably coined by Pepys to indicate that Miss Dickens had a dark complexion.

Morena (b. possibly Mrs Horsely)
Later mentioned as a 'pretty black woman'.
   '… To church, where, God forgive me! I spent most of my time in looking [on] my new Morena at the other side of the church, an acquaintance of Pegg Pen's.' (Diary 18th December 1664)

Goody Mulliner (unknown)
Lived opposite Magdalene College, Cambridge and from whom he apparently purchased prunes.

Nan (unknown)
Maid to an old woman in Pannier Alley who ruled Pepys' writing paper. Called 'black Nan', probably on account of her dark hair, '… there staid a great while with Nan idling away the afternoon with pleasure.' (Diary 2nd May 1666)

Damaris Page
Prostitute who became a famous and successful 'madam', running two brothels, one of which was frequented by men of the royal court, including the king's brother.

Elizabeth Pearse (also Peirce)

Wife of James Pearse, Surgeon to the Duke of York and Surgeon-General of the Fleet. She is said to have been an extraordinary beauty and to have borne nineteen children. The couple were long term friends of the Pepys's, although Elizabeth Pepys was jealous of her (platonic) relationship with her husband. (See also Mrs Clifford.)

Mrs Judith Pennington

Daughter of Sir Isaac Pennington, parliamentarian Lord Mayor 1642/3 and sister of Isaac, the Quaker leader. Pepys saw her regularly towards the end of 1665 after which she disappears from the diary altogether. '… and [Captain] Cock being sleepy, he went away betimes; I stayed alone, talking and playing with her till past midnight – she suffering me a hazer whatever ego voulus avec ses mamelles [to do whatever I wanted with her breasts] and I had almost lead her by discourse to make her tocar mi cosa naked, [touch my bare penis] which ella [she] did presque [almost] and did not refuse …' (Diary 26th November 1665)

Lady Margaret Penn

Wife of Admiral Sir William Penn (father of the founder of Pennsylvania) Dutch by birth and described by Pepys as being short and fat, but with more wit than her husband. Her daughter was Margaret Lowther and Pepys saw both of socially on a regular basis, when they were often 'mighty merry'. In spite of the horseplay, Pepys does not succeed in making either of them his mistress: '… and going to my Lady Batten's, there found a great many women with her, in her chamber merry, my Lady Pen and her daughter, among others; where my Lady Pen flung me down upon the bed, and herself and others, one after another, upon me, and very merry we were …' (Diary 12th April 1665)

Elizabeth Pepys (nee St Michel)

The wife of Samuel Pepys, daughter of Alexandre and Dorothea St Michel, and a sister to Balty. Elizabeth was born 23 October 1640 at or around Bideford. It is not known how Pepys and Elizabeth met, but the couple married when Elizabeth was 15 years old. Shortly after their marriage, but prior to the Diary period, the couple had unspecified differences and separated for several months. By the start of the Diary, the two were reunited and living in Axe Yard.

Elizabeth is known solely through the eyes of Pepys as none of her letters survive. Apparently the marriage had difficulties and periods of jealousy appeared on both sides. Pepys was regularly unfaithful to Elizabeth and although there was no indication that she was ever unfaithful to him, he often let his jealousy get the best of him.

Elizabeth's health was an ongoing issue throughout the Diary. She often suffered from a recurring abscess, believed to be a Bartholin's cyst, which often made sexual relations difficult for the couple. The couple had no children, and the cause of their infertility could easily have been Pepys operation to remove his stone, as he never fathered any children with any of his many mistresses either.

Shortly after the Diary ended, the Pepys's traveled together to Paris with Elizabeth's brother Balty. Upon their return home Elizabeth developed a severe fever and died on the 10th November 1669. Pepys never remarried although he had a life-long relationship with Mrs Mary Skinner.

Mrs Pett
Wife of Mr Pett, a shipwright. 'So to Mr. Pett's, the shipwright, and there supped, where he did treat us very handsomely … his wife a proper woman, and has been handsome, and yet has a very pretty hand.' (Diary 14th January 1660)

Doll Powell (nee Lane)
Sister of Betty Martin. Pepys had a sexual relationship with both of them over many years. The regularity of his association with Doll are illustrated clearly on one occasion when, '… Doll, who went for a bottle of wine, did come home all blubbering and swearing against one Captain Vandener, that pulled her into a stable by the Dog tavern, and there did tumble her and toss her, calling him all the rogues and toads in the world, when she knows that elle hath suffered me to do any thing with her a hundred times.' (Diary 6th July 1667)

Mrs Shrewsbury
Wife of William Shrewsbury, a bookseller. 'Here did I endeavour to see my pretty woman that I did baiser [kiss] in las tenebras [in the dark] a little while depuis [since]. And did find her sofa [alone] in the book [shop], but had not la confidence para alter a elle [offer her anything]. (Diary 24th April 1668)

Mrs Frances Tooker
A neighbour of Pepys' landlady Mrs Clerke when he stayed with her in Greenwich during the plague; '… so home, and to my papers for lack of company, but by and by comes little Mrs. Tooker and sat and supped with me, and I kept her very late, talking and making her comb my head; and I did what I will with her et tena grande plaisir con ella, [took great pleasure of her] tocando sa cosa con mi cosa, [touching her thing with my thing] and hazendo la cosa per cette moyen. [Doing the thing in this way.] So late to bed.' (Diary 5th January 1666)

Mrs Elizabeth Turner
Wife of Thomas Turner, General Clerk at the Navy Office.

'They gone, Mrs. Turner staid an hour talking with me and yo [I] did now the first time tocar her cosa [touch her thing] with my hand and did make her do the like con su hand [with her hand] to my thing, whereto neither did she show any aversion really, but a merry kind of opposition, but yo [I] did both * and yo do believe I might have hecho la cosa too mit her [done more with her] * So parted, and I to bed.' (Diary 20th September 1668) [* The shorthand in the diary is apparently unclear at these points.)

Mrs Jane Turner
Pepys cousin married to John Turner.

'She was dressing herself by the fire in her chamber, and there took occasion to show me her leg, which endeed is the finest I ever saw, and she not a little proud of it.' (Diary 3rd February 1665)

Sarah and Frances Udall
Sarah and her sister Frances were serving maids at the Swan inn, New Palace Yard, where Pepys regularly drank. Sarah (described by Pepys as his 'petite moza' – little miss) was married in 1666.

'So it being not dinner time, I to the Swan, and there found Sarah all alone in the house and I had the opportunity a hazer what I tena a mind á hazer con ella [to do what I had a mind to do with her], only con [with] my hands -- but she was vexed at my offer a tocar la under sus jupes [to touch her under her skirts]; but I did once, nonobstant [despite] all that.' (Diary 27th November 1665)

Jane Welsh or Walsh (maid to Richard Jervas, Pepys' barber)
From September 1664, Pepys lusted after Jane for several years to no avail, for although she agreed meetings, she invariably stood him up. She eventually married a Mr Harbing, a fiddler, who turned out to be an impoverished bigamist with a family.

Elizabeth Whittle
Pepys confessed that he had 'a great opinion' of Elizabeth when a boy and flattered her by making anagrams on her name, although we know nothing further about their relationship. She was destined to become the grandmother of Charles James Fox, the great anti-slavery campaigner.

Mrs Woolley
The wife of Robert Woolley, a broker in Mincing Lane. An example of how Pepys can blow hot and cold on women for no apparent reason: 'Woolly's wife, who is a pretty woman.' (Diary 28th October 1666)

'Woolly's wife, a silly woman, and not very handsome, but no spirit in her at all.' (Diary 11th November 1666)

Appendix E

Female Servants in Pepys' Household
During the Diary Period

Alice (cookmaid) *Surname unknown 1665/66*
'A good servant whom we loved and did well by her.' (Diary 30th March 1666)

Anon (a. cookmaid) *Name unknown 1663*
'This day, our cook-mayde (we having no luck with maids nowadays), which was likely to prove a good servant, though none of the best cooks, fell sick and is gone to her friend, having been with me but four days.' (Diary 10th September 1663)

Anon (b. maid) *Name unknown 1666*
'… gone home, the very same day she came'. (Diary 28th April 1666)

Anon (c. maid) *Name unknown 1668*
'… who is lately, about four days since, gone away, being grown lazy and proud.' (Diary 20th October 1668)

Anon. (d. maid) *Name unknown 1669*
'… and this day came another new mayde for a middle-mayde, but her name I know not yet.' (Diary 5th April 1669)

Ashwell, Mary *1663/64*
Daughter of one Mr Ashwell, who worked at the exchequer, with whom Pepys had socialized in 1660 when they were both clerks.

Barker, Miss (maid/companion) *1666/67*
A destitute young girl whose singing voice was admired by Pepys and a relative of Mr Falconbridge (Fauconberg). In 1666 she was hired as a maid and companion for Elizabeth and to sing with the family and guests. She was dismissed in 1667 for insolence and lying.

Bridget (cookmaid) *Surname unknown 1668/69*
'This day also, our cook-maid Bridget went away, which I was sorry for; but just at her going, she was found to be a thief, and so I was less troubled for it.' (Diary 29th March 1669)

Doll (a. chambermaid) Surname unknown 1661
'... I am sorry to find my wife displeased with her maid Doll; whose fault is that she cannot keep her peace, but will always be talking in an angry manner, though it be without any reason and to no purpose.' (Diary 30th October 1661)

Doll (b. cookmaid) Surname unknown 1669
A 'blackamoore' (i.e. black), a servant of William Bateliers', borrowed by Pepys.

Dorothy (maid) Surname unknown 1661
'This morning our maid Dorothy and my wife parted – which though she be a wench for her tongue not to be borne with, yet I was loath to part with her.' (Diary 27th November 1661)

Edwards, Jane (Birch, maid) 1658/61
A maid in the Pepys household from 1658 to 1661 of whom Pepys was very fond, in spite of the fact that he had sometimes occasion to thrash her. She married his clerk, Tom Edwards, in March 1669 and Pepys was godfather to their son, Sam, born in 1673. She was widowed twice and in 1690 Pepys settled a £15 annuity on her.

Elizabeth (chambermaid) Surname unknown 1663/65
'... I saw Besse go away – she having, of all wenches that ever lived with us, received the greatest love and kindness and good clothes, besides wages, and gone away with the greatest ingratitude.' (Diary 6th March 1665)

Gentleman, Jane (chambermaid) 1663/64
Recommended by her kinswoman Mrs Mary Harper: '... Mrs. Harper and her cousin Jane came, and we treated and discoursed long about her coming to my wife as a chamber-maid; and I think she will do well.' (Diary 14th August 1663)

Hannah (cookmaid) Surname unknown 1663
The heroic cook (and cleaner-up-after) of the 1663 feast in honour of Pepys's 1558 stone-cutting, who well deserved the 12d (5p) tip that the guests gave her that 4th April but later proved to be a thief and was summarily dismissed: '... and after dinner comes our old maid Susan to look for a Gorgett that she says she lost by leaving it here; and by many circumstances, it being clear to me that Hannah, our present cook-maid, not only hath it but had it upon her neck when Susan came in and shifted it off presently upon hr coming in ...' (Diary 17th August 1663)

Jane (cookmaid) Surname unknown 1664/65
'This morning, my Taylor [sic] brought me a very tall maid to be my cook-maid ...' (Diary 27th May 1664)

Jinny (maid) Surname unknown 1663
Ran away the day after she was employed, taking her new clothes with her. She was apprehended and Pepys arranged to have her whipped in the Bridewell: 'Thence to my brother's, and there told him how my girl has served us which he sent me, and directed him to get my clothes again, and get the girl whipped.' (Diary 21st August 1663)

Luce (cookmaid) Surname unknown 1666/67
Replacement for Mary (d) '… and another (Luce) come, very ugly and plain, but may be a good servant for all that'. (Diary 26th June 1666)

But was later dismissed for drunkenness '… and by and by home and there find our Luce drunk, and when her mistress told her of it would be gone, and so put up some of her things and did go away of her accord, nobody pressing her to it, and the truth is, though she be the dirtiest, homeliest servant that ever I kept, yet I was sorry to have her go, partly through my love to my servants, and partly because she was a very drudging, working wench, only she would be drunk.' (Diary 18th May 1667)

Mary (a. cookmaid) 1661
Acquired from Pepys' cousin, W. Joyce on a months' trial, but left of her own volition at the end of her probation.

Mary (b. chambermaid) 1663
'… I found Mary gone from my wife, she being too high for her, though a very good servant.' (Diary 27th April 1663)

Mary (c. chambermaid) 1665/66
'… and so home and there find our new chamber-maid, Mary, come; which instead of handsome, as my wife spoke and still seems to reckon, is a very ordinary wench I think – and therein was mightily disappointed.' (Diary 6th March 1665)

Mary (d. cookmaid) 1666
Left of her own volition (but on good terms) after less than three months.

Mary (e. under-cookmaid) 1667
'… a good, big girl … this wench's name is Mary'. (Diary 21st May 1667).

She left on the 10th July of her own volition '… declaring that she must be where she might earn something one day, and spend it and play away the next …' (Diary 10th July 1667)

Mercer, Mary (maid/companion) 1664/6
17 years old when hired by Elizabeth Pepys in August 1664, Mary was the daughter of William Mercer, in whose house Will Hewer had been living. 'I like her well and I think will please us. My wife and they agreed and she is to come the next week.' (Diary 29th August 1664)

Matt (chambermaid) 1669
'The new maid's name is Matt, a proper and very comely maid; so as when I was in bed, the thought de ella [of her] did make me para hazer in mi mano [do the thing with my hand].' (Diary 29th March 1669)

Nell (a. maid) Surname unknown 1661/62
'This morning came several maids to my wife to be hired; and at last she pitched upon one Nell, whose mother, an old woman, came along with her; but would not be hired under half a year, which I am pleased at their droleness.' (Diary 16th October 1663) Nell later proved to be 'a simple slut' and a 'cross-grained wench' (Diary 15th December 1663)

Nell (b. cookmaid) Surname unknown 1667/68
'This day, Nell, an old tall maid, came to live with us, a cook maid recommended by Mr. Batelier.' (Diary 2nd September 1667)

Payne, Nell (cookmaid) 1667/69
'I have lately played the fool much with our Nell, in playing with her breasts.' (Diary 17th June 1667)

Sarah (chambermaid) Surname unknown 1661
'… my wife and I had another falling out about Sarah, against whom she has a deadly hate, I know not for what, nor can I see but she is a very good servant.' (Diary 2nd December 1662)

Susan (a. maid) Surname unknown 1662/63
'Susan beginning to have her drunken tricks, and put us in mind of her old faults and folly and distractednesse, which we had forgot, so that I became mightily troubled with her.' (Diary 19th August 1663)

Susan (b. maid) Surname unknown 1663
Replacement for Jinny who ran away with her new clothes; '… and a new one came.… which I think will prove a pretty girl – her name, Susan'. (Diary 21st August 1663)

Deb Willett (maid/companion) 1667/69

Pepys grew very fond of her and gradually persuaded her to engage in mutual masturbation, until his wife caught him 'in flagrante', kissing her with his hand under the girl's skirts. The love affair almost ended his marriage. In 1670 Deb later married a theology graduate named Jeremiah Wells and Pepys later helped him obtain a position as a ship's chaplain. The couple had two daughters, Deborah born in 1670 and Elizabeth born in 1672. Sadly, Deb died in 1678 at the age of 27. Her husband died 18 months later.

Bibliography

Akroyd, Peter, *London – The Biography*, Chatto & Windus, 2000.

Bastable, Jonathan, *Voices from the World of Samuel Pepys*, David & Charles 2007.

Bedoyère, Guy de la (ed.), *Particular Friends – The Correspondence of Samuel Pepys & John Evelyn*, Boydell Press, 1997.

Bedoyère, Guy de la, *The Letters of Samuel Pepys*, Boydell, 2006.

Berriedale-Johnson, M., & Driver, Christopher, *Pepys at Table*, Bell & Hyman, 1984.

Bevan, Bryan, *Nell Gwyn*, Robert Hale, 1969.

Bray, William (ed.), *The Diary of John Evelyn*, Chandos, 1887.

Brome, Vincent, *The Other Pepys*, Weidenfeld & Nicolson Ltd, 1992.

Bryant, Arthur, *Samuel Pepys* – i. The Man in the Making, ii. The Years of Peril, iii. The Saviour of the Navy, Cambridge University Press, 1933–1938.

Burford & Shulman, *Of Bridles & Burning*, Hale, 1992.

Carlton, William J., *Bibliotheca Pepsiana Pt.4*, Sidgwick & Jackson, 1960.

Cavendish, Richard, 'Death of Samuel Pepys', *History Today*, Vol. 53 2003.

Chappell, Edwin, 'Samuel Pepys – A Lecture', Society for Nautical Research, 1933.

Cleugh, James, *The Amorous Master Pepys*, Frederick Muller Ltd, 1958.

Cumming, Valerie, *A Visual History of Costume – The Seventeenth Century*, B.T. Batsford Ltd, 1984.

Davidson, Caroline, *A Woman's Work is Never Done*, Chatto & Windus, 1982.

Delaforce, Patrick, *Pepys in Love*, Bishopsgate Press, 1986.

Emslie, Macdonald, *Pepys's Songs & Songbooks in the Diary Period*, Bibliographic Society, 1957.

Evelyn, John, *Fumifugeum – The Smoake of London*, Ashmolean Reprints, 1930.

Fraser, Antonia, *The Weaker Vessel*, Weidenfeld & Nicolson Ltd, 1984.

Hanson, Neil, *The Dreadful Judgement – The True Story of the Great Fire of London*, Doubleday, 2001.

Hardy, W. & Reckitt, G., (eds), 'Bucks Session Records 1694 to 1705', Aylesbury County Council, 1939.

Knighton, C.S. (ed.), *Pepys's Later Diaries*, Sutton Publishing Ltd, 2004.

Latham & Matthews, *The Diary of Samuel Pepys* – complete 11 volumes, G. Bell & Sons Ltd, 1971/6.

Laurence, Anne, *Women in England 1500–1760*, Weidenfeld & Nicolson, 1994.

Lincoln, Margarette (ed.), *Samuel Pepys – Plague, Fire, Revolution*, Thames & Hudson, 2015.

Magdalene College, Cambridge University, *The Pepys Library*, (Undated Guide).

Pullar, Philippa, *Consuming Passions*, Hamish Hamilton, 1970.

Richardson, R.C., '*A Maidservants Lot*', *History Today*, Vol.60 No.2, 2010.

Tanner, J.R. (ed.), *Private Correspondence & Private Papers of Samuel Pepys 1679–1703*, George Bell & Sons, 1926.

Tomalin, Claire, *Samuel Pepys – The Unequalled Self*, Viking, 2002.

Trease, Geoffrey, *Samuel Pepys & his World*, Thames & Hudson, 1972.

van Yelyr, Prof. R.G., *The Whip & the Rod*, Gerald G Swan, 1941.

Wheatley, Henry B., *Pepysiana*, George Bell & Sons, 1899.

Wilson, Derek, *All the King's Women*, Hutchinson, 2003.

Wilson, John Harold, *The Private Life of Mr. Pepys*, Robert Hale Ltd, 1960.

Index

Allbun, Dr. (also Allbon), 130
Allen, Mrs Becky, 139, 164, 168
Allen, John, 139
Archer, Betty, 16, 164
Archer, Mary, 16
Ayloffe, John, 148
Aynesworth, Mrs, 16–17, 162, 164

Backwell, Mary, 165
Bagwell, William, 100, 104, 108, 111, 114, 161
Bagwell, Mrs, viii, 44, 63–4, 68, 70, 80, 100–117, 152, 154, 161, 165
Bales (also Bowles) Mrs, 81
Balthasar (Balty), St Michel, 72
Bartholomew Fair, ix
Batelier, Mary, 165
Batelier, William, 118–19
Batten, Sir William, 2–3
Batters, Mrs, 113
Birch, Jane, 40
Bishop, Sir Edward, 120
Bowyer, William, 62
Braybrooke, Lord, vii
Brown, Tom, 47
Bryant, Arthur, vii
Burrows, Lieutenant Anthony, 78, 110
Burrows (also Burroughs), Mrs Elizabeth, 36, 49, 68, 70–2, 75, 78–83, 98, 107, 110, 120, 122, 166
Burrows, Mrs (senior), 80–1
Butler, Mrs Frances, 34, 165

Campbell, Archibald 9th Earl of Argyle, 149
Carpenter, Elizabeth (see Knepp, Elizabeth), 85
Carteret, Jemima (b.Montegu), 57
Castlemaine, Lady (see Palmer, Barbara)
Cavendish, Margaret, Duchess of Newcastle, 30
Clerke, Mrs (a), 48–50, 166
Clerks, Mrs (b), 166

Clifford, Mrs, 166
Coke, Frances, 24
Cony, John (also Conny), 140
Cox, Captain (also Cockes), 44, 48, 85
Cragg, Mrs (probably Alice), 74, 77, 167
Creed, John, 29, 53, 78, 102, 150
Crisp, Diana, 167
Crofts, Mrs, 78, 110
Cromwell, Oliver, 6, 12, 147

Daniel, John, 50
Daniel, Mrs, 48–53, 114, 167
Davenport, Hester, 84, 122, 167
Davis, Mary (Moll), 84
Delkes, Robin, 167
Dillon, Cary, 34
Dolling, Tom, 55
Downing, George, 58
Drumbelby, Mr. 96, 112
Duchess of Cleveland (see Palmer, Barbara)

Eastwood, Mrs, 36, 68, 79, 168
Edwards, Tom, 40, 135
Evelyn, John, 4, 9, 22, 24, 27, 144, 147, 156

Fairbrother, Mr William, 54
Fane, Mrs, 144
Female Servants (see Appendix E)
Fenton, Mrs, 36, 68, 79, 168
Ferrer, Captain Robert, 127
Finch, Sir Henry, 153
Foster, Mrs, 115

Gibbon, Christopher, 94
Greeting, Thomas, 14
Gwynne, Eleanor (Nell), 32, 47, 82, 88, 168

Haines, Joseph, 91
Hale, Sir Matthew Lord Chief Justice, 153
Hall, Betty, 168
Hare, Mrs Alice, 58
Harmond, Sarah (see Udall, Sarah), 80

Harper, Mrs, 39
Harrison, Major-General, 6
Hatton, Lady Elizabeth, 24
Hawley, John, 55, 58–60, 62
Hayls, John, 14
Hely, Mrs, 17, 168
Herbert, William, 151
Herbert, Mrs, 60
Hewer, William (Will), 3, 43, 88, 121, 131–6, 155
Hickes, George Dean of Worcester, 155
Hinchingbrooke, Lord (see Montague, Edward 2nd Earl of Sandwich)
Holder, Thomas, 81
Holder, Mrs Thomas, 81
Hollier, Thomas, 10, 127
Howlett, John, 73
Howlett, Betty (see Mitchell, Betty)
Howlett, Mrs, 56, 59, 81, 96, 99
Hughes, Peg, 168
Hunt, John, 58

Jackson, John, 144, 155
James, Duke of York (see Stuart, James)
Jeffries, Judge, 6
Jervas, Richard (also Gervas), 18, 34, 105, 140–41
Jonson, Ben, 4, 9
Jowles, Henry, 139
Jowles, Rebecca (see Allen, Becky)
Joyce, Katherine (Kate), 81

Killigrew, Tom, 82
King Charles I, 6, 54
King Charles II, 13, 29, 147, 149, 153, 157, 159
King James II, 13
Kite, Margaret, 1, 15
Knepp, Christopher, 85
Knepp, Mrs Elizabeth (also Knep, Nepp, Knip, Knipp), 32, 44–5, 47, 82–91, 110, 115–16, 122, 124, 169

Laby, George, 149
Lane, Mrs. Betty (also Mrs. Betty Martin), viii, 18, 34, 54–63, 65, 92, 100–101, 103, 108, 150–2
Lane, Doll (also Mrs Powell), 70, 72, 74–7, 111
Latham, R.C, vii
Lennox, Charles, 1st Duke of Richmond, 148

Linsay, Lady Sophia, 149
Lowther, Mrs Margaret, 18, 23, 52, 115, 169

Manly, Major John, 140
Manuel, Mrs, 88
Markham, Mrs Nan (b. Wright), 122, 169
Martin, Mrs Betty (see also Mrs Betty Lane), 26, 34, 36, 62–78, 80, 82, 98, 119, 151, 170
Martin, Samuel, 60–3, 70–1, 77
Matthews, W, vii
Mercer, Mrs, 8
Mercer, Mary, 7–8, 42, 90, 95, 109, 114–15, 121, 170
Mitchell, Betty (b.Howlett), 23, 35, 56, 58–9, 66, 71, 74, 76, 81, 92–9, 108–109, 111–12, 170
Mitchell, Elizabeth (1), 98
Mitchell, Elizabeth (2), 98
Mitchell, Michael, 93–9, 112
Montague, Edward, 1st Earl of Sandwich, 12, 29, 54, 124, 127
Montague, Edward, 2nd Earl of Sandwich, 127
Montague, Sir Sidney, 1
Mordaunt, Penelope, Countess of Peterborough, 30, 170
Morena (a), Elizabeth Dickens, 170
Morena (b), (possibly Mrs Horsley), 37, 170
Mulliner, Goody, 16, 170

Nan, Black, 171
Noble, Mrs, 81

Page, Damaris, 27, 171
Palmer, Barbara, 1st Duchess of Cleveland (also Lady Castlemain), 38, 46, 148, 166
Palmer, Roger, 1st Earl of Castlemain, 148
Palmer, Mrs (landlady), 20
Pearce, Mrs Elizabeth (see Pierce, Elizabeth)
Penn, Lady Margaret, 171
Penn, Margaret (Peg) b. Jasper, 34, 43
Penn, Sir William (also Pen), 2, 18, 45
Pennington, Sir Isaac, 48
Pennington, Mrs Judith, 8, 48–9, 51, 171
Pepys, Aunt Wight, 69, 80
Pepys, Elizabeth, 1, 3, 7, 18, 22, 24, 30, 32–3, 38–40, 42–4, 51, 63–4, 69, 80–1, 85, 87, 91, 93–4, 104, 109, 112–13, 118–38, 143–5, 171–2
Pepys, John (brother), 111
Pepys, John (cousin), 17

Pepys, John (father), 1–2, 15, 20
Pepys, Paulina, 1
Pepys, Richard, 1
Pepys, Talbot, 1
Perk, Anne, 149
Pett, Mrs, 172
Pierce (also Pearse), Elizabeth, 44, 85–90, 115, 124, 171
Pope, Alexander, 4
Powell, Mrs Doll (*see also Lane, Doll*), 36

Queen, Catherine of Braganza, 38, 56

St Michel, Alexandre, 19
St Michel, Dorothea, 19
St Michel, Elizabeth (*see Pepys, Elizabeth*)
Sandwich, Lord *(see Montague, Edward)*
Saunderson, Mary, 84
Sheldon, Thomas, viii–ix
Shelston (prob. Robert), 29
Shrewsbury, Mrs William, 122, 173
Sidley (also Sedley), Sir Charles, 90
Skinner, Daniel (father), 145
Skinner, Daniel (brother), 145
Skinner, Mrs Mary, 143–6, 155
Smith, Sir J, 44, 136
Stuart, James Duke of York, 27, 124, 149

Steward, Mrs, 56
Swayne, William, 60

Taylor, John, 5
Tooker, Frances, 173
Turner, Betty, 3, 88, 122, 173
Turner, Jane, 173

Udall, Frances, 67, 81, 87, 141, 150, 173
Udall, Sarah (*see also Harmond, Sarah*), 67, 72–3, 80, 141, 173
Unthank, John, 63

Vandener, Captain, 74
Venner, Dr, 69
Verney, Sir Ralph, 25
Villiers, Sir John, 24

Walsh, Jane *(also Welsh)*, 34–5, 140, 174
Wells, Jeremiah, 138
Wheatley, Henry B, vii–viii, 39, 55
Whittle, Elizabeth, 17, 174
Wilkins, Dr John, 11
Willett, Deb, viii, 3, 41, 46, 114, 116–38
Wilmot, John Earl of Rochester, 148, 159–60
Woolley, Mrs Robert, 174
Wren, Matthew, 136